RELIGION AND THE STATE,

OR,

THE BIBLE AND THE PUBLIC SCHOOLS.

BY

SAMUEL T. SPEAR, D.D.

NEW YORK:
DODD, MEAD & COMPANY, PUBLISHERS,
751 BROADWAY.
1876.

CONTENTS.

STATEMENT OF THE QUESTION.

THE GENERAL ARGUMENT.

THE SPECIAL ARGUMENT.

PREFACE.

The contents of this volume were originally published as a series of articles in the correspondence columns of THE INDEPENDENT. During their publication the author received numerous letters from various parts of the country, expressing a strong interest in the discussion, and suggesting that, at the completion of the series, the whole should be given to the public in the form of a book. The approval of the articles thus indicated, the references occasionally made to them by the secular and religious press, and the insertion of some of them in other newspapers, led the author to conclude that their collection and publication in a volume might possibly contribute some help to the public mind in arriving at the true solution of the much debated School question. They now appear just what and as they were at their original publication, with the exception of a few changes made in their titles.

The School question has for years past excited no little attention among the people, and it will probably continue to do so for years to come. It is only a branch of the larger question that relates to the proper attitude to be assumed and maintained by civil government with reference to religion. In respect to this larger question, the American people, alike in their constitutions and laws, have adopted a policy entirely antagonistical to any union between Church and State. Shall this policy be applied to the public school, organized and managed by State authority, and supported by general taxation? Shall this school, like the State itself, be exclusively *secular* in its purposes and processes, or shall it, in addition to the secular element, be made the instrument of *religious* instruction and worship?

The object of this volume is to answer these questions. As to the correctness of the conclusion, and the pertinency and power of the argument to sustain it, the reader can fairly judge only by perusing the entire series of essays. If he will turn to the last number, entitled "The Conclusion," he will find a summary of the whole discussion, and be the better able to judge of the relations of its several parts to each other. No one aspect of the question exhausts it; and no examination of it can be deemed at all thorough or complete that does not carefully consider the principles and ends of civil government, especially as constitutionally established in this country.

It being granted that civil government should confine itself exclusively to the attainment of secular and temporal ends, and it being further granted that the political system of the American people is based on this principle, and also granted that the public school is an institution of the State, and not of the Church, then the only conclusion, at all consistent with the premises, is that the school should be a fair expression of the character of the State. This is the conclusion adopted by the author; and his main effort in this volume has been fully to state the premises and show that they prove this conclusion. The argument is addressed to the people as *citizens*, and not as religionists, whether Protestant or Catholic. In the latter aspect they can never agree upon a common school policy: yet in the former they should agree by fully respecting each others' rights as citizens, and hence by asking nothing of each other which they do not as cheerfully concede.

BROOKLYN, September, 1876.

RELIGION AND THE STATE,

OR

THE BIBLE AND THE PUBLIC SCHOOLS.

STATEMENT OF THE QUESTION.

THE NEW POLITICAL PROGRAMME.

Ex-Speaker Blaine, in his letter of October 20th, 1875, addressed to a gentleman in Ohio just after the election in that State, suggested an amendment to the Constitution of the United States, which he has since submitted to the House of Representatives in the following form :—

"No State shall make any law respecting an establishment of religion, or prohibiting the free exercise thereof ; and no money raised by taxation in any State for the support of public schools, or derived from any public fund therefor, shall ever be under the control of any religious sect ; nor shall any money so raised ever be divided between religious sects or denominations."

The first clause of the First Amendment to the Constitution declares that "Congress shall make no law respecting an establishment of religion, or prohibiting the free exercise thereof." Mr. E. P. Hurlbut, formerly one of the Judges of the Supreme Court of the State of New York, in a pamphlet published some years since, and entitled "A Secular View of Religion in the State," suggested that this amendment should be so altered as to read as follows: "*Neither* Congress *nor any State* shall make *any* law respecting an establishment of religion, or prohibiting the free exercise thereof." The words in italics are the ones which Judge Hurlbut proposed to add. If there be good reason for imposing such a restriction upon Congress, there must be an equal reason for imposing it upon the several States. While Congress has no power except such as has been delegated to it by the Constitution, the States possess *all* governmental powers except such as the Constitution denies to them or grants exclusively to the General Government. There is nothing in the fundamental law of the land to prevent them from establishing Protestantism, Roman Catholicism, Judaism, or even Mormonism, according to the will of the majority, and imposing special disabilities and burdens upon the dissenting minority. Mr. Blaine proposes to withdraw this power from the States, and subject them to the same restriction that now applies to Congress.

The only difficulty that we feel in regard to this part of the amendment respects the extent of its application. Does the language reach and inhibit all religious tests as qualifications for voting or holding State offices, and all exercise of the power of taxation in support of religious institutions? The constitutions of some of the States contain religious tests; and those of New Hampshire and Connecticut provide for a tax levy as the means of sustaining Christian societies. Those who believe in the absolute divorcement of the State from religion, and who think it expedient to place this doctrine in the organic law of the land will, of course, approve of Mr. Blaine's proposition, so far as it goes; yet they will naturally raise the inquiry whether it is not too narrow in its scope. In their view it is less, except by a very liberal construction, than the whole truth; and for this reason they are likely to regard it as defective.

The other part of the amendment relates specifically to the School question. Its provision is that "no money raised by taxation in any State for the support of public schools or derived from any public fund therefor shall ever be under the control of any religious sect, nor shall any money so raised ever be divided between religious sects or denominations." This language clearly comprehends and precludes all propositions for a division of State school funds among religious sects, or placing any portion of such funds under the control of any such sect. Would it settle the much-debated School question? It would do so in part, since it would put an end to all discussion about any division of money "raised by taxation in any State for the support of public schools, or derived from any public fund therefor." This certainly would be a very important point to gain ; and possibly it is all that ought to be sought in an amendment to the National Constitution. Yet it manifestly does not cover the whole question in controversy. The manner of conducting public schools, including the subject of Bible-reading and religious worship therein, which is one of the sharpest issues between the Catholic and the Protestant, would be still left to the discretion of each State. So also there would be no inhibition upon the use of public funds for sectarian or religious purposes, raised by taxation or held by the State, unless they were so raised or held "for the support of public schools." The money that is the subject-matter of the restriction is *public* money, either raised by taxation or derived from some public fund therefor ; and this, and this only, is the money that must not, according to the proposition, be placed "under the control of any religious sect," or "divided between religious sects or denominations."

So much we offer in explaining the programme of ex-Speaker Blaine. If he designed to arrest public attention, he certainly has the satisfaction of having achieved a decided success.

The President also in his Message to Congress, December 7th, 1875, called the attention of the public to the same subject. In the Message he says :—

"I suggest for your earnest consideration, and most respectfully recommend it, that a constitutional amendment be submitted to the Legislatures of the several States, for ratification, making it the duty of each of the several States to establish and forever maintain free public schools, adequate to the education of all the children in the rudimentary branches within their respective limits, irrespective of sex, color, birthplace, or religion, forbidding the teaching in said schools of religious, atheistic, or pagan tenets, and prohibiting the granting of any school funds or school taxes, or any part thereof, either by legislative, municipal, or other authority, for the benefit or in aid, directly or indirectly, of any religious sect or denomination, or in aid or for the benefit of any other object, of any nature or kind whatever."

In addition to this, the President says : "I would suggest the taxation of all property equally, whether church or corporation, exempting only the last resting-place of the dead, and possibly, with proper restrictions, church edifices." In his recapitulation, at the close of his Message, the President names the following questions which he deems of "vital importance, which may be legislated upon and settled at this session" :—

1. "That the States shall be required to afford the opportunity of a good common-school education to every child within their limits."

2. "No sectarian tenets shall ever be taught in any school supported in whole or in part by the State, nation, or by the proceeds of any tax, levied upon any community. Make education compulsory so far as to deprive all persons who cannot read and write from becoming voters after the year 1890—disfranchising none, however, on grounds of illiteracy who may be voters at the time this amendment takes effect."

3. "Declare Church and State forever separate and distinct, but each free within its proper sphere; and that all Church property shall bear its own proportion of taxation."

The President's programme fills a larger space and embraces more particulars, than that of Mr. Blaine. What he says about the taxation of Church property would be very appropriate in a Governor's message, addressed to a State Legislature; but we do not see that Congress has any thing to do with the question in the exercise of its taxing power, or in that of proposing amendments to the Constitution. The President is right in his opinion that Church property should be taxed, in common with all other private property; yet the whole genius and spirit of the Constitution leave this question to be determined by the respective States. So, also, the President's theory as to an intelligence qualification for voting, may be very sound doctrine; yet there is not the slightest probability that two-thirds of Congress will propose the theory in the form of an amendment to the Constitution, or that three-quarters of the States would ratify such an amendment. The principle is adopted in the constitutions of only three States in the Union ; and this one fact is quite sufficient to settle the point in the negative. The question, moreover, is one which, according to the general policy of the Constitution, should be determined by each State for itself.

The plan of the President in regard to the public schools is both positive and negative. The positive part consists in making it the constitutional duty of the States to establish and maintain such schools and to give adequate opportunity for "the education of all the children in the rudimentary branches within their respective limits, irrespective of sex, color, birthplace, or religion." The public would be interested to learn from the President how such a duty would be enforced in case a State failed to comply with it. Without some method of enforcement it would be practically of but little consequence. Whether a State shall have a public school system or not is purely and absolutely a State question—as much so as the question whether it shall have a prison or a police system ; and it should be left to the sovereign discretion of every State. The General Government was not organized to educate the people, or take the superintendence of their education.

The negative part of the President's plan substantially coincides with the amendment proposed by Mr. Blaine in respect to the use of school funds, and goes beyond it in prohibiting the teaching of religious, sectarian, atheistic, or pagan tenets in any school sustained in whole or in part by the State. Whether Bible-reading, opening the school by prayer, and singing religious hymns would come within the prohibition, would be a question of construction, in regard to which we here express no opinion, because the President has not given the exact words of the amendment which he desires to have adopted. All he has done is to indicate the subject in general terms, showing very clearly the drift of his own mind, but not showing the precise thing which he would have accomplished.

The only other idea in the President's programme in relation to religion is the one which "declares Church and State forever separate and distinct, but each free within its proper sphere." This language is altogether too general, too ambiguous, and too susceptible of diverse constructions to be of any practical service. The way to gain the end is not to delegate the powers which in their exercise involve a union of Church and State, or prohibit specifically the exercise of any powers which necessarily lead to the result. A mere general dogma on any subject will not do for a constitutional law. Making constitutions which are to be the basis of powers to be exercised, or restraints to be imposed and enforced, is a work that demands the utmost accuracy in the use of words.

Taking, then, ex-Speaker Blaine's proposed amendment, and the President's general suggestions together, it seems by no means improbable that they will give a new impetus to the discussion of the principles, political and religious, that are involved in the School question. The editorials of newspapers, the numerous letters of correspondents, and the conflicting sentiments expressed by different persons, show that the discussion has already begun with renewed earnestness. Precisely what shape the question will take, and to what extent and in what manner it may be allied, if at all, with the policy and movements of political parties, especially in the approaching Presidential election, is a point not now determinable with any certainty; yet it would not be at all surprising if the Republican party should think it expedient to court, and, if possible, make an issue with the Democracy on this subject. The Democratic party depends largely upon Catholic votes for its hopes of success; and it is well known that the attack upon our public school system, and the clamor for a division of school funds, come mainly from Catholics. They, of course, will not be likely to look with favor upon Mr. Blaine's amendment, or upon the views of the President; and, hence, the difficult problem for the managers of the Democratic party to solve is to decide what shall be its attitude on this subject. Shall they accept or oppose the amendment proposed by Mr. Blaine?

With such an issue, if made, as a mere matter of party strategy between Republicans and Democrats, we have no concern. Yet the great principles which are involved in the question, and which in their various applications bring to the surface the whole subject of Church and State, civil government and religion, in their relations to each other, are matters of the very deepest interest. Some years since the attention of the public was strongly called to this subject, by the action of the Board of Education at Cincinnati. At that time the author of this article expressed his views on the question in a series of communications published in *The Independent.* He proposes now to renew the discussion in another series, regarding himself as at liberty to make any use which he thinks proper of the published results of previous labors. The present seems an opportune moment for asking the people to think upon a question which, if ever settled rightly and finally, must be settled in accordance with the principles that lie at the foundation of our political system.

II.

THE ROMAN CATHOLICS.

The Roman Catholics of this country, considered as a class, and especially as represented by their clergy and their religious journalists, are by no means pleased with our American public school system as an instrumentality for the education of their children. It is not what they want, or what they would make it, if they had the power. Justice to them demands that we should correctly understand and fairly state the grounds upon which they base their dislike of this system.

First of all, we should remember that, in the view of Catholics, no educational system applied to children is or can be right, whatever it may be in its secular character, that is not also distinctively religious. The secular without the religious element gives a "godless" and atheistic education; and, hence, a school organized on this principle is a "godless school," periling the soul while attending to the comparatively insignificant knowledge that relates purely to the interests of time. It is far more important that children should learn to pray and worship God, and be instructed in the tenets of religion, than that they should learn the multiplication table, or how to read and write, or to speak the English language correctly. No Christian certainly will make any issue with the Catholics as to the importance of a religious education: it is not possible to overstate this importance, or evince too much zeal in regard to it; and yet, whether they are right in denouncing every school system that does not meet this specific demand, is quite another question. A system may be very good for some purposes, and for this reason deserve to be supported, while it may not comprehend all desirable ends.

The next thing to be borne in mind is that, when the Catholic speaks of a religious education, he means an education after the specific type of his own faith. He means Catholicism in its tenets, ceremonies, usages, and forms of worship. Give him this in the public school, and not another word of complaint will be heard from either priest or layman to the end of time. Put into the school religion after the Protestant model, in either its character or its tendencies, and this for his children is the next thing to a "godless" school, if not quite as bad, since it teaches them "damnable heresies." The danger is that it will make them Protestants, or prevent them from being Catholics, and in either event ruin their souls. The reading of King James's version of the Sacred Scriptures, opening the public school by prayer, and singing a religious hymn will not satisfy the Catholic, for two reasons: First, as an educational *régime* it is, in his view, exceedingly defective in *quantity*, and in this respect he is entirely right; secondly, not being Catholic, but, so far as it is anything, Protestant in its character and tendency, it is still worse in *quality*. It is no relief to his conscience, and no answer to his objections, to supplement secular with this kind of religious education. Between a purely "godless" school and one that in his estimate is Protestant, he sees very little to choose. Neither meets the requirements of his faith. He desires to protect his children against the evils of both.

We see nothing strange or mysterious in this general position of the Catholics, if we look at the question as one of ecclesiastical and religious policy. Intense and exclusive ecclesiasticism is both a sentiment and a policy of their Church life—a conviction and a practice thoroughly fostered by their religious teachers. As religionists, they are educated to have no fellowship with Protestants or extend to them any Church recognitions. They are *the* Church, and there is no other Church upon the earth. Protestants are heretics; and wherever the Catholic creed is fully carried out there heresy is a *crime*, punishable by the civil power. Moreover, the Catholic clergy seek to make hatred of Protestantism a part of the religion of their people. This they do in order to isolate them as a distinct order of religionists by themselves, and, as far as possible, to make them *clannish*, and thus guard them against all dangerous contact with Protestant heretics. Their policy is to husband their own resources by taking the best possible care of the religious faith of their own people, and that of their children; and it is but just to say that they are skilful adepts at this business. No Church organism has ever existed that in the unity and singleness of its purpose, and in the persistency of effort with which it is worked, will at all compare with that of the

Catholics. It makes Churchmen of the most intense type and developes the purely Church theory with immense efficiency.

The managers and manipulators of this organism—the persons who do the brain-work, and who are almost exclusively the clergy—understand very well that Catholicism in this country depends for its life and progress upon two conditions: first, a large and continuous importation of foreign-born Catholics; secondly, home production, by educating the children of Catholics into the faith of their parents and the faith of the Church. Take away either of these sources of supply, and especially the latter, and conversions to Catholicism from the outside world among the adult population would by no means replenish the losses by death. The clergy are too sagacious not to see that, on this soil and in this atmosphere, a school system in which their creed is not made a primary and elementary part of the education of Catholic children will not meet the stern ecclesiastical necessities of Roman Catholicism in these United States. Ignorance and despotic control are historically the strongholds of Catholicism. It is not, never has been, and until greatly modified never can be the religion of popular enlightenment. Surrounded as it is in this country by a predominant non-Catholic influence, and brought in contact with the institutions of free and independent thought, "the holy Roman faith" has a very hard battle to fight; and, hence, the most zealous care over the education of Catholic children is with it a matter of life and death. This care it must give, or run the hazard of not being transmitted in the line of family descent. It must bring the children under its power in their earliest years; and anything that does not meet this necessity fails at a most vital point.

This statement of the question, as it respects Catholics, proceeds from no ultra-Protestant spleen against them, and no wish to call in question their sincerity or in the slightest manner to abridge their rights. We have no sympathy with, and hardly any respect for, that stupid and furious Protestantism which sees nothing good in Catholicism, and brands it as evil and only evil, and that continually. The best apology that can be made for it is its sheer ignorance. Nor do we intend to place a low estimate upon the value of a religious education. On this point we heartily agree with the most strenuous Catholic, however widely we may differ from him as to what is such an education, or as to the means by which it should be furnished. Nor, again, do we desire to curtail the privileges of the Catholic in the freest and fullest propagation of his own faith, by whatever means he chooses to adopt, in consistency with the laws of the land, provided always that *he also chooses to pay his own bills.* The law secures to him this right, in common with all other citizens, and defends him in its exercise. This is a free country for Catholics, as well as for Protestants, and both would do well to keep this fact in mind.

When, however, the leaders and teachers of the Catholic host make war upon our public school system because it does not answer their Church purposes; when they identify all true religion with the Catholic faith, as the sole measure and criterion thereof, and, hence, denounce all education as "godless" and "irreligious" that does not inculcate this faith; especially when they ask a subsidy from the school funds of the State or demand from the State a portion of these funds as the means of supporting schools one of whose prime objects shall be to teach Catholicism—yes, when this is the programme of the Catholic clergy and the Catholic press, there certainly can be no harm in looking at the philosophy of the movement. Such a programme, whatever may be its reasons in the minds and hearts of Catholics, or however necessary it may be for their purposes, brings before the American people a series of the very gravest questions. These questions are to be thoughtfully considered.

We confront the whole programme, as an aggregate and in all its parts, with the generic proposition that the public school should be made neither a Catholic nor a Protestant machine, any more than it should be made a Jewish, a Mormon, or an infidel machine. It should be a State machine, and this only, supported by general taxation and conducted under the exclusive authority of the State; and this one principle furnishes an unanswerable reason why it should have nothing to do with the Protestant, as such, or the Catholic, as such, and should deal with both on precisely the same terms, knowing them only as citizens, and, hence, knowing nothing about them as religionists or about their respective creeds. This is the true theory of the American public school system, and to the theory the practice should conform. If there be anything in the practice inconsistent therewith, then let it be corrected, no matter who may be offended thereby. The Protestant has just as many rights in the public school as the Catholic, and *no more;* and the latter has in it just as many rights as the former, and *no more.* Either can send his children to this school, and have them there educated in the common branches of useful secular knowledge, at the public expense; and this is all that either should ask at the hands of the State.

Catholics, however, and, we regret to say, some Protestants, are not satisfied with such a plan of State education. The reading of King James's version of the Scriptures in the public schools is demanded by a certain class of Protestants; and to it the Catholic objects, as an offense to his conscience. What he wants is the Douay version; and this is just what these Protestants do not want, and would not for a moment tolerate. Though the Catholic claims that *this* kind of Bible-reading shall be discontinued, yet his plan is much broader and deeper than the simple expulsion of King James's version from the public schools. What he wants is to have Catholicism formally and methodically taught to his children in the school which they attend; and, inasmuch as this cannot be done in the public school under present arrangements, he desires that the State should in some way so modify its system as to gain this end at the expense of the public. Such a division of the school funds as would give him a certain proportion thereof, and allow him to use it for the support of Catholic schools would just meet his wishes. This, or the nearest possible approach to it, is the ultimate point at which he aims.

The system of parochial schools after the Catholic model, is burdensome to those who have to pay its expenses; and, although Catholics, especially in large cities, have on this subject shown their faith by their works, still it would be a most welcome relief to them if the State would in some way secure to them the substantial ends of the parochial system without its charges—in a word, if the State would *pay the bills* and let them regulate the teaching. Such a plan would secure the whole end of the Catholic agitation about the public school, so far as the question of ways and means is concerned. The entire agitation converges at last to this one practical point: *Shall Catholics pay the cost of their own ecclesiastico-*

educational propagandism, or shall the State pay it? Here the question is one of dollars and cents.

The amendment proposed by ex-Speaker Blaine answers this question by declaring that "no money raised by taxation in any State for the support of public schools, or derived from any public fund therefor, shall ever be under the control of any religious sect, nor shall any money so raised ever be divided between religious sects or denominations." Though this would not dispose of all the issues involved in the School problem as debated by religious sects, yet, if the amendment were placed in the fundamental law of the land, one question, and that too a very important one, would receive a final settlement. The Rev. Thomas S. Preston—one of the most considerate and able writers on the Catholic side of the question—in a pamphlet published by him a few years since, took the ground that education and religion are inseparable; and that the State should adopt a system by which "every religious denomination which has its own schools shall draw its proportion of the sum raised by general taxation, according to the number of children whom it educates." We shall have occasion hereafter to examine both of these propositions; yet for the present it is sufficient to say that ex-Speaker Blaine's amendment gives an emphatic and unqualified negative to the latter proposition; and if Congress will propose, and the State Legislatures will ratify the amendment, that will be the end of all schemes for a division of school funds among religious sects.

III.

THE PROTESTANTS.

The term Protestant, used as a title of distinction from Catholics, applies to all the professedly Christian sects of this country. These sects may be regarded as forming one great body of religionists, in the aggregate more numerous and influential than the contrasted Catholic sect. Considered, however, relatively to each other, they are divided into several branches, or religious denominations—as Baptists, Congregationalists, Episcopalians, Lutherans, Methodists, Presbyterians, the Reformed Church in America, Unitarians, Universalists, and other smaller sects—all agreeing in being Protestants, as distinguished from Catholics, and yet thus divided, as the result of differences in doctrine or polity or both. They all claim the Christian name, and all profess to rest their religion, either wholly or in part, upon the authority of the Bible. Their number, their intelligence, their general standing as citizens, their Church wealth, their religious zeal, and their instrumental agencies for operating upon the thoughts of men, invest them with great power in reference to any public question. Taken as a whole, they unquestionably form the best and most useful portion of the American people. The religion, the moral influence for good, and the numerous charities of the land, are largely identified with their efforts.

There is one aspect of the School question in respect to which these Protestants march together as nearly a solid host. However much they may be divided among themselves, they are, with very few exceptions, an absolute unit in opposing the Catholic programme in regard to the public schools. Submit to them the question whether any portion of the school funds shall be placed in the hands of the Catholics for the support of their sectarian schools, or whether the public schools shall be so conducted as practically to be Catholic schools, or whether the school funds shall be divided *pro rata* among religious sects, according to the number of pupils taught in their respective denominational schools, and the overwhelming mass of Protestants would promptly reject each of these propositions. It is quite possible that some High-Church Episcopalians would accept the last proposition; yet the School question can be placed in no form that will be satisfactory to Catholics, without at once awakening the earnest and most intense opposition of the great majority of Protestants. While the latter are willing that the former should organize and conduct as many parochial or private schools as they choose to support, they are not willing to be taxed for any such purpose; and any political party that should place them in this position would be swept from power, at the very first opportunity. With some this opposition is largely a matter of anti-Catholic prejudice; but, with the more intelligent Protestants, it rests on the palpable inconsistency between what the Catholics desire and the whole genius and nature of our political institutions. Nothing can well be more certain than that the Catholics cannot Romanize our public schools or foist their own sectarian schools upon the State for support, as a general thing, unless they immensely increase the number of their voters. They are met at every point of the contest by a nearly-united opposing Protestantism. Here Protestants are of one mind, having little if any ground of debate among themselves.

When, however, we change the issue from the purely negative form of resistance to Catholics, and ask these Protestants to give us a positive scheme of their own, their unity and harmony very speedily disappear. The great mass of them may be conveniently arranged into three classes:—

1. A small number, as compared with the whole, take the ground (advocated by the Rev. John Miller, of Princeton, in a letter published in the New York *Tribune*, December 9th, 1875) that the whole system of State schools for popular education is a mistake; and that the true solution of the School question consists in dropping the system altogether, and remitting the entire business

to the family and such auxiliary agencies as it sees fit to employ. This was the view held by the late Gerrit Smith. The theoretical basis upon which it rests is that the education of children, especially in a democratic republic, does not lie within the normal functions of government at all. The constitution of things assigns this duty to the family; and the State might as well undertake to stand in *loco parentis* in respect to the discipline and government of children as to do so in reference to their education. Education is the proper work of parents, and not that of the State. This theory is supplemented by adding that education and religion cannot be separated, and that the moment the State attempts to give the former it necessarily becomes involved in the latter; that, on the whole it will be best for the State and best for the people to leave education to the family and to voluntary effort; and that the State cannot participate in the work without becoming entangled in the collisions and jealousies of religious sects, making itself more or less a party thereto, and perhaps doing injustice to some, if not all of them.

These are among the reasons assigned by this class of Protestants for abandoning the whole scheme of government education. The State has travelled beyond its proper sphere as really as it would if it should undertake to be a banker, a manufacturer, a merchant, a grocer, or a pedler; and by so doing it has gotten itself into difficulty and the people into difficulty. The remedy is to retire from the business, and let that alone which it should never have touched. The various sects will then settle the School question, just as they do all other questions of religious propagandism, and give the State no trouble on the subject. These views have so few advocates, as compared with the whole body of the people, that they scarcely enter at all into public discussion.

2. The second class of Protestants embraces those who believe that the State should have a system of popular education supported by general taxation, and managed exclusively by its own authority; and that the system should be rigidly confined to the secular sphere of knowledge, leaving religious instruction and worship to be attended to by other agencies. Those who adopt this view deny that education and religion, so far as the former comes within the province of the State, are inseparable; and they also deny that an American State, founded in its government not on the principle of theocracy, but on that of a representative democracy, can properly have anything to do with teaching, regulating, controlling, or patronizing any or all of the different systems of religion which may be embraced or practiced by its citizens. On this subject they sweep the whole deck of all forms of State religion, and plant themselves upon the doctrine of an absolute and unqualified divorce of the State from things spiritual. They are *secularists* in

respect to the ends and functions of civil government—as much so as they are in respect to the ends and functions of a bank corporation or a railroad company: and they are equally secularists in regard to the purposes and, hence, the management of the public schools. The State, in their view, cannot pass beyond its sphere here without a self-contradiction.

The exact number of Protestants who take this ground it is not possible to tell; yet the view is widely held by the membership of the professedly Protestant sects in this country. The discussion of the School question, within the last twenty years, has added largely to the number of its advocates. Many of the religious papers and most of the secular papers of the country support the view, as impartially just to all parties, and the only thing that is so.

3. The third class embraces those Protestants who, while they believe in the necessity and wisdom of State education, and also utterly protest against the Catholic programme in respect to the public schools, nevertheless, insist upon the reading of the Bible in these schools, without note or comment, as one of the standard exercises thereof, and would be glad to supplement this reading by opening the schools with prayer and the singing of a religious hymn. The Bible-reading is the main thing which they demand. By this they mean the reading not of the Douay version, used by the Cath-

olics, and not the version made some years since by a portion of the Baptists, but King James's version of the Old and New Testament, in common use among Protestants. This is the Bible about which they are talking, and upon which they concentrate their zeal.

And, inasmuch as they belong to different sects—some of them being Presbyterians, others Congregationalists, others Methodists, others Baptists, and so on through the whole list—and, still further, inasmuch as they cannot agree as to any system of special teaching out of the Bible and upon its authority, or cannot trust the Bible-reader to expound and enforce those views upon which they are agreed, they compromise this matter among themselves by agreeing that the Bible shall be read without note or comment. Read it must be; but explained and applied it must not be, lest perchance the latter should in some way be tinged with a specific sectarian proclivity, to the advantage or disadvantage of some one or more of these sects. If, for example, a Baptist teacher and reader should attempt to make the Bible teach immersion by putting upon it the Baptist construction, or an Episcopal teacher and reader should seek to make it teach apostolical succession, or a High Churchman should undertake to make it teach a system of ritualism, it would not be long before these advocates of Bible-reading in the public schools would be at serious odds with each other. Any such experiment would give rise to a new School question. The only thing to which these Protestants can agree is the *bald* and naked act of reading, without any verbal comment that will touch a single one of their denominational peculiarities. And, since the book read is non-sectarian as between *them*, so also this reading process as between *them* is and must be non-sectarian.

This statement is not made for the purpose of caricature, and certainly not for that of offense. We simply mean squarely to state the position of these Protestants, without the slightest impeachment of their motives. Many of them rank among the theological and religious lights of the land. They hold the doctrine, and they hold it earnestly, that the reading of King James's version of the Sacred Scriptures, without note or comment, should be a daily exercise in all the public schools of the country. They protest against the exclusion of this use of *this* Bible from these schools. This they have done over and over again as individuals, and by the resolutions and deliverances of ecclesiastical bodies representing their views. They form by no means a small and insignificant portion of those who belong to the various Protestant sects, if they do not constitute an actual majority.

We design hereafter to examine the merits of this view somewhat at large; and, hence, now content ourselves with the single remark that these Protestants *substantially ask for themselves in respect to the public schools what they deny to Catho-*

lics. They would not for a moment consent to substitute the Douay version for that of King James. Make the substitution, and they would very generally demand the expulsion of *that* Bible. The Bible upon which they insist is the one which Catholics regard as the *Protestant* Bible, and which certainly is such in its use. Now, do they not know that this Bible to the Catholic and the infidel is a sectarian book, as really as the Westminster Catechism or the Prayer-Book of the Episcopal Church ; and that the New Testament portion of it is a sectarian book to the Jew ? This is the fact ; and they ought to have the consideration to see it, and the candor to admit it. King James's version is all very well for *them*, since they are agreed in accepting it ; but it is not so for these other parties, who are taxed in common with them for the support of public schools, and who under our theory of government have just as many and just as sacred rights as they have in these schools. The very terms of their doctrine commit them to a species of self-preference in the schools of the State, which they claim for themselves, but will not concede to anybody else. Whether they are in favor of Bible-reading depends upon *what* Bible is to be read. Let the Catholic select the book to be read, and then he will favor the reading of that book ; and this in principle is precisely the doctrine of these Protestants. The religious *meum* and *tuum* in this matter form a very significant part of the whole question.

It so happens, too, that, outside of Protestants and Catholics, there is a large body of citizens who have their peculiar religious notions, represented by neither, yet who are voters and taxpayers. There are Jews, Swedenborgians, Shakers, Spiritualists, Deists, Pantheists, Positivists, Atheists, and multitudes who can hardly be said to have any settled faith on religious subjects. All these people are citizens, belonging to the State, if they do not to the Church ; and they have as much proprietorship and right in the common school as the most devout Christian, whether he be Catholic or Protestant. The public school is the common property of the *whole* people, and not exclusively of any portion of them. The argument to show that no Christian should be taxed to support infidelity is just as good to show that no Deist should be taxed to support Christianity, unless we adopt the theory that one of the functions of civil government is to decide what religion is true, and then provide for its maintenance.

The discussion of the School question, as the reader will readily see from the simple statement of it, draws within its own circle the great question of the ages. It involves the whole subject of the province of civil government, considered in relation to religion. In the principles relating to it, and by which it is to be determined, it is one of the most elementary and far-reaching questions of human society. If the State may properly undertake the work of religious propagandism *anywhere* or at any point of its action, then it may, in its discretion, do so *everywhere.* If religion comes within its sphere, then it has as much right to establish a State religion, and to teach and enforce it, as it has to establish a State prison for convicts. If we concede the principle, we must accept its consequences. The extent to which it shall be exercised is simply a matter of legal discretion. Dr. Ralph Wardlaw declares that "the province of the State in respect to matters of religion is that it has *no province at all*"; and if we adopt this view, then we must accept its consequences.

IV.

THE SCHOOL PROBLEM.

The attitude of religious sects, especially the Catholics and a portion of the Protestants, in respect to the public schools of this country, creates the necessity of inquiring in what way the difficulties that beset the system can be best solved.

One solution of the problem is to abandon the system altogether and remit the whole work of education to private and voluntary effort. The great objection to this view is that the remedy is far worse than the disease. The country can much more safely get along with the sectarian quarrel about the public school, if there must be such a quarrel, than it can without the school. Popular education in some form, gratuitously afforded and managed by the State, has so many advantages, meets so large a sphere of wants, rests on so broad an experience of its utility, and is so intimately identified with the perpetuity, safety, and success of our republican institutions, that its total abandonment is not a thing to be thought of for a moment. Such a course, by involving a vast reduction of educational opportunities and entirely withdrawing them from a large number of the poorer classes, would be practically equivalent to a plan for lessening general intelligence. The statement of the idea supplies its own refutation. The necessity and wisdom of public schools are as thoroughly established in the convictions of the American people as the doctrine of liberty itself. The system is virtually a part of the doctrine. We, hence, spend no time in proving that it ought not to be abandoned in order to escape from the difficulties which attend its continuance.

A second solution of the problem, strongly urged by the Catholics and favored by some Protestants, is the distribution of the public school money, either the whole or a part of it, among religious sects, to be used by them for the support of their own denominational and sectarian schools. This idea is totally inconsistent with the public school system as at present organized, and would in the end prove its destruction. Moreover, it would be exceedingly difficult, if not wholly impracticable, to make the distribution according to equity. How much should the Catholics receive? The number of children taught by them would not answer this question, since it would be no index to the tax paid by them, especially when we remember that the great majority of them pay no taxes at all. Their tax contribution is all that they could justly claim, unless it is proposed to educate their children in the Catholic faith with funds derived from other sources. The plan would add to the cost of education by an unnecessary increase of machinery, would lessen its opportunities in sparsely settled districts, and would almost certainly make the education inferior to that given in the public schools, with the single exception of the religious element. If the principle of distribution is good for Catholics, then it would be equally so for all the other sects; and if generally adopted, the public school would disappear altogether. So also the whole tendency of such a plan would be toward the disintegration, and not the unification of the American people, by planting elements of antipathy, antagonism and religious bigotry in the bosoms of children, unfriendly to the interests and duties of a common citizenship in after years. And, finally, the State through its taxing power would become the supporter and patron of religious sectarianism, and compel the people indiscriminately to pay the expenses thereof.

The proper answer to this distribution theory is a plump and unqualified negative. The money raised by general taxation belongs to all the people, and the State through its own agents should control its uses to the last dollar. It should open its schools to all children of suitable age, free of charge; and if Catholics or Protestants choose to have their children educated elsewhere, then this is their business, and not that of the State. The plea that they are thus subjected to a double taxation, and, hence, that the State ought either to give them a portion of the school money or omit to tax them for school purposes, is false. Their self-imposed burdens for sectarian purposes are not taxation at all, and no reason for tax exemption. They choose to have it so, and, hence, they must patiently take the consequences. The State might just as well exempt those from taxation who for other than religious reasons choose to send their children to private schools at their own expense. The general public surely cannot abandon or modify a good system to suit sectarian necessities or proclivities. The system should have in it no just ground of objection; and then it should be firmly maintained, whether Catholics or Protestants like it or dislike it.

A third plan is that of a *supplementary* system of religious teaching, added to the public school, by classifying the children according to the faith of their parents and giving the instruction, not in the regular school hours, but at a special period set apart for this service, either before or after these hours. We do not see that this mends matters at all, since the real difficulty is not with the *time* of giving religious instruction, but with giving it *at all* in connection with any school which the State controls and the people support by general taxation. The State, in its school system, has nothing to do with the hours which precede or those which succeed the regular period assigned for the application and use of that system, and, hence, should make no arrangement with religious sects in respect to them. If Catholic or Protestant or Jewish parents want to have their children instructed in their respective creeds, then let them attend to this business in their own way, and at their own time ; yet let them not attempt to make the State a party either to the process itself, or to the character of the instruction. If the State is to go into the business of religious and sectarian instruction at all, then let it do so openly, without any indirection, and not shove it into a corner.

A fourth plan is to establish schools by law, and then remit the whole question of religious teaching, as to kind, quantity, and method, to the several school districts, leaving each district to decide for itself by a majority vote. If Protestants have the majority in a given district, then the school would be Protestant ; and if Catholics have the majority, then the school would be Catholic. So, if Infidels form the majority, they might make the deism of Thomas Paine the religion of the school, and use his "Age of Reason" as the text-book for teaching it. All must be taxed in each district, and the local majority is empowered to decide what and how much religion shall be taught, and to its decree the State affixes the seal of public authority.

What, then, is this school district? Simply a small division of the State—a creature of State power, exercising such powers and such only as the State sees fit to confer. Were the School question remitted to such districts, or to the towns, villages, or cities of the State, the Legislature would abdicate all direct control over it. This would settle nothing and establish no general policy. If the whole people as represented in the Legislature, cannot wisely dispose of the subject, is there any prospect that the people acting in these divisions of the State will be able to do so? The plan would beget animosities and strifes in the school districts and lead to a general war of sects over the public schools. The stronger sect or sects would prevail, and the weaker would have to succumb to their views. In some places the school would be stamped with Catholicism, and in others it would be distinctively Protestant, and might be Presbyterian or Methodist or Baptist in its specific type; and whatever it was in its religious and sectarian character, it would be such by the authority of the State. Catholics, when in the minority, would be taxed to support Protestant schools; and Protestants, when in the same position, would be taxed to support Catholic schools; and it is possible that, in some cases, both would be taxed to support Infidel schools. The actual result would be the virtual support of some kind of religion or some species of infidelity, under the sanction of State authority. The School war, so far from being terminated, would go on with increased intensity and bitterness. The question is one that belongs to each State as a whole; and we are persuaded that nothing is to be gained by remitting it, as an undetermined problem, to its minor divisions, and leaving each division to adopt its own mode of settlement. There should be some general law as to the management of public schools, applicable to the whole, and governing all its parts.

If, then, these four plans for solving the School problem should be rejected, what shall be done? The answer of a certain class of Protestants is that the reading of King James's version of the Sacred Scriptures as an opening exercise, either with or without prayer and religious singing, is the proper thing to be done, provided that the reading be without note or comment; and this is a fifth solution of the problem. To this the Jew objects, alleging that the New Testament part of this version is not true, and that he does not want to have his children taught religious error. The Catholic also objects, declaring that the version is not only not correct, but is a Protestant version and adapted to promote Protestantism, and that he does not wish to have his children taught in the Protestant faith. The Infidel also objects, saying that the whole version is a mass of fictions ; and that he ought not to be taxed to support religious superstitions, and that the public school for which he is taxed ought to be available for his children, without this objection.

All these objectors happen to be citizens of the State in which they reside, and under our political system they stand upon the same level with Protestants. They share in the burdens of government and are amenable to its laws. The State of which they are citizens, considered as a civil power, existing and acting for temporal purposes, is no more Protestant than it is Catholic, and no more Christian than it is Jewish or Mohammedan. It is simply a *political* body ; and, as such, it has no religion to teach or sustain or compel the people to sustain. Such is the essential character of an American State ; and such it should be, since it is only by this feature that the rights of conscience in respect to religion are guaranteed against encroachment. The objection, therefore, of the Catholic, the Jew, and the Infidel against any Protestant *régime* in the public school is a valid one, and admits of no answer unless we abandon the fundamental principles of our republican system. It is as much an act of tyranny and wrong to tax a Catholic or a Jew to support a religion in which he does not believe as it is to apply the same principle to a

Protestant. There is essentially no difference in the two cases. Mere numbers can never make a difference, unless religious liberty is a question of numbers, which is not the fact.

Discarding, then, as we must, by the stern demands of logic and, as we believe, by the demands of a true religion, this fifth solution of the School problem, we still press the question: What shall the State do? But one answer is left, and that answer constitutes the sixth solution, which is the one we adopt and describe as follows:—

The State, by which we mean the people acting in their organic capacity through the machinery of law, should say to all the religious sects, to all anti-religionists, and indeed to all classes of citizens, that its ground as to the public schools is the one of absolute and impartial "neutrality" with reference to the doctrines and tenets of religion, whether drawn from the Bible or elsewhere; that the ends for which it exists do not include such doctrines and tenets, either as a means or an end; and that the only aspect in which it can consider Protestants, Catholics, Jews, Rationalists, Infidels, indeed, every man, woman, and child subject to its jurisdiction, is simply that of citizenship, without any discrimination for religious reasons. The public school is not a Church, or a synagogue, or a theological seminary; but a piece of State machinery, organized and supported for purely temporal ends —as really as a court of justice, a constitutional convention, or a legislative body. Its function is not to make or unmake Christians, or predispose children to this or that form of religious faith. It does not propose a *complete* education ; and does not propose a *religious* education at all, either partial or complete. It proposes to do a certain thing, on the ground of its necessity and utility to the State, and to stop there, by not entering that field which lies beyond the purview of civil government. In short, it proposes a *secular* education, and that only—an education that would be needful and useful in this life, if there were no God and no future for the human soul.

This we believe to be the true ground on which to place a school system organized and conducted by the authority of an American State. It is the proper language of the State to the Catholic, and just as proper to the Protestant, the Jew, or the Infidel. It is the one answer to be given to everybody who asks the State to use its school system for any other purpose than that of *secular* education. To all such claimants and all such petitioners the State should turn a deaf ear, and confine its system of education within the limits of the ends for which it exists as a State. They should all be practically taught that the State will protect them in the exercise of their religious liberty, and will not on the subject of religion extend its agency the breadth of a hair beyond this point.

The general argument on which this doctrine

rests will be presented in its proper place. Yet it may be well here to say that the objections to the doctrine urged by those who dissent from it, when traced to their final application, are simply objections to *the system of government* which the American people have chosen to adopt and under which they are now living. The objectors, in effect, find fault with the theory of a State that has no religious creed to teach, support, or enforce. Their argument, if good at all, is good to rehabilitate the machinery and prerogatives of a state religion. They really object to the American doctrine of a State. We do not; but heartily accept it as true, being willing, without qualification or reservation, to extend it to all its legitimate applications. As a Protestant and a Presbyterian, we have no objection to the reading of King James's version of the Sacred Scriptures in the public schools, and should have none to the teaching of the "Shorter Catechism" there, regarding it as a most excellent compendium of Christian doctrine; yet, as an American citizen, taxed in common with all others for the support of these schools, we ask for no such tribute to our faith in distinction from the faith of the Catholic or the Rationalist, and concede no such claim to any religious sect or creed.

The Supreme Court of Maine, in the case of Donohue *vs.* Richards (38 Maine Reports, p. 401), expressly rejected the idea that Christianity, before the law, is entitled to any higher or other privileges than those that are common to "the Pagan and the Mormon, the Brahmin and the Jew, the Swedenborgian and the Buddhist, the Catholic and the Quaker." This is simply carrying out the American theory of civil government by an impartial application of its principles. Those who are not willing that an American State should occupy this position either do not understand the theory of such a State or are not content to abide by its fundamental doctrine.

V.

SECULAR EDUCATION.

Bishop Butler remarks that "the constitution of human creatures, and, indeed, of all creatures that come under our notice, is such as that they are capable of naturally becoming qualified for states of life for which they were once wholly unqualified." This presents the fundamental law of human improvement. The first and for a considerable period the only form of its action we find in the nursery, where infant children gain that stock of information and those mental and physical aptitudes by which they become miniature men and women. Speedily they quit the nursery and enter upon the sterner and more methodical task of a higher culture. What meets them in the outset is *common* education, in distinction from academic, collegiate, literary, or professional. The great mass of them stop with this, and for their sphere it is sufficient. A common education is such as the average man needs for daily use in the average work of life. More would be no disadvantage to him; yet he has not time to obtain it, and also do the other things which must be done according to his programme of existence.

It is the specific function of the public school, organized and supported by the State, to meet these graduates from the nursery with the facilities for a common preparatory education before they become men and women, and, indeed, before they acquire those special arts the prosecution of which is to be the business of their after-lives. The public school is just what its name imports—a public school, a school to give a certain amount of education to all the children of the land that have reached and not exceeded the appropriate age. It does not support these children, or divorce them from home government, or in any way supersede or disturb the *régime* of the family; but it does take the daily charge of their education during a certain number of allotted hours, and during these hours places them under the discipline and government of the school teacher. It thus comes to the aid of the family, and supplies what without it in a large number of cases would not be supplied at all.

The State, appreciating the importance of such

education to the general community, deems it a just and needful exercise of its power to devise a system for this purpose, to establish school-boards, to build school houses, to hire teachers, to adopt certain general rules in application to the subject, and charge the cost thereof to the people by compulsory taxation. Most of the States of this Union have such a system. The constitutions of some of the States make it the duty of their respective Legislatures to establish common schools, and in no state is the power denied to the Legislature thereof. The system is a State system ; and, however much the General Government may be profited thereby, it has nothing to do with it and no control over it. Any interference with it or attempt to regulate it by the authority of Congress would be simply an act of legislative usurpation, because without any warrant in the Constitution of the United States. Whether the schools shall be what are called "mixed schools," or separate schools, in which different races shall be educated separately, is a matter for each State to determine in the exercise of its own discretion.

As to the *quantity* and *quality* of the education thus provided for, it is conceded on all hands that at the very least, it should embrace reading, writing, spelling, arithmetic, and grammar. These are the branches of knowledge which the people have most occasion to use. To them the State may, according to the scope of its policy, add other branches—as geography, history (especially of the United States), natural philosophy, physiology, book-keeping, the lower grades of mathematics, the system of American jurisprudence in its general principles, and perhaps the simpler forms of mental and moral science. Precisely how near the common school should come to the higher academy and the college is an interesting and important question of public policy; but it is not the question in dispute among religious sects.

The public school, by the very terms of both the process and the end, naturally and necessarily involves the element of *moral* education. The children form a society for the time being, and for that time the school-house is their dwelling place. In it they spend their school-hours, in constant intercourse with their teachers and subject to their authority. These teachers, if what they should be, are discreet and well-behaved persons, having a good moral character, cleanly in their habits, pure and chaste in their language, and honest and upright in their discipline. It is their province to preserve school order, to subject their scholars to wholesome restraints, to commend and encourage them when they do well, to condemn and rebuke them when they do wrong, to see to it that they accomplish their task; and thus develop in this theater a set of *school* virtues, in the habits of patience, diligence, industry, steadiness of application, submission to authority, respect for superiors and for the rights of each other, cleanliness of person, good manners, self-control, truthfulness, honesty, and the like—habits which in kind have their basis and sanction in our moral nature, and which, moreover, are just the habits to fit and dispose them to act well their part in maturer years. These virtues are State virtues, social virtues, business virtues, and are also in constant demand for the purposes of this life, independently of any considerations that respect the future, and may be powerfully enforced by arguments that relate purely to the interests of time. They are certainly good for this world, and good for citizenship, whether there be any hereafter or not.

Such elementary moral principles have existed in human thought and to some extent in human practice, wherever man has been found. They attach themselves to his nature and relations. They are not peculiar to Christendom or Christianity; but rather belong to man *as man.* His depravity has never sunk so low as to involve their total absence. Christianity fosters these virtues and begets others of a higher grade; but it is a grave mistake to suppose that those who administer Christianity, repeat its precepts, teach its doctrines, and preach its sanctions, whether in the pulpit or out of it, are the only apostles of morality in the world, or that they have any exclusive monopoly in this kind of teaching. This is not true, never has been, and never will be true.

Morality, in the large sense, is a spontaneous outgrowth of human nature and human relations, notwithstanding the terrible depravity that has infected the race. It is a thing of home, of the street, of the public lecture, of business intercourse, of the State, of the court-room, of the jury-box, of the school-room—yea, of the ten thousand influences that operate in the formation of the human character—as really as it is of the ministry or the Church. The State itself is a moral teacher, by legislative enactment and judicial administration. There is a generic morality, whose usefulness no one questions, that comes within the province of the public school, just as really as do the spiritualities and higher sanctions of religion come within that of the ministry and the Church; and to it nobody objects, whatever may be his religious creed. For the want of a better term, let us call it *secular* morality—a morality that has its basis in the natural dictates of conscience and its direct sphere in the relations and actualities of the present life. Any theological creed that cannot see it needs reforming. It is certainly the kind of morality which the State is immensely concerned to secure; which makes the orderly, the peaceful, and law-abiding citizen; and which also forms one of the primary objects and great blessings of the public school.

We give this outline sketch as a definition of what we mean by a common school *secular education.* It is not religious in the sense of relating to

God or the duties we owe to him, or of affirming or resting upon the authority of the Bible, or adopting or denying any specific system of religious belief. It is just what it is—*secular* education—and as such distinct from the dogmas of religious sects, whether true or false. It omits to consider these dogmas, just as chemistry does not determine mathematical questions and as political economy does not discuss any theory in geology. It is neither Protestant nor Catholic, heterodox nor orthodox, Christian nor Pagan, because the matters indicated by these terms do not come within its scope.

The public school, as the instrumentality of an American State, whose creature it is and for whose purposes and by whose authority it exists, is sufficiently explained and justified by being patterned after the State. There is nothing in it more dreadful than there is in the State itself. If the people can be content to live under the one, they ought to be content with the other. In having no religious system to teach and in denying no such system it fairly represents the State—not the Christian or the Infidel, the Protestant or the Catholic ; but a State that in its organic being has no religious creed and no rule or form of worship. It is all that such a State can make it in consistency with its fundamental principles. A theocratic State might go further ; but a democratic State cannot, without self-contradiction.

But it is objected that this is not a *complete*

education, since it does not include religion. Who ever said that it was so? No system of education is absolutely complete. Neither the pulpit nor the Sabbath-school furnishes such a system, since neither teaches all which it is desirable to know. Education involves a division of labor, and no system undertakes to comprehend every possible kind of knowledge. The incompleteness of the secular education of the public school is no objection to it that would not equally apply to that of the sanctuary or the theological seminary. Though not complete, it is certainly good as far as it goes.

Again, it is said that such a system, by not including religious teaching, omits the most *important* part of education. This is true, and equally true of every system that does not include religion. The transcendent importance of religious education does not prove it to be either necessary or wise to combine such education at the same time and by the same agency with every other process of educational culture. A young man may very properly study book-keeping, without at the same time studying the Catechism, or going through the discipline of the Sabbath-school. We see no just objection to an arrangement which assigns the teaching of arithmetic to the schoolmaster, and leaves religious teaching to other agencies. The schoolmaster has not the entire charge of the children, and certainly does not undertake their *entire* education. The fact that he teaches what is secular does not preclude others from teaching what is distinctively religious; and it does not in any way imply that the latter, our whole existence being taken into the account, is not far more important than the former. The importance of things spiritual, as compared with things temporal, supplies no reason why the State should give its attention to the former in the public school system that would not be equally pertinent to show that it should give the same attention in the Church system. This, indeed, is one of the old arguments for Church and State which the people of this country profess to have outgrown. It may be (in the sequel of this discussion we expect to show the fact) that things spiritual lie outside of State jurisdiction altogether; and that civil government is not an agency fitted to take charge of them, and cannot do so without more evil than benefit. And if this be a fact, then the importance of these things does not bring them within the purview of the State at all.

We are again told that a school system confined to secular instruction is "godless" and "irreligious." There is a sense in which this is true, and in that sense there is nothing in the objection. A merchant makes out a bill for the sale of goods to his customer, with not a word about religion in it. That is a "godless" bill, in the negative sense. A young man attends a medical school, and there hears nothing about theology. That is a "godless" school, in the same sense. So one listens to a lecture on astronomy, in which no reference is made to God. That is a "godless" lecture. A boy works eight hours per day in a factory, in which no religious instruction is given. That is a "godless" factory. So a child goes to the public school, and while there is exclusively occupied with secular branches, and not religious studies at all. That is a "godless" school in the same and in no other sense.

The impression, however, meant to be conveyed by the terms "godless" and "irreligious," when applied to the secular public school, is that the school is *anti-religious,* and must be so unless it makes religious teaching one of its functions. In this sense the statement is utterly and absolutely false, unless the religion had in view be of a kind that will not stand the test of popular enlightenment; and, if so, the sooner the world gets rid of it the better. So far from being hostile to *true* religion, the secular culture which the child gains in the public school, the power to read and understand the meaning of words, the discipline of the intellectual faculties, the increased grasp and activity of mind, and the moral habits there acquired, not only place no impediment in the way of religious teaching, but actually prepare the mind for it, by supplying important conditions, if intelligence is favorable to religion. The drill of the day-school is a very good drill for that of the Church and the Sabbath-school. It is by no means certain that the latter will not be more profitably and successfully performed by not being combined and mixed up with the routine of the former. Be this as it may, the public school is no enemy to true religion, because teaching religion is not made one of its objects.

We see, then, nothing in a purely secular system of education, established and conducted by the State and modeled after the type of its own organic life, that should create the slightest alarm in any reasonable mind. Ignorance, bigotry, sectarianism, intense ecclesiasticism, and a domineering priestcraft may lift up their hands in holy horror ; yet a sober common sense, serenely, if not pitifully, contemplates the spectacle. Must an American State change its essential nature to accommodate religious fanatics? Must it virtually become a theocracy, and that, too, by no higher authority than that of the people, in order not to be the enemy of God ? Is religion such an article that it is put in jeopardy by the acquisition of knowledge in respect to things temporal ? Does it harm religion, to teach children to read, to cipher, to reason, to practice good manners, to deport themselves well in school hours, and submit to school discipline and authority? Does this impair the power of the Church, or that of the family, or interfere with the zeal and success of those who choose to embark in the work of religious instruction according to their own methods, at their own charges, and in conformity with their own ideas of truth ?

Those who are suspicious that an educational system which simply does *not* teach religion, but for sufficient reasons leaves it to be taught elsewhere, is and must be hostile to religion, pay a very poor compliment to the thing they are so anxious to preserve. Those who think that the public school must be "irreligious" in the bad sense if it has not the Bible, or the Catechism, or both in it, must also think an American State to be "irreligious" in the bad sense because it has no Bible or Catechism in its fundamental organization, and, hence, makes no distinction among its citizens on any religious ground. The effectual way for them to cure the difficulty is to reform the State, and thus strike at the evil in its source, by producing a theological or theocratic State. Religious teaching, by its authority, would then be in order; and so also the destruction of individual religious liberty would be in order. The hanging of witches would be in order. The religious persecutions of the Dark Ages would be in order. Every man ought to thank God that our political system does not provide for this kind of order.

VI.

RELIGIOUS TEACHING BY THE STATE.

Religion, considered as a communicable system, consists in a body of beliefs or forms of thought whose objective center is God. As an experimental system it consists in the emotions and affections awakened and sustained by these ideas or beliefs. As a practical system it consists in the embodiment of both elements in outward action. Thoughts first, emotions and affections next, and outward action last—such is the order of nature in respect to religion. The power of the religious teacher lies mainly, if not exclusively, in the first of these categories. He cannot awaken emotion or affection, or influence action, except by using the ideas which supply the occasion for both. The thoughts which he transfers constitute his means of religiously impressing others.

Such a teacher must, of course, have something to teach—something which he knows or thinks he knows, at any rate, believes; and this something, be it more or less, true or false, is his creed in regard to God, and the duties which men owe to him. Religious teaching, measurable by no standard, analyzable into no elements, and definable by no quantity or quality, is merely a name. Something must be taught, or there is no teaching. This something must be in the teacher's mind; and, in order not to be a deceiver, he must himself believe it. He ought to be, at least, a decent illustration of his own creed, since otherwise he will practically contradict it. Irreligious, immoral, and profane teachers handling the things of godliness present an incongruity which human nature declines to fellowship. Hypocrites succeed only by not being known.

If, then, the *State*, in its corporate capacity and in addition to the other things which it must do, undertakes the work of religious teaching, whether in the public school or elsewhere, it must comply with the conditions of the process. One of these conditions is a creed of doctrinal beliefs adopted by the State as the basis and guide of the instruction to be given under its patronage and direction. A State without a creed, seeking to do the work which demands a creed, is an absurdity. What shall the creed be? The State is the only party that can authoritatively answer this question. It so happens that the term religion is a word of many meanings as to the ideas indicated by it. The State must, hence, give a specific import to the term, and thus define its own religion; and, in order not to be a trifler, it must fix upon that religion which it holds to be true, and upon this bestow its sanction. The State surely should not propagate heresy; and, since there are many heresies in the world, it must separate the wheat from the chaff, rejecting the latter and using only the former in its educational system. Let us have sound doctrine from the lips of the State through its legally authorized teacher.

If, for example, the theology of the Bible, taken as a whole, be that which the State adopts, then let its ideas be made a living and practical power in its educational system. Let the work be done effectually. And, to this end, let the legal agent of the State be commanded to teach the religion of the State as found in the Bible ; to catechise the children in the name and by the authority of the State ; and employ all the forces of the living voice and the active mind to impress its ideas upon their hearts. There surely can be no just objection to this course, provided the work belongs to the State. Never mind the disputes among religious sects, since the Bible, being adopted by the State, is the State book on the subject of religion, and to it on this subject the infallible rule of State faith and State practice. The State, for its own purposes, has decided that this book contains the true religion, and also what version is the true translation of the original Scriptures. And now, having settled these points, it should not hesitate to wield the power of the book to the fullest extent. To limit the teacher to the mere reading of the Bible, without comment and without any explanation, is to aim at the minimum rather than the maximum of power. No such practice is adopted in teaching arithmetic or grammar ; and no such practice should be adopted in teaching religion, provided it be the purpose of the State to do the work in the best manner. If the work is to be done at all, let it be well done.

And then again, the selection of proper teachers to do this work is quite as important as the creed to be taught. These teachers should be *orthodox* according to the standards of the State, not only well versed in the secular branches of knowledge, but competent teachers, and at least respectable examples of the religion of the State which they are expected to teach. And, to guard against any mistake on this point, they should be thoroughly examined by a board of State theologians, not only as to their general competency and character, but also as to their religious and doctrinal views, especially as to their understanding and acceptance of the religious creed of the State, and their aptness to explain and apply this creed ; and no one should be appointed to the service who upon such an examination is found deficient. No ecclesiastical body will put its seal upon a candidate for the ministry whose theology does not substantially accord with its own. And surely the State can follow no better rule in appointing its teachers of religion. If the religion of the State be Protestantism in its generic sense, or in any of its sectarian senses, then let the teachers be selected in accordance with this idea. So if the religion of the State be Roman Catholicism, then Roman Catholics, and these only, are the proper persons to be appointed.

Dissenters who form the minority are not to be heard or considered in this matter. Indeed, they ought not to exist at all ; and if they will exist, the best that they can expect is mere toleration, provided they are peaceable. The State in its sovereign capacity has a will and a religion of its own, and with both the majority coincides. The minority may be taxed to help pay expenses; but its views must bow to those of the majority, both as to the doctrines taught and as to the persons teaching them. The minority, of course, cannot expect to furnish the teachers, any more than a defeated political party can expect offices. Dissenters are not orthodox; and this is a good reason why they should not be trusted with the theology of the State, in the pulpit, in the public school, or anywhere else.

There is not the slightest objection to these procedures on the part of the State, provided always that the work assumed to be undertaken by it, comes within its province. To treat the idea of religious teaching in its school system as one of great importance; to magnify it in sermons, essays, editorials, and speeches; then in practice to shrink from its vigorous application, and shear it down to the smallest significance for the sake of dodging the jealousies of religious sects; thus to make but little of the idea except in public discussions about it: this is not at all our notion of teaching religion by State authority. If we are to have the thing, then let us *have* it, with the right sort of doctrines, with the right sort of teachers, with no heretics among them, and in a manner and to a degree worthy of the State and worthy of the thing itself. Let the State put honor upon the office whose duties it assumes and professes to perform. Ecclesiastical bodies, from the local church up to the highest judicatory, are wont to be careful and circumspect as to doctrines and teachers; and for this they are to be commended. Should not the State, having a theological doctrine for its educational system, be equally careful and circumspect? Indifferentism poorly becomes a State that has a theological creed to administer and propagate; and as a matter of history, it has seldom been chargeable with this kind of delinquency.

These statements, the reader may be assured, are not made for mere sarcasm. We write precisely as we think. Concede the principle that religion, either as an end or a means, falls properly within the administrative agency of the State, and the inference is irresistible that the State must have a religion to administer; that it must determine what that religion shall be; and that it must and should appoint suitable persons to do the executive part of the work. We have no difficulty with the natural and necessary modes of making the principle effective—none whatever—since they result from it by inevitable sequence. Nor have we any scruples about the so-called rights of dissentient minorities, since there are no such rights, provided the principle be a sound one. They have no right to be talking about the rights of conscience against the just exercise of the powers of the State. They are by the very terms of the case mere grumblers. The administration of religion being one of the functions of the State, then the

State must, of course, follow its own conscience, just as it does when it hangs a murderer; and the individual who, on the score of his private conscience, gets in the way of the State conscience, must get out of the way or be crushed by it. He has no right to arrest or control the action of the State conscience with his private judgment, since the former is only exercising its legitimate powers and discharging its duty. It is a mere farce to talk about the rights of an individual and unofficial conscience against the operations of a government that is acting within the scope of its appropriate powers. There can be no such rights in consistency with the existence of government. Where a government has jurisdiction it must judge of its own duties. Grant that religion comes within this jurisdiction, and that is the end of the question. The procedures in asserting and exercising it follow as a matter of course.

Our great difficulty with the doctrine of those who demand that the State shall become a religious propagandist in its school system is with the *principle* that lies at its bottom, and not at all with the details of its execution, however stringent or seemingly severe, provided they are necessary to the end. Their doctrine logically commits them to the principle of State jurisdiction and State duties in respect to things spiritual; and if they refuse to accept the consequences, no matter whether they are Protestants or Catholics, then they are afraid of their own creed. If, on the other hand, they carry out the principle and make it a living and operative power, and not a mere sham for the sake of appearances, then, alas! for the real rights of conscience and the liberties of men, they land us, body and soul, into the system of *State religion*—namely, religion defined by the State, taught by the State, supported as a charge upon its treasury, and if necessary, penally enforced by the State. This is all very well for *them*, since they always assume their religion and that of the State to be identical. How would it be if the fact were just the reverse? This question bigotry, whether in a Catholic or a Protestant bosom, seldom has time to consider. When Protestant and Puritan New England hung witches and persecuted Quakers, and when Roger Williams was banished from his home on pain of death, things moved along very finely for the religionists in power; but not as smoothly with the victims of their mistaken and maddened zeal. The principle upon which these religionists acted, being conceded and developed, with no limitations except those furnished by itself, sets the State to doing a thing which does not belong to it and which, if it be true to its own position, will be sure to make it a persecuting power.

Macaulay well says that "the experience of many ages proves that men may be ready to fight to the death and to persecute without pity for a religion whose creed they do not understand, and whose precepts they habitually disobey." Many a dark chapter in history confirms the truth of this remark. The moment religion is in any way armed with the civil power the fatal step is taken.

We deny the rightfulness of the power in this connection by entering a universal demurrer to its action. We deny that the State has the right to tax the Jew to propagate Christianity, or to make Infidels help to liquidate the expense account of a religion which they repudiate. We place this denial on the broad ground that religion in itself, in its very nature, in the processes of its culture and promotion, in its relations to God and the interests of another life, lies above and beyond the jurisdiction of the State, unless God himself has constituted that State. The State is not an exhorter or a persuader or a debating club, but a positive law power for secular purposes; and, hence, when it attempts to administer religion it must of necessity give to it the law force, deciding what religion is true and by what methods it shall be promoted. There is no escape from this result if we admit the principle from which it springs; and, the principle being true, then the result is right. If religious teaching is really one of the proper functions of the State, then all that is necessary to the end, of which the State itself must be the judge, is included therein. Moreover, the implications of the function need only to be fully drawn out to cover the whole ground of State religion, with all its ways and means.

To the authority of the State when acting within its appropriate sphere every citizen should cheerfully bow, supporting it, if necessary, by the sword. If it be a democratic State, the will of the majority, legally expressed, should be the rule for the whole. But when the State engages in the work of religious teaching, whether in the public school or elsewhere, and does the things which must be done to realize the end, then it not only disowns the elementary principles of a democratic government, but is guilty of a legal usurpation, against which every lover of liberty, be he saint or sinner, Protestant or Catholic, ought to protest in thunder-notes. Not a few Protestants in dealing with the School question, and especially in their zeal to resist the demands of the Catholics, have reasoned as if our American State Governments were Protestant State Governments; as if Protestantism were a part of their public law; and, hence, as if Protestants had some rights which are not common to all the people. We entirely sympathize with them in their opposition to the Catholic demand; but we utterly dissent from the political heresies with which they seek to sustain it. We believe them to be radically wrong in asking the State to assign any religious work to the public school system. If it does not make a sham of the work by the manner of its performance, it will be sure to do injustice to somebody.

VII.

THE BIBLE IN THE PUBLIC SCHOOLS.

The question of the Bible in the public schools, in order to be properly understood and discussed, needs explanation. What are these schools? They are not at all private institutions; but wholly the creatures of State authority, and, as such, supported by general taxation. The property, including school-houses and their sites and the fixtures and appurtenances thereof, is public property. School-boards and trustees and teachers are officers, provided for by law and subject to its regulations. The whole machinery, from beginning to end, is exclusively a system of State machinery for educational purposes; not the less so because local divisions of the State—as cities, villages, and school-districts—directly work it. These divisions are only parts of the State, acting by its authority and under its supervisory control. What they do the State does through them.

The term Bible, as used in connection with these schools, does not mean the Sacred Scriptures of the Old and New Testament in the form of Hebrew and Greek, since these languages are unintelligible to the great mass of the people. The Bible, or the book involved in this discussion, is simply a version of these Scriptures. Two such versions are in use—the one known as King James's version, used by Protestants, and, hence, sometimes designated as the Protestant Bible ; the other being the Douay version, and used by Catholics, and, hence, called the Catholic Bible. Each of these parties claims for the Bible it uses the greatest perfection, and that the Bible of the other does not, in several important respects, correctly represent the original Scriptures. The consequence is that the Bible of each is a sectarian book to the other, as really as is the Westminster Confession of Faith such a book between the Presbyterian and the Methodist.

Both versions—that of King James and the Douay version—claim to teach a supernatural religious system given to the world by the inspiration of God, hence, bearing the stamp of his authority and having for its object the instruction and salvation of sinners. These features mark the original Scriptures, and they fully appear in both of these versions. The distinctive characteristic of each is that of a *religious* book, demanding human belief and obedience upon the warrant of God. No matter which version we use, and no matter whether we accept or reject its authority or that of the Scriptures of which it is a translation, still we cannot fail to recognize the fact that religion, and not science, constitutes the subject treated of. By religion we mean a system of truths purporting to be supernaturally given to men, in which God is revealed to them and their duties to him made known, and in accordance with which he will judge them and appoint their destiny in the final day. We here raise no question as to the truth of what is thus alleged, since the argument in hand does not turn at all upon the answer. We believe in the truth of the system; yet we should reason in the same way if we did not thus believe.

This explanation of the public school as a *civil* institution of the State, and of the Bible as a *religious* book, shows that, if the State is to employ the latter in conducting the former, it has several very grave questions to settle. First of all, it must decide whether it will do so *at all*, and in deciding this point it must, except upon a supposition that will be specified in the sequel, determine whether it will undertake to be a propagator of religion at the expense of the general public. If it decides this question in the affirmative, then it must also determine *what form* of religion it will propagate. Shall it be Roman Catholicism, and for this purpose shall the Douay version or the Catholic Bible be used? No, says the Protestant, declaring that he does not wish to have his children taught in or disposed toward that system of faith, and that he has no idea of being taxed for its support. Very well. Shall it be Protestantism, and shall King James's version or the Protestant Bible be the book used? No, says the Catholic, affirming with equal emphasis his rights as against any such instruction. It seems then that these parties cannot agree as to the Bible to be used, to say nothing now about the manner of the use. Each wants his own Bible, and neither wants that of the other.

Shall this difficulty be solved by taking the ground that the religion to be taught shall be Protestantism when and where Protestants are in the majority? Yes, say a certain class of Protestants, always assuming Protestants to be the majority, and either wittingly or unwittingly committing themselves to a principle which would make the religion of the public school Catholicism, or Mormonism, or Judaism when and where Catholics, or Mormons, or Jews form the majority. If the majority doctrine is good for Protestants in settling the *kind* of religion which the State shall propagate at the expense of the whole when Protestants are in the majority, then it is just as good for these other parties when they happen to be the majority. Is not this the very principle that has been adopted by kings and priests and popes in forcing their own religion upon the minority? Did not our Pilgrim Fathers quit their English homes, cross the ocean, and come to this then western wilderness in order to escape from the tyranny of the religion of the majority? If the State is to determine the religious question by the number of persons who are the adherents of a specific religion and put its stamp upon the religion of the majority, then its ground is that on which all State religions have rested, and under the color of which religious proscription and persecution have been perpetrated and justified. The religion of the majority has never been persecuted, and in the nature of things never can be. Persecution strikes at the religion of the minority.

We thus see that this question of using the Bible in the public schools involves very important matters for the State to decide; that it cannot decide affirmatively to use the Bible without deciding *what* Bible it will use and, so far, what religion it will propagate; that it cannot satisfy all the parties that are disputing over this question; and that it cannot adopt the religion of the majority as its rule without accepting a principle which has, in all ages, been the enemy of religious liberty. We more than suspect that the State had better say to all these parties that it is a political and not a religious organization, and that the public school is simply a *civil* institution, for certain temporal purposes; and, hence, that it cannot be used as the instrument of any religious propagandism. We do not see what else an American State can say without contradicting the fundamental theory of its own existence. The State, in taking this ground, which is the shortest and simplest road out of the difficulty, disposes of the whole question by its own absolute neutrality on the subject of religion, and its refusal to be a party to any of the religious creeds of its citizens. It simply lets these creeds alone, neither patronizing nor persecuting them.

If, however, the State decides to have the Bible in the public schools, and decides *what* Bible to have there, then another series of questions relating to the *manner* and *extent* of its use at once arises for settlement. To put the Bible there in the merely physical sense would be a farce. What shall be done with the book? This question admits of three answers.

The first answer proposes that the Bible shall be used as a *common reading* book, for the single purpose of teaching the art of reading—just as Hesiod, Homer, and Virgil are used as college classics, to teach the Greek and Latin languages, or as the spelling-book is used in the public school to teach the art of spelling. Such a use would have no reference to the religion to be taught; and, hence, it would not involve the question of religion at all. It would, however, raise the inquiry whether the Bible, taken as a whole, and used simply for the purpose of discipline in the art of reading, is a book well suited to this end. We frankly say that we think not. It was not written to answer any such end. Many portions of it would be eminently unsuitable; and those parts most appropriate would have to be selected, and the State would have to make the selection by charging the school teacher with this duty, or by appointing a committee for the purpose. Moreover, this use of the Bible would be an act of the State justly offensive to those who regard it as a divine revelation. It would not be a proper use, since it would sink the book to the level of the grammar or the spelling-book; and, by making it a common book used for a merely secular end, dispossess it of its distinctively sacred character. It would not impress the mind with the divine authority of the book, without a sense of which nearly all its power is lost. We can hardly think that any Christian would insist that the Bible shall be in the public school merely as a reading classic. This, surely, is not the theory upon which the newspapers and the ministry have been discussing the question of the Bible in the public schools.

A second answer proposes that the Bible, as such shall not be used at all; but that a selection of passages therefrom shall be made, and that a portion thereof shall be read in the public schools as a daily exercise, or at stated periods, for moral and religious purposes, either with or without other religious services. This excludes a part of the Bible and includes a part, and employs the included part as the means of religious instruction, and of course commits the State in the public school to this work. Several questions here arise. By what authority shall the selection be made, and from which of the two versions shall it be made? What part of the Bible shall be thus selected? How far shall the selection embrace the peculiar doctrines of the Bible in relation to the person and work of Christ? Shall we have the Christian morals of the Bible without the Christian motives furnished by the doctrines, or shall we have the morals and the motives together; and if the latter, then shall we have the whole system of doctrines, or only a part of it, and if merely a part, then what part? If it be said that such parts should be selected as embody the principles of our common Christianity, which all Christian sects are agreed in accepting, this only creates the necessity for further questions. What are the principles of our common Christianity upon which these sects are agreed? What passages of the Bible contain these principles and nothing else? How many sects are included in these Christian sects? Are the Universalists, the Unitarians, and the Quakers included? What is to be done with the opinions and preferences of those who do not come within the limits of these sects, yet who, being citizens and taxpayers, have some rights in the public school?

Upon all these points the State must act, provided it attempts to put in practice the selection theory. It must affirmatively settle these two propositions: first, that the public school shall, upon its authority, be in part a religious institution on the basis of the Bible; secondly, that the religion there taught shall be of a defined quantity and quality, indicated by the selection. How much would this come short of State religion? We say State religion, because no such system can be adopted without or against the authority of the State, and because no such system can be practiced and not be a State religion.

The third answer is that a portion of the Bible, to be selected by the teacher, should by him be read, "without note or comment" as a daily opening or closing exercise, either with or without prayer and singing. This in theory, whatever might be the practical result, would be a process of religious worship and instruction. It would conform to the usages of the country in respect to public worship. When Christians assemble for this purpose the devout reading of the Bible is a part of their worship. Singing and public prayer have the same character. Those Protestants who insist upon this use of the Bible in the public school are content with it, provided always that King James's version be the Bible used, and that it be read without note or comment. A great many who are not Protestants are not thus content; and many who are Protestants think it not only inexpedient, but practically unjust to a portion of the community.

The one feature marking this use of the Bible we have in the fact that it transfers to the public school, on a small scale and for a short period each day, a part of the ordinary worship of Christians on the Sabbath. Who makes the transfer? Not the teacher who reads the Bible and conducts the worship, since he is a subordinate officer; not the Board of Education, except as exercising powers bestowed by the State; but the State itself, in its sovereign capacity. The State governs the public school by laws enacted in regard to it. According to this theory, it makes religion a part of its school system, derives that religion from a book called the Bible, and then taxes all the people for the support of this public-school State religion. The direct agency may be by boards of education ; but the ultimate authority is that of the State itself. It establishes a religious system in its public school, and makes that system Christian in its generic character, and Protestant in its specific type, if King James's version be the book used. And this is just what those Protestants demand who insist that the Bible —namely, King James's version—shall be thus used by a democratic State.

The result, then, that we reach from this analysis of the question is simply this :—that, by using the Bible in the public schools, unless the use be merely that of a reading-book, an American State, founded on the principle of the strictest impartiality towards all religious sects and of making no discrimination between them, undertakes to create and does create a religious establishment in these schools at the public expense, and after the Christian model, either Protestant or Catholic in its specific type, and to this end affirmatively determines all the questions and institutes all the agencies necessary to make it a fact. This, in plain English, is just what the proposition means, and what those demand who advocate it. The public school is what it is by State authority; and so far as religion is there, whether as a matter of instruction, or worship, or both, it is there by this authority, and there established by being included in a State school system. We do not overstate the proposition, but simply state it according to the fact.

Now, whether this is a good or a bad system, congruous with the nature of an American State or contradictory thereto, just to all the people or grossly unjust to a portion of them, is a question that cannot be wisely settled by one's prejudices, and surely ought not to be settled by furious clamor, either in the pulpit or out of it. It is a question that cannot be correctly answered without considering the ends and province of civil government, and especially the nature of the civil governments established in this country. This series of articles on the School question, of which the present one is the seventh, has been gradually advancing to the point where these governmental questions come to the front, and demand a hearing. He who attempts to solve the School problem as a mere *ecclesiastic*, fired only by religious and perhaps largely by Church zeal, may as well stop before he begins. His vision is not broad enough clearly to apprehend, or thoroughly discuss, the real points that lie in the problem.

THE GENERAL ARGUMENT.

VIII.

THE UNCHRISTIAN METHOD.

It is a rule, alike of common sense and Christian morality, that no end, however good in itself, should be sought by unlawful and improper means. We are not to do evil that good may come. In obeying one law we are not to violate another. Christianity neither needs nor approves of any unchristian methods for its propagation. It permits no one to contradict any of its own principles on the theory of serving its interests, or making it the minister of human benefits. It is, hence, pertinent to inquire whether those who demand that our public school system shall be used as one of the means for teaching and propagating Christianity, and who to this end insist that the Bible shall be read, and other religious services shall be had in the public schools, are not amenable to the charge of seeking a good end in an improper manner. It will be well for them not to assume that they are infallible, or the only persons who have any genuine religious zeal, who believe and reverence the Bible, or upon whom God has placed the seal of his favor. It may be that they are entirely wrong as to their *method*, and that the wrong involves a trespass upon the rights of others; and whether such is the fact or not, is certainly a fair subject for honest inquiry.

We propose, then, to consider this point, and for this purpose quote, as follows, the language of Judge Welch, in delivering the opinion of the Supreme Court of Ohio in the case of The Board of Education of Cincinnati *vs.* Minor and Others (23 Ohio State Reports, Granger, pp. 249, 250):

"If it be true that our law enjoins the teaching of the Christian religion in the schools, surely then all the teachers should be Christians. Were I such a teacher, while I should instruct the pupils that the Christian religion was true and all other religions false, I should tell them that the law itself was an *unchristian* law. One of my first lessons to the pupils would show it to be unchristian. That lesson would be: 'Whatsoever ye would that men should do to you, do ye even so to them, for this is the *law* and the Prophets.' I could not look the veriest infidel or heathen in the face and say that such a law was just or that it was a fair specimen of Christian republicanism. I should have to tell him that it was an outgrowth of false Christianity and not one of the lights which Christians are commanded to shed upon an unbelieving world."

In another part of the opinion (p. 253), Judge Welch said:—

"Government is an organization for particular purposes. It is not almighty, and we are not to look to it for everything. The great bulk of human affairs and human interests is left by any free government to individual enterprise and individual action. Religion is eminently one of these interests, lying outside the true and legitimate province of government."

In another part of the opinion (p. 248), the Judge also said :—

"*Legal* Christianity is a solecism ; a contradiction of terms. When Christianity asks the aid of government beyond mere *impartial protection* it disowns itself. Its essential interests lie beyond the reach and range of human governments. United with government religion never rises above the merest superstition ; united with religion government never rises above the merest despotism ; and all history shows us that the more widely and completely they are separated the better it is for both."

In still another portion of the same opinion (p. 249), the Judge further said :—

"Properly speaking, there is no such thing as 'religion of State.' What we mean by that phrase is the religion of some individual or set of individuals, taught and enforced by the State. The State can have no religious opinions; and if it undertakes to enforce the teaching of such opinions, they must be the opinions of some natural person or class of persons."

It is not at all surprising that the Court, holding these views of government considered in relation to religion, should have spoken of the enforced teaching of Christianity in the public schools as being "*unchristian*"—yea, as a method of teaching alike inconsistent with the system itself and the legitimate province of civil government. The Court decided that Ohio had no such "unchristian law," and that the Board of Education of Cincinnati, when resolving to discontinue "religious instruction and the reading of religious books, including the Holy Bible," in the public schools of that city, was simply exercising a power vested in the board by law.

It is well to keep in mind in all our reasoning upon the School question that the State, as a political organization, has never been trusted by the Divine Founder of Christianity with the duty of its propagation. He never said to the State: "Go ye into all the world and preach the Gospel," or "Lo! I am with you alway, even unto the end of the world." He said these things to his apostles, and to those who through them should believe on his name. The apostleship of his Word he located in his disciples and followers, and not in kings, governors, rulers, senators, or legislative assemblies. To the former he gave his commission, and on them imposed its duties, forewarning them of persecutions for his name's sake, and promising to be their helper. An apostle sums up the whole idea when he speaks of the Church—the company of believers and confessors of the faith—as the pillar and ground of the truth. Jesus presented the same thought when speaking of his disciples as the light of the world, and commanding them to let their light so shine before men that they might see their good works and glorify their Father who is in Heaven.

What, then, according to the express plan of Christ, has the State to do with teaching or propagating his religion? Absolutely nothing whatever. It has no commission or warrant to touch the work at all. The duty is assigned to another and different agency. It is, hence, true, as said by Judge Welch, that a law enjoining the teaching of Christianity in the public schools, which are purely State institutions, sustained by general taxation and governed by the civil power, would be "an *unchristian* law"—unchristian in the sense of changing and contravening the policy established by the Son of God himself. It would employ the State power for religious and spiritual purposes; and this certainly was not the theory of Christ. It would be anti-Christian; and, hence, those who propose to serve God in this way are, in our judgment, gravely mistakened in their method. Their plan is to call into action a power that has no commission to do the work, and never attempted to do it without far more damage than benefit.

This, however, is not the whole case, since the teaching of Christianity or any other religion by the State, and, of course, at the public expense, in a community of diverse religious beliefs as is the fact with the American people, is "unchristian" in the sense of violating the golden rule of equal and impartial justice, as laid down by Jesus himself; and in this sense it becomes a *positive* wrong, if injustice be a wrong. Let us see how this matter stands in a practical operation.

The teaching of Christianity in the public schools, for example, in the Protestant form, must be paid for by taxation, and all the people who have any taxable property must share in the burden. Now, are they all Christians and all Protestants? By no means. There is a great diversity among them as to their religious opinions; and yet they are all citizens, and, as to their citizenship and their respective religious faiths, they are, by the guaranteed rights of our political system, and by the rule of right reason, just equal before the laws. No one class tolerates all the rest, since they are equals. Is it, then, just for the State in its public schools to extend the hand of favoritism to Protestantism and Protestants, and tax Catholics, Jews, Infidels, Rationalists, Swedenborgians, etc., to pay the expenses thereof? Others may answer this question as they think best; yet we pronounce it grossly unjust. It makes a distinction by State authority which cannot be made without violating the rule of equal justice; and when the Catholic, or the Jew, or the Infidel protests against the distinction, he has justice on his side. He may be voted down, but he cannot be reasoned down. No amount of zeal can sanctify the injustice or make it anything but injustice.

The same injustice in kind would be perpetrated if Catholicism or Judaism were thus taught in the public schools. The only difference would be that Protestants would be among the parties suffering the wrong. There is no doubt that they would very readily perceive it, and loudly declaim against it, however willing some of them may be to have the injustice inflicted upon others. No one who will look at this question candidly can maintain that any religious *régime* in the public school can be put into practice in this country of diverse religious beliefs without violating the rule that "whatsoever things ye would that men should do to you, do ye even so to them." The Saviour himself, by the plain meaning of the rule, stamps the practice as wrong. It is not simply a mistake. It is more. It is a *moral wrong*, because it is not equal justice to the rights of all the people; and because the State makes a discrimination as to the religious faith of its citizens and taxes all to support one of the forms of such faith. It is Church and State in the public school.

But should not the *majority*, either in the school district or in the State, settle the question as to *what* form of religion shall be taught in the public school? We shall have occasion in another connection to consider this majority doctrine; yet here we say emphatically: No! The rule of the majority within the limits of those objects which properly come under the jurisdiction of civil government is a good rule ; but, when civil government exceeds those limits by undertaking to do things in respect to which it has no rightful jurisdiction, then the rule ceases to be operative. Majorities may then become the oppressors of minorities ; and this is precisely what happens when the majority, whether in a State, a city, or school district, imposes upon a minority the legal necessity of contributing to the support of a religion from which it dissents. There are no rights more sacred than those which relate to one's religious faith ; and there is no injustice more abominable than that of compelling a man to aid in the support or propagation of a religious system which he regards as false. It is the very climax of legal tyranny. The object of the various clauses in regard to the rights of a religious conscience found in the bills of rights of the several State constitutions is to protect the minority in the matter of religion. They are designed to take this one subject out from the jurisdiction of government entirely, and leave it to individual conviction and choice, with simply an equal and impartial protection of the rights of all. We, hence, utterly reject the majority rule as a rule for civil government in relation to religion. It has no application to the question and can never cancel the wrong of compelling the minority to pay taxes for the propagation of the religion of the majority.

We are, however, reminded by Catholics, and also by some Protestants, that a public school in which religion, and that too, of the kind which they approve is not taught at all, is an offense to their consciences, and hence, an invasion of their religious rights. These parties do not complain of what such a school positively is or of the secular knowledge which it imparts, since this is certainly good as far as it goes; but they do complain that it does not go far enough. It is defective because it does not, by including religion, sweep the whole circle of education. We submit the following answer to this sort of religious conscience, if such it may be called:—

1. A public school in which no religion is taught invades the religious rights of nobody. It taxes no one to teach religion. It simply lets this one subject entirely alone, and justifies its existence and support by general taxation on grounds which have no reference to religion, and in respect to which all have a common interest, however widely they may differ in their religious opinions.

2. This so-called conscience assumes that it is the province and duty of the State in its public school, if it sees fit to establish one, to discharge the religious duty which the constitution of things and the law of Christianity assigns to the family and the Church. Now, where did these Catholics or these Protestants learn that any such duty is imposed on the State? Certainly not in the Bible, and certainly not out of it by right reason. Unfortunately for the assumption, the State is neither

a father nor a mother, and is not charged with the special duties of either. The State is not a Church or, at least, should not be, and has no apostolic commission to fulfil. Civil government holds no such relation to God or man that the propagation of religion, whether among the young or the old, is one of its duties. That is, indeed, a very singular conscience which asserts a personal grievance and injustice because the state does not do what does not belong to it.

3. This conscience, when sifted to the bottom, is merely an *opinion* that the State should have religious teaching in its public school, and clearly involves no right of conscience that such teaching should be there. We do not deny the right of any man to have such an opinion; yet when he presents the omission of the State to undertake the work of religious teaching as a violation of his rights of conscience he assumes that his conscience is the proper guide for determining the positive duties of the State. How much this comes short of sheer stupidity we leave the reader to judge.

4. What the State does by secular education for the common good of the whole body politic, and, hence, by general taxation of the whole, in no way interferes with religious education by such agencies as parents or the Church may choose to employ. It simply does not enter this field; yet it does not shut it up against others, or control it in any way. Religious education is to the State

unoccupied territory, left entirely open to all who choose to enter it. The territory which it does occupy comes within the scope of its powers; and the occupancy furnishes sufficient advantages to the whole people to justify it at the public expense.

5. If parents, for religious or other reasons, do not choose to use the advantages for a secular education afforded by the State, then this is and must be their own matter. The State, by the very terms of the case, puts nothing into the public school in conflict with any right of religious conscience which they possess; and if, nevertheless, they do not like the school, then they are at liberty to dislike it, and, if they thus choose, to educate their children elsewhere, at their own charges. This is their privilege; and if they avail themselves of it, then so be it. Let them, however, not stultify common sense by saying that their religious rights are outraged, because they are taxed to support a public school whose single object is *secular* education—an object in which all the people, including themselves, have a common interest.

The conclusion that we reach from this examination of the question is this: A public school system planned on the principle of secular education, and, hence, excluding all religious teaching and religious worship is, in a community indiscriminately taxed for its support and in which there are diverse forms of religious faith, the only State school system that is just, that does not violate the fundamental theory of the Saviour in respect to the propagation of his Gospel, and that accords with the golden rule of doing to others as we would have them do to us. It respects the rights of all, and commits no encroachment upon the rights of anybody. Accepting this conclusion, we necessarily accept another, which is this: those who demand religious teaching and religious worship in the public schools of this country are justly amendable to the charge of seeking a good end by an *unchristian* method. We bring this charge not against their motives, but against what they propose.

IX.

GOVERNMENTAL JURISDICTION.

Jurisdiction is a law term used to denote the idea of governmental authority over persons and things within the scope of its action. No such authority is absolutely universal as to the persons subject to it, or as to the territory over which it extends, or as to the matters which it embraces. Many things are so entirely private in their nature or so little concern the general public that they are by universal consent left exclusively to individual choice, without any attempt to regulate

them by law. Governments exist for particular purposes, which by no means include the entire bulk of human affairs.

How, then, is it with religion considered as a faith or a worship, as a spiritual exercise or a social expression thereof? Does it come within the rightful jurisdiction of human government? Does it properly belong to any such government to regulate, administer, propagate, or in any way take charge of the religion of the people? The answer given by history is that most of the governments of the world have assumed that religion lies within the scope of their regulating and administrative agency. The legislation consequent upon the assumption, whether more or less liberal, or more or less oppressive, will be according to the general civilization of the people. Pains and penalties, discriminations on religious grounds, special immunities granted or denied on these grounds, compulsory taxation for the support and propagation of religion, the appointment and control of religious teachers, religious tests as qualifications for civil office or to testify in a court of justice—these are among the things which the assumption carries along with it, and by which it makes itself operative. The principle is the same in all cases, varying only in the extent to which it is applied.

It seems not a little strange that a principle fraught with so much evil and so essentially false, as well as absurd, should have lasted so long and spread so extensively among the nations of the earth, and that even now the discovery of its falseness should be limited to so small a portion of the human family. Its victims usually perceive the wrong when they feel its burden; yet it has often happened, as was the case with our Puritan Fathers, that they no sooner cease to be victims than they are ready to become oppressors—forgetting, "as victors, the lessons which as victims they had learned." One would think that so simple a proposition as that which affirms the existence and inalienable character of the rights of a religious conscience as above and beyond all human authority ought to have been among the earliest and most widely-extended discoveries of the race. The fact, however, is sadly the reverse. Of all the forms of wrong which men have suffered from each other, none have been less reasonable or more merciless and unrelenting than those of religious zeal armed with the civil power. There is no darker chapter in the history of governments than that which chronicles their misdeeds in the attempt to administer and propagate religion. The attempt is essentially a horrible human tyranny begun, and every step of the process is that tyranny continued.

The doctrine of a *personal* God, related to men as their Creator and Preserver, being received into the mind as the *objective* basis of religion, naturally connects itself with the idea of this God as a supreme *lawgiver*, to whose authority we are directly subject and from whose administrative control no power can release us. His will, no matter how ascertained is the final law. Peter and John were simply true to universal thought when they said: "We ought to obey God rather than men." Daniel was true to the same thought when he disregarded the edict of a king rather than violate that of his God. The martyrs who took joyfully the spoiling of their goods and cheerfully died at the stake for what they regarded as obedience to God were true to the doctrine that God, and not man, is the supreme ruler, and that the authority of the latter—whether that of the parent, the magistrate, the legislative assembly, or the king—when in conflict with that of the former, is not for a moment to be regarded. No human law can outlaw the law of God. There is but one supreme authority in the universe, and this is exclusively vested in God himself. No one disputes this proposition who believes in the existence of a personal God. It is one of the first truths of all religion.

Now, as to the question whether there is such a God, thus related to each individual man, and, if so, as to what are His laws and what duties He requires us to perform; and as to the further question whether this God has made a supernatural revelation of His will to men, and, if so, as to what that revelation contains—as to these questions no human being, unless directly inspired by God himself, can authoritatively judge for another. What others think may be a source of light, and, in this sense, of value; but it is no rule to the individual, unless he thinks the same thing. He must adopt their thoughts before they can become his rule; and in doing so it is not possible for him to disown his own reason or his own conscience. These faculties form his best light, and necessarily imply a negation of the authority of any other human being to govern his thoughts, or the right of any human power forcibly to interfere with their peaceable exercise. God has established no ecclesiastical bureau in any earthly government to take the religious charge of the individual reason and conscience, to supersede their personal functions, and dispense truth and piety to men according to order. All such bureaus, whether managed by kings or popes, invade a province exclusively occupied by the Divine Government, and, hence, insult the majesty of Heaven while they outrage the rights of earth. Each individual soul must and does think for itself upon its own direct responsibility to the King of kings; and that too, no matter how ignorant or how much superstition may have warped the understanding. What it thinks is necessarily a law whose jurisdiction no merely human opinion or authority can either displace or destroy. It is sovereign for the individual.

Moreover, religion consists essentially in *voluntary* homage and obedience rendered to God by a rational and accountable being. Its spiritual phenomena belong to a realm to which no human authority can extend. Such authority may punish their outward expression or the want of such expression; but the seat of religion lies beyond its agency. No parent can lash his child into piety and no king can make his subjects devout toward God by commanding them to be so. Religion was never forced into any soul, or forced out of it. Whoever worships and obeys God, worships and obeys the God of whom he thinks, and in whose existence he believes. He does so under the inner guidance of his own reason and conscience, and not under the authority of the reason and conscience of another. This is the immutable law of his own being, as well as of the character of the service rendered.

It follows, then, from the very nature of religion, as a matter between the soul and its God, from the absolute and supreme authority of God and from the necessary supremacy of the individual reason and conscience in determining the religious question between God and the soul, that civil governments cannot extend their agency to the administration or regulation of religion without committing a trespass upon the rights of God and man at the same time. They cannot make its laws, since here God himself is the sole lawgiver. They cannot add to its sanctions or modify or cancel its claims. They cannot coerce men into piety, since the service itself admits of no coercion. They cannot destroy the authority of the individual reason and conscience, since this authority is indestructible by any human power. Each soul, as to its faith, its thoughts and affections, and the obligations which bind it to God, is as free from the rightful control of human authority as it could be if no such authority existed. And this is what is meant by religious freedom—freedom not from God's authority, but from man's authority, so that each one is left to follow the dictates of his own conscience.

This statement needs to be qualified by the remark that no one, as a member of civil society, has a right so to exercise his religious liberty as to make himself a trespasser upon the rights of others, or act in a manner inconsistent with the good order and safety of that society. While free to think what he pleases, and equally free peaceably to express and propagate his opinions, he is not free to commit acts which society cannot, in consistency with its own welfare, permit to be done with impunity, for any reasons. It is the province of just and enlightened legislation to fix the limits within which individual liberty must move, and beyond which it must yield to the general good. It is possible to err here; yet without such limits fixed somewhere the community would be at the mercy of every man's superstition, and each would be licensed to do what he pleased under the color of religion.

Society cannot, as an organism regulated by law, exist upon any such principle. A penal code to protect the rights of men by preventing crime is, hence, not repealed by the doctrine of religious liberty.

Restraining, then, the outward exercise of this liberty within the limits established by sound reason and impartial justice, human governments have but a single additional duty to perform; and this is to *protect* it. Protection here does not mean patronage, or support, or regulation of religion in any way; but it does mean that no one, no matter who he is, or what may be his religion, or whether he belongs to the majority or the minority or stands absolutely alone, shall be interfered with when peaceably worshipping God according to the dictates of his own conscience or when peaceably imparting his religious convictions to others, and that no one shall be compelled by law to perform any religious duty or be subject to any disability on the ground of non-performance, or be required by compulsory taxation to contribute to the maintenance or propagation of any religious system. It does mean that, within the limits demanded by the rights of others, each individual shall be left absolutely free as to his religion and as to its social expression, being protected in his person against oppression and in his property against religious exactions. It does mean such a complete, universal, and impartial equality before the laws as excludes all discriminations among citizens on religious grounds, and permits every one to judge for himself as to what religion he shall adopt, or whether he shall adopt any, and then as to what he shall do or omit to do within the bounds of decency and social order. It does mean —if law, as it justly may, authorizes the existence of *civil* corporations whose purposes are religious—that it should protect the rights of these corporations in their civil character, without any discrimination among them, and let their religious functions and purposes entirely alone. Protection is the one word that defines the whole duty of civil government in respect to the religion of its citizens. This is all they need, all to which they are entitled, and the utmost that a just government can consistently render.

But what has this discussion as to the jurisdiction of human governments to do with the School question? We answer that the public schools of this country are supported by *taxation;* that taxation is a *compulsory* process; that as such it involves one of the highest attributes of government; and that if these schools are made the instrument of religious instruction then this instruction, both as to quantity and quality, and also as to agency, is established there by the authority of the State, and that the people are compelled by law to pay the expenses thereof—and that, too, whether they believe the religion taught to be true or to be a mass of superstition. Religious instruction in the public school is, in respect to the taxpayers, a *coerced* support of religion. Among the "things which are not lawful under any of the American constitutions," Judge Cooley, in his "Constitutional Limitations," p. 469, specifies "*compulsory* support, by taxation or otherwise, of religious instruction." He immediately adds: "Not only is no one denomination to be favored at the expense of the rest, but *all* support of religious instruction must be entirely *voluntary*." This principle is clearly violated by the state if it makes such instruction a part of its public school system. The support is then not voluntary, because the taxpayer has no option whether to render it or not.

Judge Welch, of the Supreme Court of Ohio, in delivering the opinion of the Court in the case of The Board of Education of Cincinnati *vs.* Minor and others (23 Ohio State Reports, Granger, p. 250), said that the teaching of the Christian religion in the public schools "violates the spirit of our constitutional guaranties and is a state religion in embryo; that if we have no right to tax him [the citizen] to support worship, we have no right to tax him to support religious instruction; that to tax a man to put down his own religion is of the very essence of tyranny: that, however small the tax, it is a first step in the direction of an establishment of religion; and I should add that the first step in that direction is the fatal step, because it logically involves the last step."

Mr. Horace Mann in his twelfth report on the schools in Massachusetts, says: "But if a man is taxed to support a school where religious doctrines are inculcated which he believes to be false and which he believes that God condemns, then he is excluded from the school by the Divine law, at the same time that he is compelled to support it by the human law. This is a double wrong. It is politically wrong, because, if such a man educates his children at all, he must educate them elsewhere, and thus pay two taxes, while some of his neighbors pay less than their due proportion of one; and it is religiously wrong, because he is constrained by human power to promote what he believes the Divine Power forbids. The principle involved in such a course is pregnant with all tyrannical consequences. It is broad enough to sustain any claim of ecclesiastical domination ever made in the darkest ages of the world." The only escape from the adoption of this principle is for the state to abandon its school system altogether, or to exclude religious instruction from that system, on the ground that such instruction does not come within the proper jurisdiction of civil government. The latter, and not the former, is the course we advocate. It is the only course possible in a State school system supported by compulsory taxation that is consistent with the religious rights of the people.

No man has a right to say that *his* religion, in distinction from that of his neighbor, shall be taught in a school for the support of which both are taxed in common. What the State should say is that the religion of neither shall be taught, and that the support of religion, whether it be true or false, shall not anywhere or to any extent be made a charge upon its public treasury. This is fair and just to all. Any other ground assumes a jurisdiction in the State which cannot exist in consistency with the rights of conscience, and which, if it be conceded at all, logically covers the whole ground of a State religion.

X.

STATE THEOLOGY.

The term *State* means any distinct and independent body of persons occupying a given territory and united together under some form of civil government. The governmental organization of a State for the purpose of enacting and administering law, is practically the State itself. It is such as the agent of its legal operations. By the term *theology* is meant the science of God, embracing what is assumed to be known in regard to him and consisting subjectively in human beliefs with reference to the Supreme Being. What men thus believe is their theology; and if they believe in the doctrine of God at all the natural sequel is some form of religious worship. The combination of the ideas indicated by these terms gives a *state theology*, or a government in which the State asserts a legal doctrine or creed in regard to God and stamps the same with its own authority. The State, then, is a theological State. Its opinions, whether in respect to God himself or the duty and mode of religious worship, form a part of its laws: and this distinguishes them from *individual* beliefs or convictions that rest merely on private judgment, and, hence admit of no coercive enforcement.

The natural and, as a most ample experience shows, the sure result of State theology is either such an identification of Church and State that the two are practically the same thing, or such an intimate legal union of the two that they mutually act through each other. In the one case the State is the Church and the Church is the State; and in the other, though formally distinct as organisms, they are, nevertheless, blended in a common set of functions in respect to religion. In both cases we have the union of ecclesiastical and civil powers, and in both we have religion with the sanction of human law impressed upon it.

Every State theology must necessarily have some *specific* character; and as to what it shall be—whether Pagan or Christian, and, if the latter, whether Catholic or Protestant—the State itself must be the judge. Its opinion on this subject it expresses through the edict of a king or the vote of a legislative assembly. It does the work of a theological professor, adding thereto the power of the civil arm. It teaches by command. Its dogmas are laws. All the reasons which demand or justify a State theology at all equally demand that it should be put into effective action. If it be the right and duty of the State to have a theology, then it is its duty to be governed by it and to govern the people by it. The least that it can do is to devise the ways and means of asserting, perpetuating, and enforcing it. If it is worth anything it deserves this tribute. State patronage, State disabilities or penalties for dissenters and State administration are the logical corollaries. To this there can be no just objection, since if the State *ought* to have a theology, then it ought to use the necessary means to maintain and administer it. It should see to it that not only the children in the public schools, but also the adult population—indeed, all the people—enjoy the benefits thereof. That would be a very queer theology which the State first adopts and legalizes and then leaves to shirk for itself. We hold it to be the duty of the State to sustain its own theology, provided always that theology comes within its proper sphere.

This, moreover, would be practically an easy task if all the people thought exactly alike and their common thoughts were faithfully represented by the theology of the State. Such, however, does not happen to be the case.

What, then, shall be done with those who dissent from this theology and decline to conform to its requirements? This question the State must answer, and generally does so answer as to involve the principle of proscription or persecution. It is a fact wide as the world and spread all over the records of history that State theologies have with great uniformity been persecuting theologies. Christ and his apostles and their followers were persecuted by the State theology of the Jews. Pagan Rome had such a theology, and for three bloody centuries she wielded its power against the Christians. Constantine established Christianity as a State theology and made it a persecuting power. The State theology of the Roman Catholic and that of the Protestant show the same record. State theology drove the Puritans out of England and murdered the Huguenots in France. It made our Puritan fathers persecutors. Mohammedanism as a State theology and Paganism as such are marked by the same feature. The missionary efforts of modern times to propagate Christianity among the heathen meet with one of their most formidable obstacles in State theologies, and the same was true of like efforts in the apostolic age. It is a general fact that the moment theology allies itself with the State and commands its powers it becomes persecuting in respect to all who dissent from it, and that, too, whether it be Pagan or Christian, Catholic or Protestant. History paints this fact in lurid colors.

Nor is there anything strange or unnatural in such a fact. It results from the very nature of the case. The theology of the State is a part of its organic or statute law, and, of course, it should be sustained by its authority and power. Heresy is, hence, a *crime*, as really as murder, and as such it should be punished. So the State reasons, and that, too, correctly, provided we accept the doctrine of State theology. Catholic States and Protestant States have reasoned in this way. What we call religious persecution State theology calls punishment to prevent crime. What we call religious liberty it calls a dangerous exercise of private judgment. Saul of Tarsus was a conscientious persecutor, regarding himself as doing God service; and it is but just to say that State theologies have generally been conscientious in their deeds of murder and blood. They have not looked upon themselves as ruffians and outlaws, but rather as the conservators of the divine honor and the true interests of souls. The thoughts of an after and a wiser age were not their thoughts when they trampled the religious rights of men into the dust and shocked Heaven, if not earth, with their cruelties. Religious zeal misdirected is a terrible passion: and all State theologies, because administered by men, are apt to have this zeal.

We present, then, the disabilities, the persecutions, and the martyrdoms, which are so conspicuous in the history of State theology, as more than suggesting that there must be some radical mistake in the doctrine itself. A doctrine that can by perversion turn the mild and genial religion of Jesus into a flaming persecutor, and make it a ferocious enemy to religious liberty as vested by God in individual souls; a doctrine that undertakes to adjudicate upon questions lying exclusively between the soul and its Maker; a doctrine that substitutes carnal for spiritual weapons; a doctrine that resorts to the law of force, where nothing is pertinent except the peaceful persuasion of argument and the gentle and loving voice of entreaty; a doctrine that in practical execution becomes an abominable despotism exercised over the bodies and attempted over the souls of men—yes, such a doctrine has written upon its face in letters of light the glaring evidence of being essentially and fundamentally wrong. Judging it by its fruits, we find it difficult to use terms sufficiently intense to describe the degree of that wrong. Its prevading principle is hostile alike to God and man, although it professes to be the servant of both.

It is, moreover, a significant fact of history that Christianity has always prospered most in the true sense when it has had least to do with the State and the State has had least to do with it. For the first three centuries it was the theology of individual conviction, resting simply on its own evidence, holding no other relation to the State than that of a persecuted religion, and doing its entire work by the use of spiritual means; and then it was that it spread itself among the nations of the earth with a purity and power that have never since been exceeded. Then it was that venerable and pompous systems of Paganism yielded to the resistless energy of its moral march. Afterward it became a State theology; and then, in the hands of the State, it was not only corrupted and half-paganized, but at once assumed, and for centuries maintained, the character of a persecuting religion. All the persecutions of the Romish Church, and, indeed, all the persecutions that have existed in the name of Christianity, have had their basis in State theology. If God should be pleased to constitute a theocracy on earth, and by inspiring it guarantee its infallibility, then it would be the duty of men to bow to its authority; but until we have this fact established by appropriate evidence the conclusion drawn from history is that the State should confine itself exclusively to things temporal, and leave theology to the individual convictions and private judgments of men. This is certainly the truth in respect to Christianity.

There can be no doubt that a true theology in the heads and hearts of the people is a very important and much-needed influence for good in relation to civil government; yet it does not follow that the State is the proper party to take care of this theology, to define it, to teach it, to support it, or in any way invest it with the sanction of law. Those who set up the proposition that religion is essential to morality, and also the further proposition that morality is essential to good government, and then infer that the State should establish and support religion are guilty of a palpable *non-sequitur* in logic. The truth of their premises does not prove that of their conclusion. It may be true (facts show it to be so) that the State will receive the largest and purest contribution of morality founded on religion when the latter is left entirely to the educational influences of the family and the Church ; and if so, then State theology is not only a superfluity, but a positive damage to the best interests of the commonwealth. The morality as derived from religion which the State needs will be best supplied by the confinement of its agency to things temporal and the entire omission on its part of any attempt to administer things spiritual. The State can do religion no favor so great as to have nothing to do with it, and itself no favor so great as to let religion alone. The moment the two are put in alliance with each other both are injured.

Those who drew the plan of our National Government built the system upon the principle that religion and civil government were to be kept entirely distinct; and, for the most part, all the State governments are constructed upon the same theory. The general character of both is that they neither affirm nor deny any doctrine in respect to God and that they command no duty as a religious duty. They deal with the temporal rights and obligations of citizenship, without any reference to the question whether the citizen is a religionist or not. His religious faith is no part of his citizenship and no criterion of his rights. It confers upon him no immunities and imposes no disabilities. It is a matter between himself and his God, and with it the civil authority does not concern itself. He is not forbidden to be an atheist and not commanded to be a Christian. He forfeits no rights by being the one and gains none by being the other; and as between these two extremes of opinion, the State does not undertake to decide which is the true and which is the false opinion. Such is the great American principle in respect to the sphere of civil government. This principle, being the exact antipodes of State theology, admits of no reconciliation with it.

We submit this summary of thoughts in regard to State theology for the consideration of those who insist that the public school system of this country shall be made the instrument of religious education. Catholics, in respect to their own children, desire that the education should be thoroughly religious in the sense of teaching the Catholic faith; and to this there is no objection if they will give it at their own charges and not ask the State to be a party thereto, either by remitting taxes in their favor or appropriating public money for the purpose. A very considerable number of Protestants who are agreed in being opposed to any teaching of Catholicism by the State also desire that the amount and kind of religious education in the public school should be equal to that naturally furnished by reading King James's version of the Sacred Scriptures in these schools, either with or without the supplement of prayer and religious singing. Both classes, while widely at variance as to what the religious teaching shall be, nevertheless, want the teaching by the authority of the State and at the expense of the general public.

The practical meaning of this demand is that an American State shall in its public school adopt the principle of State theology. Have those who make the demand well considered the fact that they logically ally themselves with all the religious despotisms that have ever existed among men? They in effect accept and advocate a principle which has in all ages been the enemy of religious liberty, against which heroes have fought, on whose cruel altars martyrs have bled, and whose historic enormities are sufficient to startle the world. They assume that an American State has a theology to teach and support; and in this one assumption they pass the Rubicon, and grant what never did anything for Christianity but to corrupt and weaken it as a moral and spiritual power.

The question of Bible reading and other religious exercises in the public school, when sifted to its bottom, is really a question of State theology. It comes to this at last. And, to say nothing now about the conflicts of opinion as to what the theology shall be and the utter impossibility of satisfying all the parties with any theology, we are opposed to the whole underlying theory, anywhere and everywhere, whether applied to men, women, or children, in a school system or a church system. If the State will simply take care of the *citizen* in his rights as a human being and a member of the body politic, the religionist will have all the care that he needs and certainly all to which he is entitled. It cannot connect its authority with the religionist or his faith as such without exceeding its own proper jurisdiction and without immensely more mischief than benefit. In order to be a democratic State, governed by the rule of equal and impartial justice, it must leave the religionist and his creed to take care of themselves, concerning itself only with the *citizen*. The moment the State abandons this ground the elementary law of a democratic government is gone.

XI.

CIVIL GOVERNMENT.

It is of the utmost importance to society that human rights as to person and property should be defined and protected by the authority of law; that the public peace should be preserved; that crime should be punished; that controversies among individuals should admit of settlement by legal arbitration, and that the people should be defended against encroachments by foreign enemies. For these and similar temporal purposes, civil government in some form is a necessity, in the sense that either they cannot be secured at all or cannot be so well secured without it. Though not absolutely perfect and though capable of great abuses, it is, nevertheless, the best machinery for these ends that human wisdom can employ. No other can take its place or do its work. No government was ever so oppressive that it was not far better than anarchy. The total absence of all government would be the very extreme of the savage condition.

The purposes of government, as thus specified, are *moral* in kind, since they relate to the rights of life, liberty, and the pursuit of happiness. They are also *temporal* in their scope, since they have no reference to what may or may not await us after death. The present advantages of civil government are sufficient to vindicate its propriety, even if no other and higher interests were attached to human nature. The atheist ought to believe in its necessity and wisdom. The things of time do not cease to be real and do not lose their value while they last because they are limited to this life.

And yet, if we concede the doctrine of a personal God, to whom we owe duties, and that of a future state, to which death consigns us, then what are called things *spiritual*, in distinction from things *temporal*, form immeasurably the largest and most important field of human thought. Our chiefest interests must lie in the former. It has, hence, been inferred that civil government, being so necessary and useful in the sphere of things temporal, should extend its regulative agency and supervision into the higher sphere of our spiritual relations, and, in so doing, define, teach, and enforce religious duties. State religion—namely, religion allied with and sustained by the civil power—is the formal expression of this idea. Those who demand that our public school-system—a system which is purely governmental, because ordained, established, and conducted by State authority—should be the instrument of *religious* as well as of secular education, in logical effect, commit themselves to this doctrine. They ask the State to be the minister and propagator of religion in the public school, and thus grant the principle that the civil power may and should extend its action into the sphere of things spiritual. Their argument is essentially the one which has in all ages been urged in behalf of State religion. We object to both the argument and the conclusion, whether applied to a public school system or anywhere else.

The fact that civil government is the best possible agency to attain certain temporal ends does not prove that it is equally well adapted to spiritual and religious ends, or that it is at all adapted to the latter purpose. To show that a thing is good in one relation and for one object clearly does not show that it would be good in another relation and for a different object. Macaulay, in his review of Gladstone's work on Church and State, says: "It is of very much more importance that men should have food than that they should have piano-fortes. Yet it by no means follows that every piano-forte maker ought to add the business of a baker to his own; for, if he did so, we should have both much worse music and much worse bread."

A society of men organized for one purpose may, as thus organized, be well adapted to its attainment; but if it were to add some other purpose, and attempt to accomplish both at the same time, it might fail in respect to both, as it would not in respect to the first purpose if its action had been strictly confined thereto. So civil society, acting through government and wielding the forces of legislative, judicial, and executive power, may be and is a most appropriate organization to maintain public order, to establish justice, and punish crime; but it does not follow that it is equally well fitted or fitted at all to undertake the cure of souls, to teach religion, and prescribe rules for the observance of men in their relations to God. The transcendent importance of things spiritual, as compared with things temporal, furnishes in itself no reason why government should embrace the former in its sphere of action. It may be that they will be best promoted by being let alone, so far as government is concerned, and that its duties in the temporal sphere will be best discharged by exclusive confinement to them.

No human government is omnipotent or omniscient, and, hence, no such government can give its attention to everything that concerns the welfare of society. The effort would not only overwhelm it with the magnitude of the task, but so interfere with the freedom of individual action as to produce more evil than good. Society may be as much damaged by being governed too much as by being governed too little. The things which governments can wisely do are few when contrasted with that vast bulk of things which must be left to individual thought and enterprise. The care of infant children in the family is a very important interest ; yet nobody pretends that government should regulate the nursery, beyond the general prevention of crime. What men eat and drink, as to both quantity and quality, is also important ; but no one claims that government should establish rules of personal hygiene. The business which men pursue and their manner of pursuing it are most vital questions ; yet government cannot assume the work of managing the industries of society, beyond the general function of protecting individual rights. The great mass of human interests must be left and by every wise government are left to the spontaneous and self-imposed care of those whom they specially concern.

Religion, considered as a faith in regard to God or as a practice in the expression of this faith, evidently belongs to this class of interests. It is in its very nature a matter between the individual soul and its God, and, hence, placed beyond the appropriate jurisdiction of civil government. It is not possible to conceive of anything more entirely foreign to that jurisdiction.

Moreover, all civil governments act authoritatively and sustain their authority by the compulsory law of force. They grant to the subject no discretion. They assume their own infallibility, as against the right of the individual practically to dispute it. They put their opinions into execution, if necessary, by the sword. Where, then, is there any proper place in things spiritual—things that have their center in God and refer mainly to the interests of the after-life—for any merely human government to exercise its authoritative power over the individual will? Shall it adopt a creed for the people, and thus decide what creed they shall adopt? Shall it regulate their mode of worship? Shall it tax them for the support of a religion which it thinks to be true, but which some of them may think to be false? Shall it make its conscience the law for their conscience? There is no religious belief and no religious duty to which it can add the civil sanction without invading the inalienable rights of the individual conscience; and, at the same time, assuming an authority which belongs to God only. It may justly require that no one shall make his religion an excuse for crime against the temporal good order and safety of society, and so it may protect every one in the free and peaceable exercise of his religion; but beyond these two points it cannot go without taking the fatal step which logically involves the whole principle of State religion.

Concede religion to be one of the ends for the attainment of which governments exist among men, and all laws necessary and proper for carrying this end into effect follow as a matter of course, and this is in its very nature the essence of religious despotism. Every step in this direction places the religious liberty of the individual at the pleasure of the government, armed with the whole power of society to enforce that pleasure. If government may tax him to support and teach religion, then it may establish for him a religion which he must observe whether he believes it or not. The only escape from this result is that theory of civil government which limits it to things temporal and denies to it any jurisdiction or any duties beyond impartial protection in the sphere of things spiritual. This, and this only, secures religious liberty, as against any oppression by the civil power.

The correctness of this theory is strongly confirmed by the general fact of history that when religion and civil government are legally united neither derives any benefit from the union, but both are seriously damaged by it. The most characteristic feature of such a union is that of a bad religion and a bad government at the same time, each being harmed by the other. Let it be remembered that the governments of the world have almost always been wrong on the subject of religion; that the majority of them have been opposed to the religion of the Bible and quite often persecuted it; that they have generally used religion for selfish and ambitious purposes; that by uniting it with the State they have corrupted both; and that, for a rule, their religious propagandism has been mainly that of error, rather than truth. These facts prove most conclusively that civil government is a failure when it attempts to administer and regulate religion; and, hence, in the interests of pure religion, as well as those of good government, every Christian, every statesman, and every citizen should protest against any theory that carries even a single drop of State religion in its veins. We cannot import rulers from the skies or impart to earthly rulers the inspiration and infallibility of the skies. Governments must be managed by men; and if history proves any thing, it proves that men are very poor managers when they exercise the civil power in relation to religion. Their positions make them despots in theory, and in practice they often become demons incarnate, treading under foot the rights of conscience with a ferocity as reckless as it is cruel.

The theory which unites government and religion and makes the latter one of the ends to be pursued by the former, if good at all, is equally good for *all* governments—for "the powers that be" in

Turkey, Japan, and China, as really as for those of these United States. Apply the theory in China, and it means State power employed to sustain, propagate, and enforce Buddhism and idolatry. Apply it in Turkey, and it means the same power thus employed in the interests of Mohammedanism. It so happens that the world is fruitful in religious systems ; and, unless we adopt the doctrine that all these systems are equally true or equally false, the theory, as thus applied, would lead to the most opposite results and entirely confound the distinction between the true and the false. If when applied to Christianity it would promote the truth, it would, with equal certainty, promote the grossest superstition and error when applied to Paganism. A change of circumstances often gives one a view of things otherwise not so readily taken.

Let us then suppose a Protestant to transfer his residence to China and to become subject to the government of that country. While in this country, we will further suppose, he belonged to the class demanding that religion shall be included in the educational *régime* of the public schools, and was horrified at the idea of not having King James's version of the Sacred Scriptures read in these schools for religious purposes. How does he reason when the principle comes to be applied to him in China ? The Chinese Emperor agrees with him in his principle, and proposes to tax him, not to support and teach Protestant Christianity, but to support and teach the religion of China, which he regards as an abominable idolatry. This would probably open his eyes to the nature of his own doctrine. Yet, if it is the right of one government to enter the province of things spiritual, and tax the people to support and propagate religion, then it is the right of all governments to do so.

The principle, if valid at all, is just as valid for Paganism as it is for Christianity, for idolatry as it is for the purest worship, for the most superstitious form of Roman Catholicism as it is for the most enlightened Protestantism. No Protestant would ask for its application in any other than a Protestant country; and this is a good reason why he should not ask for it there. If it is not good in China or Catholic Spain, it is no better in these United States. The principle is the same, no matter to what religion it is applied, or whether Pagans or Christians, Catholics or Protestants form the majority of the people. It is the principle of State religion, good everywhere or good nowhere. If Protestants were in the minority in this country and Catholics in the majority, the former certainly would not advocate a public school system, to be supported by general taxation, in which Catholicism should be taught.

The conclusion from this line of thought is that civil government, though the best possible machinery to secure certain ends connected with our temporal interests, is not a contrivance adapted to secure the ends that relate to our spiritual welfare. "Surely," says Macaulay, "if experience shows that a certain machine, when used to produce a certain effect, does not produce that effect once in a thousand times, but produces in the vast majority of cases an effect directly contrary, we cannot be wrong in saying it is not a machine of which the principal end is to be so used."

The learned essayist might justly have said that it is not a machine properly adapted to this end at all. The notorious and world-wide failures of civil government to make itself useful in the department of things spiritual, when attempting to manage and conduct them, furnish the most complete demonstration that, however useful it may be elsewhere, it is not suited to this purpose. A sledge-hammer is a very good instrument with which to break a rock, but a very poor tool with which to mend a watch or perform a delicate operation in surgery. So civil government is a very good agency within certain limits and for certain objects; but beyond these limits and objects it has no function to perform, and when its powers are extended beyond them they are found in practice to be immensely more injurious than beneficial to the very interests they seek to serve.

Mr. Madison was right when he said: "Religion is not within the purview of human government." He was right again when he said: "Religion is essentially distinct from human government and exempt from its cognizance. A connection between them is injurious to both. There are causes in the human breast which insure the perpetuity of religion without the aid of law." In a letter addressed to Gov. Livingston, July 10th, 1822, he further said: "I observe with particular pleasure the view you have taken of the immunity of religion from civil govėrnment in every case where it does not trespass on private rights or the public peace. This has always been a favorite doctrine with me." He certainly was not an atheist or a hater of religion; but was a profound thinker, who did more than any other man in framing the Constitution of the United States, and as such he saw that it was best for the State, and best for religion, that the two should be kept absolutely independent and distinct.

The American people have only to apply the principle avowed by Mr. Madison to our public schools, and this would be the end of the whole discussion on the subject. The conclusion would be that, as a State agency to attain certain temporal ends, the public school has nothing to do with religion, and religion nothing to do with it. The government employing it has no religion to teach, not being a government for Christians any more than for Deists, or for Protestants any more than for Catholics. It is not its business, as a government, to affirm or deny, to teach or support any religious system.

XII.

THE POLITICAL VALUE OF RELIGION.

Judge Hagans, of the Supreme Court of Cincinnati, in delivering his opinion in the case of Minor and others *vs.* The Board of Education of Cincinnati and others, said: "In a word, it is the *political value* of religion, morality, and knowledge which the State proposes to secure for its varied purposes, and that only." This utterance was preceded by an extended quotation from an article by Dr. Seelye, which appeared in the *Bibliotheca Sacra*, Vol. XIII, No. 52. In this article Dr. Seelye says that "the State has its own end," and that it "uses religion as a means to this end; but religion itself is never an end with the State. Everything relating to the moral and religious life of its subjects is of interest to the State only so far as the State can use it to its own ends." Again he says: "With the State religion is a means." He says again: "There are temporal and earthly interests for the individual, and it is to subserve these that there is a State, a community, among men. These interests are undoubtedly more perfectly secured through the agency of some religion, and hence the proper and necessary connection of religion with the State. But in this connection religion is ever the servant; never the sovereign. It is to be used to secure some end"—namely, some temporal end, that comes within the province of the State. On this ground we understand Dr. Seelye to hold to a legitimate "connection of the State with religion, and the duty of the State to maintain its religion," while he disclaims any right on its part to resort to persecution.

The substance of this theory, as adopted by Judge Hagans and more fully explained by Dr. Seelye, seems to be this: The State may and should incorporate religion into its own being as a part of its public law; not as an end, or on account of what religion is in itself, considered as a spiritual system, but solely on account of what the State can do with it as the means of promoting the civilization, improvement, and good earthly order of the body politic. The State can make use of it as a "servant," and, hence, in this character should maintain it. Its "political value" brings it within the purview of civil government.

This theory is as old as the efforts of human thought to vindicate the establishment and maintenance of religion by the civil power. There is nothing in it which limits it to Christianity in either the Catholic or the Protestant form, and it has not been so limited. It applies to any religious system, whether Pagan or Christian, true or false. Any such system, which in the judgment of the State, can be made useful for the attainment of its temporal ends may, as the means thereof, be legalized, adopted, and supported by the State. Almost any religion is, in its social effects, better than blank atheism; and, hence, it might be used by the State as a means, rather than have a nation of pure atheists, especially as no religion has ever been so bad as not to contain at least some rays of truth. Of course, it would be better for the State to adopt the true system; but, in its absence, it will be better to put its stamp on any system, and use it for State purposes, rather than be wholly without religion.

Now, in order to give this theory the benefit of the most favorable application, let us understand the term religion to mean Christianity. The case will then stand thus: The State may and should establish a connection between itself and Christianity; not because Christianity is true, not because it is a divine system in its authority, not on account of its relation to the spiritual duties and immortal interests of men, but solely on the ground of its *temporal* utility. Being an existing system known to the people, it is good for this purpose—just as revenue laws, currency laws, laws of debt and credit, patent laws, commercial laws, police regulations, courts of justice, state-prisons and indeed all the ordinary appliances of civil government are good to secure the material and social prosperity of the people. The State may, hence, maintain and use it as one of the wheels in its complex machinery, on the same principle that it maintains and uses other wheels to run its own system. Not what Christianity is, but what the State can get out of it for temporal purposes, is the single thing to be considered.

It is hardly necessary to say that Christ and his apostles did not preach the Gospel upon any such theory. They made no mention of it as the "servant" of the State. They presented it as God's supernatural interposition for the salvation of individual sinners. What the State should gain or lose by it was not their question. Salvation, and not State utility, was their grand idea. They did not concern themselves with the relations of the Gospel to Cæsar; but rather with its relations to God and sinners against his law. They preached repentance toward God and faith in the Lord Jesus Christ and warned men to flee from the wrath to come. There is a vast distance between the conception of Christianity as preached by its Author and his apostles and the conception of it as a piece of State machinery, sanctioned and sustained by the State on account of its "political value" or as the means of attaining a purely temporal end.

Let the State frankly enunciate the theory, and, hence, say that it uses Christianity as a mere instrument for State ends; and let the people, including the children in the public school, both understand and accept the theory, and who believes that the system would then have any power to gain these ends? No one ever was and no one ever will be made a Christian on the ground of State utility. No man ever made a prayer to God as the means of turning himself into a good citizen. A truly pious man will be a good citizen; but the motives that make him pious rise infinitely above the range of citizenship. The State can successfully work the theory of "political value" only by being a hypocrite, pretending one thing while seeking another.

If a general should hold morning and evening prayers with his army, or have religious lectures delivered to his soldiers, simply to make them better *fighters* in the day of battle, they would only need to understand the *sham* to treat the whole thing with contempt. Religion cannot be brought down to the level of State strategy or fighting strategy, and yet retain its power as religion. At this level it has no value for either purpose. The moment we make it the means of an end immeasurably less than itself, and so regard it, we destroy its power as religion. The man who is religious for the sake of making money is not religious at all; and so the State that uses the Christian religion simply for its "political value" adopts a theory that cannot survive its own exposure. Let the State by all means put the theory among the *esoteric* doctrines which are not to be known. Statesmen may perhaps be admitted into the secret; but it will not do to give it to the common people, and especially it will not do to tell the children in the public school that they are trained in religion and its duties in order to promote the temporal ends for which the State exists.

The theory, moreover, involves all the perils to religious liberty which ally themselves with the system that makes the regulation of religious belief and practice one of the *ends* of civil government. The distinction between the two theories may be very nicely worked out in an essay; yet, if the State may establish a connection between itself and religion as a means to State ends, then it may equally decide what religion it will so use—whether Christianity or some other system—and, having settled this point, then it is equally privileged to determine upon the methods by which it will sustain and apply the chosen system. The power to use Christianity as a means implies the power of employing all the means of using it. Whether, then, the State will simply teach the religion it uses for temporal ends, or enforce it by pains and penalties, how far it will tolerate other religions, to what extent it will tax the people for the support of its own system, and by what rules it will regulate the administration thereof—these and the like questions will be answered according to the bigotry or liberality of those who enact and apply the laws. The fatal step is taken by conceding that the State has any jurisdiction in the premises, whether religion be viewed as a means or an end.

The voice of history is that all such deposits of power with civil government, whether as a means or otherwise, are exceedingly dangerous to the liberties of the people. No small part of the oppressions which have cursed mankind may be traced, directly or indirectly, to the administration or regulation of religion by State authority. Their justification has been State necessity or Church necessity, or both put together. Even Christianity has never been able to enter into any alliance with the civil power without receiving damage and doing damage. Many pages of its history are stained with the blood of martyrs slain in order to maintain its authority and put down heresy. The framers of our National Government were eminently wise in making all organic connection between religion and that government, upon any theory or for any purpose, and, hence, all disabilities, proscriptions or persecutions on religious grounds, constitutionally impossible. There are no consequences in the way of evil attaching themselves to this doctrine in practice that in the magnitude of the evil will at all compare with the consequences of the opposite doctrine.

Christianity is a divinely-given system of religion, and, hence, authoritative over the individual conscience; yet there does not exist on all the face of the earth any civil government that has the right for any purpose to administer this authority. The assumption of the right is an act of tyranny, and every exercise thereof is simply the continuance of that tyranny. When Massachusetts, as was the fact prior to 1833, made every citizen taxable for the support of the *Protestant* religion, whether he was a Protestant or not, her constitution in this respect bore the distinctive mark of religious despotism. When, as was the fact prior to 1821, no person in Massachusetts was eligible to the office of governor, lieutenant-governor, or counsellor, or senator, or representative in the legislature, unless he upon oath declared his belief in the religion adopted and sanctioned by the State, then the same feature marked her constitution. Such provisions are virtually persecuting, no matter upon what theory they are defended.

Those who talk about the "political value" of religion as a reason why the State should maintain and teach it would do well to remember that Christianity has uniformly made its largest contribution to the State when left to depend upon the *voluntary* efforts of its friends, unconstrained and unregulated except by the law of Christ. Its brightest pages are the ones written when such has been the fact, and its darkest pages are those written when the reverse has been true. What the State really wants for its own good is the elevating and purifying power of Christianity in the hearts of the people; and all history shows that in reference to this end the State can do nothing so wise for itself as *simply to do nothing* and leave the work of maintenance and propagation to other and more appropriate agencies. It has always proved itself to be a poor preacher of the Gospel, and quite often a worse theologian. It never did the work well and it never can, because it is not well adapted to the work.

The Bible speaks of Christians, and not of the State, as the visible Kingdom of God and as the habitation of God through the Spirit. To the former, and not the latter, Christ gave the preaching and propagating commission, and never said a word implying that the civil power, as such, was to be called into his service. The simple truth is that the Church, composed of his friends and inspired with holy zeal in his cause, holding in her hands the sword of the Spirit, which is the Word of God, and, without any State battalions or State tax-gatherers, assailing the citadels of sin and error—yes, the Church, unlicensed and unpatronized by the State, yet strong in argument, patient in effort, persuasive in love, and, above all, having the assurance of divine help, constitutes the effective soldiery in this warfare. It can make more converts than the State can, and make better ones. Christianity, in itself, in its own appointments, in the inspirations which it imparts and the laws which it prescribes, contains all the necessary instrumentalities for its own diffusion; and the State can add nothing thereto with any advantage.

Granting, then, as we most cheerfully do, the great "political value" of the Christian religion as the means of producing good government, we come to a conclusion entirely different from that drawn by Judge Hagans and substantially drawn by Dr. Seelye. The surest way to realize this value is to leave the spiritual agencies of Christianity entirely to the voluntary, the self-imposed and self-directed efforts of its friends. Let them build their own churches, choose and support their own ministers, and, subject to the rules of good public order, manage their affairs according to their own discretion. Let them replenish their own money-chest and disburse their own free-will offerings. Let them organize as many religious schools as they choose, and in those schools teach what seems to them good, whether on the Sabbath or the week day, and then let them pay the expenses thereof. Let the State afford to them impartial protection, and stop there. This gives Christian truth, and its friends a fair and open field, without patronage and without State resistance. More would be bad policy, even if we concede that the State has a right to do more. By doing more it would lose rather than gain.

Elevate and sanctify the people, as individuals, by a wide diffusion of the real power of Christianity, and there will be no trouble about the State, especially under a republican government. Such a people will take care of the State, by choosing good rulers and sustaining good laws. Their intelligence and personal character will guarantee a government of righteousness. Masterly inactivity on the part of the State, in the sense of leaving the maintenance, propagation, and administration of the Christian religion entirely to the *voluntary* principle, is just the position to call forth the intensest activity on the part of the Church. It is the best position for the church, and the best position for Christianity, and equally the best for the State to derive from both the largest quantity of moral power which it is possible to apply in this imperfect world.

XIII.

STATE PERSONALITY.

One of the arguments urged in favor of religious teaching and worship in our public school system is based on the theory that the State, as such, in its political and corporate character, is virtually a moral person, and, hence, like individuals, the subject of religious responsibility. It must to some extent, at least, be a theological organism, and, as such, discharge religious duties, or be justly exposed to the imputation of irreligion and antagonism toward God. Those who adopt this view reason in regard to the State, considered as a body politic, just as they do in respect to living and conscious moral agents. A similar method of reasoning is employed by those who desire to have the Constitution of the United States so amended as to make it a religious as well as a political instrument. An organic law without religion in it, like a public school without religion in it, is an offense to God; and neither should be tolerated, especially by a people who hold to the doctrine of a personal God and the duty of religious worship. The purpose of this article is to examine the merits of this politico-religious theory.

What then, is a State, in the general sense of this term? Bouvier, in his "Law Dictionary," answers this question by saying that it is "a self-sufficient body of persons united together in one community for the defense of their rights and to do right and justice to foreigners. In this sense the State means the whole people united into one *body politic.*" Chief-Justice Chase, in delivering the opinion of the Supreme Court of the United States in the case of Texas *vs.* White (7 Wallace, p. 720, 721), said:

"It [a State] sometimes describes a people or community of individuals united more or less closely in political relations, inhabiting temporarily or permanently the same country; often it denotes only the country or territorial region inhabited by such a community; not unfrequently it is applied to the government under which the people live; at other times it represents the combined idea of people, territory, and government. It is not difficult to see that in all these senses the primary conception is that of a people or community. The people * * * constitute the State. * * * A State, in the ordinary sense of the Constitution, is a political community of free citizens, occupying a territory of defined boundaries and organized under a government sanctioned and limited by a written constitution and established by the consent of the governed."

The constituent elements of a State or nation are these: 1. A number of individual human persons. 2. The political union of these persons under a government of law vested in and administered by legal agents. 3. Their conjoint occupancy of a given territory, over which, as to persons and things, the government exercises a supreme and independent jurisdiction. Individual persons, as the primary conception, and their common subjection to the same government and common occupancy of a given territory, as the complemental conceptions, constitute a body politic or State. These persons are succeeded by others holding similar civic relations, and thus the State is perpetuated. The title of the State is simply a class-term to represent all these individuals thus united together.

Is, then, a State, considered as a whole and in distinction from the individuals composing it, a personality possessing a moral nature and subject to religious responsibility? Professor Pomeroy, in his "Introduction to Municipal Law," p. 392, says that "the State, as separated from the individuals who compose it, has no existence except in a figure; and that to predicate religious responsibility of this abstraction is an absurdity. Whatever, then, the State does, whatever laws it makes, touching religious subjects, are done and made not because the State is responsible, but simply that the people may be secure in the enjoyment of their own religious preferences." This he presents as the theory of our national and State constitutions, in accordance with which "the State, as an organic body, has nothing whatever to do with religion, except to protect the individuals in whatever belief and worship they may adopt." The word State or nation is an abstract or class-term, used to designate a mass of individuals in certain relations to each other, established and maintained by law; and to predicate personality of this numerical aggregate, or of the relations existing between its constituent parts, except as a mere figure of speech, is an absurdity. A corporate personality is simply a fiction. A person is a living and conscious moral unit, and no collection of such units, in whatever manner related to each other, can make a person.

When the Bible speaks of a State or nation it uses the title by which it is known; and this title is not the name of a person, but simply a term applicable to a whole class of persons. God blesses or curses a nation only by blessing or cursing the individuals who compose it. National character, national responsibility, and national virtue or vice exist only in the people, and independently of the people they have no existence. The only personality that even by a figure can be affirmed of bodies of men grows out of their organization into bodies, and this consists wholly in a set of *relations* which real persons hold to each other, and on account of which they are bodies politic or corporate, in distinction from miscellaneous and unrelated individuals.

Pennsylvania, for example, is a State or body politic, composed of individuals and existing as a State only through these individuals. Their joint occupancy of a given territory and their common subjection to the same government make them a body politic or State. There is no objection to speaking of a State as a *plural* person, if we keep in mind that this is but a phrase of rhetoric, used to describe real persons in certain relations to each other, and that in reality there is no such thing as a plural person. A bank corporation is a plural person in the sense of a number of real persons associated for the purpose of doing the banking business, and in this sense only. So a State is a plural person only in the sense of a number of persons politically associated under a government of law. They do not, by the association, beget a real personality distinct from their own as separate individuals.

Passing this point without further illustration, we come now to the inquiry whether individuals who as separate and distinct persons are bound to have a theology and glorify God in their bodies and spirits, which are his, may lawfully unite themselves together in social organizations that do not include religion in their objects, and, hence, do not embrace any religious creed, worship, or duty in the terms of the union? Let us reduce this general question to specific modes of statement.

May two men form a partnership whose sole business is to buy and sell goods? May bank corporations, railway companies, insurance companies, trust companies, manufacturing companies, and the like be organized for purposes which are purely temporal, and, hence, in the objects to be attained, involve no reference whatever to God or the duties which the associated persons, as individuals, owe to the Supreme Being? Must we, as moral beings, abjure every association with others which, as such, does not profess faith in the existence of God, and which, therefore, proposes no duty toward him as one of the things to be accomplished by it? Must every body of men, considered as a body, perform the religious duties which belong to them as individuals? Is the mere absence of religion in a social organization for a temporal purpose to be set down as a positive principle of irreligion?

We suppose it enough to ask these questions. Their answer lies upon their very face. No one unless a wild and impracticable fanatic, will lay it down as a principle of religious ethics that the duties which each individual owes to God morally exclude him from associating with others for purposes and objects that have no reference to God. Such a principle would forbid two men to unite their strength in lifting a stone, which neither alone could lift, unless a religious creed was stamped on the process. There are many lawful associations of men in which the alternative does not lie between religion and positive irreligion, so that it must be one or the other; and to assume that this is the alternative in respect to these associations, and then proceed to denounce them as atheistical and irreligious because they are not positively religious in their objects, may be a wonderful display of zeal, yet it is zeal at the expense of common sense.

How, then, is it with that particular organization, association, or union of persons that we call a State or body politic? Must it be positively religious in its objects in order not to be positively irreligious? Take for example, the people who in adopting the Constitution and providing thereby for the establishment of a civil government, styled themselves "the people of the United States." By this instrument they organized a great national association, whose objects, as set forth in the preamble, were "to form a more perfect union, establish justice, insure domestic tranquillity, provide for the common defense, promote the general welfare, and secure the blessings of liberty to ourselves and our posterity." The whole Constitution is limited to these confessedly *temporal* objects. It neither affirms nor denies any doctrine in respect to God or any duty of human beings toward him. It expressly declares that "no religious test shall ever be required as a qualification to any office or public trust under the United States." An atheist is, hence, just as eligible to any national office as the most devout Christian. And to put the purpose of the people beyond the possibility of dispute or doubt the First Amendment to the Constitution provides that "Congress shall make no law respecting an establishment of religion, or prohibiting the free exercise thereof."

Here, then, is a constitution, and here a civil government provided for by it, and here a great national State organized under it, with no affirmation or denial touching religion in the fundamental law.

Whether the people are Pagans or Mohammedans, Atheists or Christians, does not appear in the law. No matter what they are, considered religiously, the objects specified are such as are of common concern and importance to them all. Now, is this Constitution opposed to God and atheistical in the evil sense because it does not embrace any doctrine of God in its provisions and does confine itself and the government which its authorizes exclusively to the temporal objects named in the preamble? Is the nation a community of atheists because God and religion are not found in its organic law? We might as well say that the Constitution is opposed to the Copernican theory of astronomy, because it contains no doctrine on the subject of astronomy.

It is neither a theistic nor an anti-theistic constitution; but republican in its theory of government and absolutely secular in its ends. The State established under it, existing as a body politic and doing its work through the agency of a government, is not a theological State, any more than it is a geological or astronomical State. It is a republican organism, for purposes that relate purely to the temporal interests of men; and, as such, it has no opinions to express or enforce in regard to religion. And in this attitude of simple omission there is no opposition to God or to Christianity, and certainly no express or implied avowal of atheism as a creed.

It is true, in all cases in which affirmation is a duty, that negatives, not in the sense of positive denials, but in that of not affirming, are equivalent to positive denials. But where affirmation is not a duty, there silence is not an offense. If one is not bound to speak, there is no sin in not speaking. Let it then be shown that States, as such, and civil governments, as such, are bound to have a theology, and assert it by legal provisions, and we shall concede their sinfulness if they fail to comply with the obligation. Let us have the Scriptures, or the intuitions, or the experience on which this proposition rests. The theory of State personality furnishes no such proof, since it is nothing but a mere fiction of the brain. History shows that for governments, as such, to assume that religion is one of their proper ends, and then act upon the assumption, is among the gravest mistakes that can be made in human society. Out of this one mistake have arisen the politico religious despotisms that have cursed the race, and to a large extent the religious corruptions that have dishonored God and injured the interests of truth. There is no lesson more clearly taught by history than that civil governments are not well fitted to be creed-makers or creed-administrators in religious matters.

This being the fact, then these governments, surely, are not to be regarded as atheistical and hostile to God if they simply do not do what they are not fitted to do and what no law of God, in the Bible or out of it, requires them to do. They are not to be indicted as offenders because they limit themselves to their proper business. Well would it be for the world if all governments and States had been guilty of this kind of offence.

But should not those who enact and administer laws discharge their religious duties to God by acts of homage and obedience to his will? Undoubtedly they should; not because they are kings or rulers, but because, like all other human beings, they are personal subjects of the divine government. It so happens, however, that the duties which they owe to God do not extend to their *official* character as civil rulers in any sense that confers on them the right to prescribe the religious duties of those subject to their authority. They are not prophets of the Lord and not delegated to expound or execute the divine will. Simply as rulers, exercising governmental power, they have no right to have any religion, and cannot have any without being usurpers in theory and almost always oppressors in practice. It is quite enough for them to perform their own personal duties to God, and then concede precisely the same privilege to all others, without any hindrance or constraint. Their official responsibility has nothing to do with the enactment and enforcement of laws to regulate the religion of the people. Here they have no rightful jurisdiction and, hence, no duty to discharge to God or man.

All this clamor about atheism and positive irreligion being the necessary corollary of no religion in the State organism is either a mere play upon words or a gross blunder of the intellect. It invests the State, in distinction from the people composing it, with personal attributes, and then assumes that its duties in the matter of religion are identical with those of real persons. The individual must have a theology in his head and his heart, and, therefore, the State must have the same in its head and heart, not as an individual, but as that mysterious entity or *something* known as a State. Unfortunately for the theory, this something has neither a head nor a heart: neither a body nor a soul. All the existence which it has or can have is simply that of certain *relations* which individuals hold to each other and on account of which they are, taken in the aggregate, called a State. And to our dull apprehension if these individuals, each for himself, including rulers and subjects, do justly, love mercy, and walk humbly with God, they will in the most effectual way acknowledge and honor him. They do not need, in order not to be opposed to God, to write their religious creed in their governmental constitution or make it one of the objects for which they are associated as a body politic.

George Washington, surely, was not an atheist. The men who framed the Constitution of the United States were not atheists. The people who placed their seal upon this instrument were not atheists. They believed in God and large numbers of them were devout worshippers; and yet they adopted a constitution of government from which they excluded—not by accident, but with deliberate purpose—all distinctively religious ends and ideas. No other example of atheism and hostility to God, according to the theory we have been considering, so openly enunciated and so long continued, can be found in all the annals of mankind. The logic of this theory turns this Constitution into organized atheism of the most frightful character. Think of it! Not a word about God, or about Christ, or about the plan of salvation, or about Heaven or Hell in any part of this instrument! Forty millions of people, millions of whom are Christians, living under such an atheistical Constitution! A civil government created, and year after year conducted for now almost a century, and no religion in it!

and Presbyterians, Baptists, Methodists, Congregationalists, Episcopalians, and various other religious sects parties to this enormity! The reader need feel no alarm. The enormity is the wisest, the best, the most reasonable plan for a civil government upon which the light of day ever dawned.

XIV.

STATE CONSCIENCE TOWARD GOD.

The advocates of religious instruction and worship in the public school, whether by the simple reading of the Bible, or with the addition of other exercises, insist that the *State* ought to have a conscience toward God. This conscience should embrace and affirm some definite system of religious belief; and this is the system to be taught in the public schools at the general expense. Not to have such a conscience and not thus to express it makes the State an offender against God. The central point of this argument is furnished by the word conscience, considered as an attribute of the State. The conscience in question is that of the State and the relation had in view is the one which it holds toward God. It is not only a State conscience, but it is a State conscience toward God. The duty to God which in this case it imposes is that of religious instruction and worship in the public school, organized and governed by the State and supported by compulsory taxation. Such is the argument. What is it worth?

In order to answer this question, we need in the outset to explain the term *conscience.* The term denotes any one or all of the following facts in the constitution and operations of the human mind: 1. The intuitive perception or idea of right and wrong as opposite moral categories. 2. A rational judgment applying this idea to specific actions, either done or to be done, and pronouncing them either right or wrong. 3. The authoritative sense of obligation to do or forbear according to the decisions of this judgment. 4. The moral emotion, either of approbation or disapprobation, when an act being done, is regarded as right or wrong. 5. The sense of merit or demerit, according to the view which the mind takes of the act, instinctively disposing virtue to expect reward and vice to anticipate punishment.

All these facts exist in human nature. Universal consciousness attests their reality and all languages have words for their expression. Whether the general term conscience in any particular use of it embraces all of them collectively, or simply refers to one or more of them, we always decide by the connections in which it is employed. The facts themselves, though intimately related to each other, are distinct, and, taken as a whole, they constitute an essential part of our moral nature.

The fundamental condition of a conscience

toward God is some idea of God, of what he is, and of our relations to him. This idea connects itself naturally with that of obligation to him, and with this is associated the direct and authorative sense of duty toward God. Coupled with this is the emotion of approval or disapproval, accordingly as we judge ourselves to be right or wrong in this relation. This emotion leads to the sense of good or ill desert, as the effect of our moral attitude toward the Supreme Being. Thus all the elementary facts which are comprehensively grouped under the generic term conscience appear in human consciousness when the *subjective* in man is engaged with the *objective* in God. They are not the fancies of hair-splitting metaphysics ; but realties, ranking among the most important elements of our spiritual being. Conscience *in* man is always conscience *toward* God when the latter enters the field of vision. God seen and thought of brings conscience into action. Man in this respect is not a stone or a brute ; but a moral being, so constructed as to be impressed with the idea of God.

All the facts of conscience, whether they relate to God or man, are *personal* facts, existing solely and only in *individual* minds. There may be millions of consciences, either concurrent or divergent in what they affirm ; yet every one of them belongs to some specific person. There is no such thing as an impersonal or general conscience not analyzable into individual ones. Wherever we find a conscience toward God there we find a moral being for its home. Its individuality is as obvious as our mental identity. Dispossessed of this feature, it instantly ceases to have any existence.

The individuals in whom a conscience toward God exists may, for the purposes of this article, be arranged into two classes—the first embracing all persons who are simply *private* citizens, and are, hence, invested with no official functions in the management of government; the second embracing the *officers of law*, or those who wield the authority and coercive power of government. All persons, in every community and under every form of government, belong to one or the other of these classes. The body politic is made up of rulers and the ruled.

As to the first class, there is no doubt that every member of it ought to have a conscience toward God for *himself* and to act according to its dictates. It is the highest authority that can be established in his soul for the government of his own conduct. It is the supreme law of his inner nature. It is, however, quite enough for him to place his own actions under the control of his own conscience, and leave all others to do the same thing. He may approve or condemn the conduct of others; he may extend or withhold his personal favors according to his own sense of duty; he may seek to enlighten those whom he deems to be in error; he may remonstrate against wrong; he may exercise all his powers in the discussion of moral and spiritual questions; whether in relation to God or man; but he has no right to be a trespasser upon the rights of conscience as vested in others. A conscience toward God that possesses the character of self-assuming and persecuting bigotry may be very zealous and sincere; yet it is the conscience of a despot, who, if he had as much power as zeal, would be a monster. Human nature, alike in Catholic and Protestant bosoms, is very apt to transcend the limits within which conscience may lawfully move and beyond which it becomes the usurper of other men's rights, claiming for itself prerogatives that do not belong to it.

As to the other class—namely, *legal officers*, who wield the power of the sword and whose will in relation to others is clothed with the attributes of *law*—it is equally clear that they are bound to have a conscience toward God and to obey its dictates. They ought to rule in the conscientious and pious fear of God. The fact that they are rulers and, as such, possess authority over others, does not cancel their personal responsibility to the King of kings. God's government reaches them as really as it does the humblest citizen or subject.

When, however, the civil ruler undertakes to make his conscience toward God a *law* for the regulation of others, defining by law what shall be their conscience toward God, and thus arming his conscience with the coercive powers of his office, then the whole question is most materially changed. His conscience is then *official,* and asserts and enforces a jurisdiction over the thoughts and actions of others in respect to God. It is not simply a reasoning conscience; but a mandatory one, with the compulsions of civil government behind it. It is not an apostleship to preach; but a statute to bind. It does not deal merely with the duties which men owe to each other as members of the State; but legislates in respect to the duties which they owe to God. This sort of conscience in the civil ruler, whether Christian or Pagan, Catholic or Protestant, is an outrage to individual rights and a curse to human society. Such consciences, whether right or wrong in the creed they affirm, are always wrong in connecting with it their official power. They are the consciences of usurpers.

If, then, the term *State,* as employed in the title of this article, simply means the people who compose the State and to whom it is applied as a class term, and who as individuals are subject to the authority of civil government, then there can be no question whether the State—that is to say, the people—viewed as individuals and citizens, each by himself, should have a conscience toward God and faithfully perform the duties which it imposes. If the term means those who rule in the enactment and execution of law, then it is equally clear that they ought to have a conscience toward God and to be influenced thereby in the discharge of all their duties, whether official and public or private and personal.

If, however, the meaning of a State conscience toward God be that the general conscience of the people, as an aggregate of individuals, or that of the civil ruler, or of both put together, should be embodied in a legal statute, and thus become a *law*, recognizing a religious system and providing for its enforcement or for its propagation at the public expense, then, under the somewhat plausible phraseology of a State conscience and of seeming fidelity to God, we have a theory as old as religious despotism. Such a conscience is simply the long standing heresy of tyrants. It is a conscience that carries with it the power of compulsion. How far other consciences shall be tolerated or whether they shall be tolerated at all is a question in regard to which these *legal* State consciences toward God have never been safe judges. History gives them a very bad reputation. The vicious and evil character of their underlying principle is not to be sanctified by a pious title. Satan does not become an angel of light by wearing an angel's garb.

What *kind* of a conscience toward God shall the State, as a legislating, coercing, and taxing power, possess and put into practice? What shall it affirm as true and what shall it reject as heresy? Shall it be a Pagan or a Christian, a Catholic or a Protestant, a Trinitarian or a Unitarian State conscience toward God? These are very vital questions if, on the plea of duty to God, we are going to establish an alliance between religion and the civil power. Manifestly, we want the *right* kind of religion—the true, and not the false; and, in order to be sure on this point, we need to find somewhere a body of men, or, at least, one man, whose conscience toward God may be taken as the infallible standard for all other consciences. The best way to run the machinery of such a conscience is to get a Pope, and then persuade some œcumenical council to vote that he is infallible, and then make him the head of the Church, and either the light or head of the State, or both at the same time. The Papacy just fits this theory of a State conscience toward God, and the theory just fits the Papacy. But for Protestants to adopt it, or to use an argument which, if it means anything, implies the theory, is to contradict one of the first principles of their professed faith. State consciences toward God, in the sense of connecting with them the civil power, ought to be the exclusive monopoly of Roman Catholicism.

In respect to *whom* shall the State have this conscience toward God, and how shall it express the same? The answer to this question given by a certain class of Protestants, in the discussion of the School question, is this: The State should have a conscience toward God in respect to the *children* in the public schools, and then express the same by providing for religious instruction in these schools—not according to the Catholic idea of such instruction, but according to the Protestant notion

—namely, by the reading of King James's version of the Sacred Scriptures, either with or without other religious exercises ; and that it should then tax all the people—Catholics and Protestants, Jews and Infidels alike—to pay the expenses. Such is the State conscience toward God upon which these Protestants insist. The meaning of their proposition is that the civil authority of the people, as represented by and operating through the agency of government, should make *their* conscience towards God the rule of its action in the public school. For their *kind* of conscience they claim the preference, and demand that the State, as a body politic, should concede the claim. A Catholic State conscience toward God would not be any more satisfactory to them than is their conscience to a Catholic or a Jew. Let the public school, in the matter of religion, be what they think it ought to be, and then the State is all right, because it agrees with them. Let it be what the Catholic desires it to be, and then the State is all wrong, because it does not agree with them.

But why limit this State conscience toward God to the children and the public school? Why not extend its benefits to adults, as well as children? Why should not the State take charge of the whole business of religious instruction in the community —appoint ministers to preach to and teach the people, build church-edifices, prescribe and regulate the forms of worship, make religion according to the judgment of the State compulsory, and then pay the expense out of the public treasury? Why stop half way with the work? The argument which declares that the State should have a conscience toward God, and then give expression to it by religious instruction and worship in the public school, if good at all, is good to prove more than those who use it are willing to admit. Generalize their logic, and, unless they believe in the doctrine of Church and State, they at once abandon it themselves, notwithstanding their zeal for it in a particular application.

There is, moreover, no reason why the State should tax the people to teach a given system of religion to children that is not just as good to show that it should do the same thing in order to teach religion to adults. The latter need it as really as the former; and, hence, if the business of religious teaching belongs to the State, as a duty which it owes to God, then it should be done on a scale as comprehensive as the wants of the people. To confine the effort simply to children is to fall very far short of its whole duty. Carry out the principle, and this State conscience toward God will not stop with the public school, but will extend to the entire people. It need hardly be said that this would most radically change the nature and purposes of our whole system of State governments. We do not believe that it is the province of the State, as such, to do the work at all, either in the public school or anywhere else, and, hence, we reject as both false and dangerous all State consciences toward God that make the State a religious propagandist. Individual consciences toward God there should be. State consciences toward God, in the sense of giving to individual consciences the authority of law, there should not be.

XV.

THE MAJORITY CONSCIENCE.

Mr. Gladstone, in his work on "The State in its Relations to the Church," reasoning from the postulate of State personality, in distinction from that of the people composing the State, derives therefrom the doctrine of State religion as a duty. The *kind* of religion to be established by the State "must be that of the conscience of the governor or none." Though meaning the parliamentary and royal conscience in favor of the Church of England, he, nevertheless, admits that the same principle would equally apply to the conscience of a Mohammedan or Pagan prince. Not what is true, but what "the governor" thinks, furnishes the rule for a State religion. He must, of course, follow his own opinions, and, hence, place the seal of his authority upon the religion which he thinks to be true.

Some who have participated in the discussion of the School question in this country claim for the so-called "majority conscience," as compared with that of a dissenting minority, just what Mr. Gladstone so strenuously asserted in behalf of "the conscience of the governor." They simply substitute the former for the latter conscience. In both cases the conscience is legal and official, and not simply advisory and argumentative.

Stated syllogistically, the argument stands thus: The majority ought to rule; those Protestants who demand religious instruction and worship in the public schools by reading King James's version of the Scriptures are the majority; therefore, these Protestants ought to rule. Nothing can be more conclusive than this reasoning, if we admit the premises. But if either premise is false or needs to be materially modified, then the conclusion is not quite so obvious.

There is no doubt that Protestants, taken as a whole, are much more numerous in this country than any other class of religionists; and in this sense there is no objection to calling it a Protestant country. Christianity under the Protestant form is the prevalent religion of the land. We should, however, bear in mind that Protestants, understanding by this term the church-membership of the various Protestant sects, do not embrace one-quarter of the whole population of the United States. If they were unanimous in the opinion that Bible-reading and religious instruction should be had in the public schools of the country, this would by no means establish the truth of the minor proposition in the above syllogism. It is well known that they are not thus unanimous; that large numbers of them adopt the theory of an exclusively *secular* education in any School system which the civil authority establishes, regulates, and supports by general taxation; that infidels and free-thinkers hold the same view; and that Jews and Catholics object to being taxed for the maintenance of public schools that are Protestant in their character or tendency. The public mind is greatly divided, and so is the Christian mind of this country divided, in regard to the School question; and what is the preponderant opinion of the people is very far from being settled. It will be time enough to reason from the majority conscience, as claimed by a certain class of Protestants, when the fact is established that this conscience represents the majority of the American people.

It is well also to remember that our public schools are not institutions of the General Government at all; but of the several State governments, under whose authority they exist. The majority conscience in New York State has nothing to do with the School question in Pennsylvania. It cannot overleap State boundaries without overleaping its own jurisdiction. At the most, it is a majority State conscience. And if the States, as is the usual fact, remit under general laws the management of public schools to local agencies, as boards of education in cities and trustees in school districts, chosen by the people, then this majority conscience narrows itself down to a city majority conscience or a school-district majority conscience, as the case may be. It does not even reach a whole State, to say nothing about the whole country, except by adding all these local majority consciences together.

Whether, then, King James's version, or the Douay version, or neither shall be used in the public schools would depend either upon the majority State conscience or upon that of local majorities. Hence, before the minor premise which we are now considering can be affirmed as the basis of a general conclusion in regard to our school system, we want to understand by a thorough canvass of all the States what the majority conscience really demands. We commend this item of statistical labor to those Protestants who assume for this conscience a specific character as the means of proving a corresponding conclusion.

It often happens that by simply changing the *minor* premise of a syllogism, while retaining the *major*, we not only entirely change the conclusion, but also reveal the true character of the latter premise. Take the following example: The majority ought to rule; the disciples of Thomas Paine, who demand that his "Age of Reason" shall be read and taught in the public schools, are the majority; therefore, these disciples ought to rule. Here we have the same *major* connected with a different *minor* premise, and, consequently, a different conclusion. Are Protestants, to say nothing about Jews and Catholics, prepared to accept this conclusion, and then quietly submit to taxation for the purpose of paying the expenses of teaching infidelity? Who doubts that they would protest against it as an outrage? And yet the syllogism is just as valid when used by the disciples of Thomas Paine, being the majority in any State or any school district, as it is when used by Protestants, they being the majority. Its logical power is precisely the same in both cases, unless we assume for Protestants some special right which is not common to all citizens.

Take another example: The majority ought to rule; Presbyterians, who demand that the Westminster Confession of Faith and the Shorter Catechism shall be taught in the public schools, are the majority; therefore, these Presbyterians ought to rule. This might be very agreeable to Presbyterians; but how would it be with the Baptists, the Methodists, the Episcopalians, and other religionists, when required to pay taxes for the teaching of Calvinism according to the Presbyterian interpretation? They would complain of the injustice, and this is precisely what Presbyterians themselves would do under similar circumstances.

We might extend these illustrations through any number of syllogisms, and, by simply changing the minor premise, prove almost all sorts of conclusions. An obvious fallacy lies in the major premise, especially in assuming the rule of the majority, without any qualification. The rule itself supposes a society of human beings bound together in certain relations and for certain ends or objects; and it is undoubtedly a good rule, so long as the action of the majority is limited to these ends. A railway company is organized to conduct a specific business, and is by the terms of its charter confined to that business. The majority of stockholders, represented by the directors, may control the business within the limits of the objects for which the company exists as set forth in its charter; yet no one will pretend that the majority, simply because it is such, would have the right to undertake the work of Christian missions to the heathen and spend the funds of the company in propagating the Gospel. The answer of law and of common sense to such a proposition would be that this work, however important, does not come within the scope of the organization; and, hence, that the majority cannot wield its powers for any such end. The charter itself is the constitution of the company, and protects the rights of the minority, by limiting the powers of the majority.

The same principle applies to civil government organized according to the democratic theory. The majority are entitled to rule within the limits of the objects for which such government exists; but the moment these limits are exceeded, then the action is simply usurpation and may be an outrage to the rights of the minority. No man, surely, will pretend that majorities under our system of government have a right to do just what they please. They must act within certain limits or become oppressors.

Let it, then, be shown that religion or irreligion in any form constitutes one of the ends of civil government, as we have it in this country, and that the people have vested their government with power to propagate one or the other; let the well established principles of American democracy in regard to religion be thus reversed; and then we shall grant that the majority conscience would have the *legal* right to suit itself, and, at the general expense, provide for teaching Protestantism, Catholicism, Judaism, Mormonism, Deism, Paganism, or any religious or anti-religious system, not only in the public schools and to children, but also in the pulpit and to adults. It would then take the place of the governor's conscience in the theory of Mr. Gladstone, or the Pope's conscience in the theory of Romanism. It certainly would be no better, since we may as well have a religious pope in *one* man clothed with the civil power, as a virtual pope in *many* men.

The unqualified and unrestrained power of the majority involves a principle that is fatal to the religious rights of the minority, and leaves the latter without any protection against the abuses of power. Adopting this principle, we may as well at once dispense with constitutions and bills of rights altogether, and simply say that, for all things and all purposes, no matter what, the existing majority may lawfully do its own bidding and employ the whole power of society for its accomplishment. This would be a short cut to the doctrine of simple absolutism under a democratic form. Any one who even half understands our political institutions knows that this is not their character at all, and that religion in any form is, as to the compulsory acceptance or support thereof, among the things excepted from the jurisdiction of civil government. The people have seen fit not to trust even a majority to pass any law for the government of the whole in respect to the maintenance and propagation of religion.

If, moreover, we look at the question as one of ethics, aside from constitutional limitations, we can hardly fail to see that this majority conscience, when employed in imposing religious taxes and burdens upon a dissenting minority, is not exercising its *own* rights of conscience, but trampling upon the rights of others. This would be readily seen by Christians if the majority conscience were Pagan and should compel Christian consciences to support Paganism. Is it any less a wrong to compel Pagan consciences or any dissenting conscience to support Christianity? The rights of conscience are individual and personal, and are not to be settled by the arithmetic of putting many consciences on the one side, against a few on the other. The conscience of a single man, peaceably exercised, is for him good against he right of the whole race to invade it by any compulsory process, when religion is the matter to which it refers. There ought to be room in this world for *all* the consciences in it, without any encroachment upon the rights of each other; and there would be if *all* men, in their relations to each other, would be content to exercise their *own* rights of conscience in a reasonable manner. This would leave every man to determine the religious question for himself, and, as the necessary consequence, relieve every man from all impositions, burdens, taxes, or disabilities arising from the determination of the question by others. Though the rule is a simple one, it is, nevertheless, one of the most difficult things for bigotry to learn. The only way to learn it effectually is not to be a bigot.

It is quite true that there are some inconveniences in the doctrine of private judgment on religious subjects. Yet, notwithstanding these inconveniences, it is much better than the doctrine of State judgment, whether in the form of the governor's conscience or that of the majority. If we have the liability of aberration and diversity in the one case, we have the more formidable liability of oppression and injustice in the other. This liability of diversity is not, after all, a very frightful thing, since it implies individual activity. There is much truth, not always seen, in the following observation of Isaac Taylor, contained in his "Essays on Ultimate Civilization:" "Religious differences—well defined, firmly maintained, and fully developed, and in such a condition that they are not mere *elements*, but are *energies* within the social mass—when duly attempered, stand, if not *foremost*, quite *prominent* among the forces that are carrying us forward toward a higher civilization." The truth is, religion is just one of those things that can never be wisely run in the rut of the governor's conscience or in that of the conscience of the majority, even for the sake of unity in the faith. By so doing we always purchase the unity at too high a price. The failure to perceive this fact is one of the fundamental errors of the Papacy, and of some Protestants who are half Papists without knowing it.

God has established no visible authority among men, either in any single man or any number of men, whose decisions in matters of religious faith are a final law to every individual. Pretenses of this character, whether ecclesiastical or civil, while unproved assumptions, generally furnish the premises on which oppression, in some form, bases its conclusion and, in view of which, justifies its work. Whether the pretender appears as the governor's conscience or as the majority conscience makes no difference with the fact. Arm either of these consciences with the civil power, and then it has a power to which it almost never fails to add the fact of oppression.

THE SPECIAL ARGUMENT.

XVI.

THE DIVINE RIGHT OF CIVIL GOVERNMENT.

If by the divine right of civil government be simply meant that men naturally exist as political communities, that some form of government is the necessary adjunct of this fact, and that God has established and maintains a constitution of things leading to these results, then it may readily be conceded that civil government exists and operates by a divine right. Earthquakes and volcanoes also exist by the same right. All the relations of means and ends and all natural laws rest on the same basis. God's providence embraces the whole scheme of things; and in the scheme political society and civil government have their place by divine appointment, just as everything else has its place.

Those who affirm the so-called divine right of civil government would not accept this as an adequate statement of their doctrine. They hold that such government is not simply a natural and providential appointment or order of things; but also a divine institution, in the sense of having God's authoritative seal affixed to it. His moral government operates, in part, at least, through the civil government which he has instituted and specially chartered by vesting it with his own authority. The civil ruler is officially the minister of the divine will. God's authority stands behind his authority as its sanction and source. He is to be obeyed as the vicegerent of Heaven, and to resist him is to resist God. His right is an *official* divine right. He governs in the name and by the authority of God.

The Old Testament account of the origin and organization of the ancient Jewish nation very clearly presents such a fact. The governmental system of that people was a *theocracy*, established directly by God himself, attended by miracles as signs and seals thereof, and bearing upon its face the broad inscription "Thus saith the Lord." Its laws were divine. God was both the object of worship and the civil sovereign. Moses held the twofold relation of being his representative and the leader of the people. God appointed him to this position and supernaturally qualified him for its duties. Joshua succeeded him, and others succeeded him. The Church and the State were the same thing. The underlying theory of the whole system was that God himself was at the head of it, and that men were merely his agents.

Have we the parallel of this fact anywhere else in the history of the world? Is the fact, so far as the question of divine right is concerned, substantially a type of all governments? No one, surely, is bound to accept such a proposition until it is proved. The proper proof thereof would be historical.

Take, then, as a specimen illustration, the government of Great Britain, and subject it to the historic test. Starting with the native Britons, trace it through the Romans, then through the Saxons, then through the Normans, and then onward through a long succession of political changes, until we at last come to Victoria and the two Houses of Parliament, as forming the existing British Government, on the basis of institutions which have been the growth of more than two thousand years. Study this whole history from its earliest point to the present hour, and where will one find a leaf or even the fragment of a leaf showing that God has interposed in any special way, made any revelation of his will, wrought any miracle to prove such a revelation, appointed or inspired any ruler, or done any other thing different from the usual providence of cause and effect by which he rules in all the affairs of earth? There is not a solitary page of credible history that establishes any such fact. If, then, Victoria rules by a divine right, other than the right derived from the acquiescence and consent of the people of Great Britain, let her show her title-deed, with God's signature affixed to it. If it be said that she has inherited the throne from a royal ancestry, then let us have the king or queen who originally received the right from God, and also the "Thus saith the Lord" for its transmission in the line of family descent until it has finally lodged in Victoria, and is waiting to lodge in the Prince of Wales. The plain fact of history is that her right is simply that of *birth*, taken in connection with the established institutions of Great Britain; and there is not a king or queen on the face of the earth who can present any better title.

It happens to be a fact that all such titles are not distinguished by any divine prerogative, divine interposition, or divine inspiration, that makes them essentially different from the commission of a bank president or the head of a manufacturing company. Victoria has no higher or better warrant from Heaven to perform the duties of a queen than has a common laborer to do an honest day's work for his employer. Her providential position brings with it peculiar duties; and this is true of every man's position. She is simply what she is in the course of a natural providence; and of whom is not this equally true? The hand of God is no more really involved in the formation, constitution, growth, and government of empires than in the formation and growth of coral reefs. Both are the products of natural forces, existing and acting under Divine Providence, and giving in the one case the history and phenomena of empires and in the other those of coral reefs. The most critical study of a State, no matter what may be its form of government, merely supplies facts that run in the channel of natural events. And the same is true of "a swarm of bees or a family of beavers."

Macaulay, in his review of Gladstone's work on Church and State, has a suggestive passage upon the *manner* in which civil governments have usually become invested with their authority. We reproduce a part of it, as follows:

"A nation of barbarians pours down on a rich and unwarlike empire, enslaves the people, portions out the land, and blends the institutions which it finds in the cities with those which it has brought from the woods. A handful of daring adventurers from a civilized nation wander to some savage country and reduce the aboriginal race to bondage. A successful general turns his arms against the State which he serves. A society made brutal by oppression rises madly on its masters, and sweeps away all old laws and usages; and when its first paroxysm of rage is over, sinks down passively under any form of polity which may spring out of the chaos. A chief of a party, as at Florence, becomes imperceptibly a sovereign and the founder of a dynasty. A captain of mercenaries, as at Milan, seizes on a city and by the sword makes himself its ruler. An elective senate, as at Venice, usurps permanent and hereditary power. It is in events such as these that governments have generally originated."

This presents a true picture of the governmental divine right as usually seen in the history of the world. The right, in respect to the process of its creation and establishment, has generally been the divine right of the sword, of military conquest, of the strongest battalions, of brains circumventing ignorance and weakness, of cunning, intrigue, artifice, pillage, and outrage. The events in which the right has been cradled and out of which it has sprung are the products of *human* forces, and these forces for the most part stamped with the indelible marks of iniquity and crime. These events exist in the scheme of Divine Providence ; just as sin exists in that scheme, but without the sanction, authorization, or moral approval of God. He may, indeed, cause the wrath of man to praise him, or use one set of tyrants to punish another, or providentially overturn one despotism through the agency and ambition of another ; but this does not make him the author of the wrath, or the approver of the tyranny or any of its enormities. It is the prerogative of God to bring good out of evil and accomplish his own purposes through even the wickedness of men. The murderers of Jesus fulfilled the divine counsel ; yet it was not the less true that they slew him with wicked hands. So human governments may fulfil the divine counsel, and yet not be of God in any other sense than that of being the creations and institutions of men under his ordinary providence.

A very serious difficulty in investing the civil ruler with divine authority is supplied by the fact that the ruler himself is neither inspired nor infallible and is often a moral monster. The office, without the ruler filling it and exercising its powers, is a meaningless abstraction; and when we put the ruler there we see at once that, whatever he *ought* to be, he is not, as a matter of fact, always the minister of the divine will. The rulers of this world have been largely the oppressors of the race; and their governments, though better than anarchy, have in multitudes of instances been stupendous machines for the perpetration of cruelty and wrong. Are the wrongs of civil government committed by God's authority, and is it exercising that authority when committing these wrongs? To assert this would be to impeach his character and blaspheme his holy name. To say that governments, established by iniquity and perpetuating the iniquity in which they originated, are the executives and representatives of the divine will in any other sense than that of existing in the providence of God, and that resistance to them is a virtual resistance against God, is to place his authoritative sanction upon the most horrible abominations found on the page of history. The divine right of civil rulers would be a mere assumption without proof even if all rulers had been wise and pure; but when we put the Alexanders, the Neroes, the Caligulas, and all the bloody tyrants of history into the catalogue of civil rulers, then the doctrine is rendered impossible by the attributes and moral character of God.

If it be said that it is only when civil government does right that it acts by and represents the authority of God, then it has no more divine authority than a railway company has when doing right. All moral beings, whether kings on thrones or peasants in cottages, have a divine warrant for doing right, in the sense of being obligated thereto by the law of God. This warrant includes the civil ruler; but it has no special application that distinguishes him from other men. Justice rendered by the private citizen is as really divine as justice rendered by the magistrate.

But did not Paul, in his Epistle to the Romans, tell the Christians at Rome to be "subject unto the higher powers?" Did he not say that "there is no power but of God," and that "the powers that be are ordained of God?" Did he not say that whoever "resisteth the power resisteth the ordinance of God?" Did he not speak of the civil ruler as "the minister of God" for good? Did he not call him the "revenger of God to execute wrath upon him that doeth evil?" Did he not exhort the Roman Christians to "be subject not only for wrath, but also for conscience' sake?" This is all true; and there is no difficulty in the language, regarded as addressed to Christians subject to the authority of a cruel Pagan Emperor, and designed to inculcate upon them the general necessity and duty of obedience to his laws. Like many other passages in the Bible, it recognizes the relation of ruler and subject as an existing fact, and directs the latter to respect the authority of the former; and so far lays down a general principle of conduct applicable in all ages and under all governments. Such was the manifest intention of the apostle.

If, however, we press the language, and especially particular phrases, beyond this construction, and make "the higher powers" that then existed at Rome "the ordinance of God" for the exercise and administration of his own authority, and further make Nero "the minister of God" for good and the divinely-commissioned avenger of evil, and then take the whole as a specimen case for all human governments, we shall have for the result self-contradiction in the Bible and the contradiction of the Bible by the most obvious facts. The example of Peter and John in preaching the Gospel when forbidden to do so by the Jewish authority, and of Daniel in disobeying the edict of a king, refutes such an interpretation of Paul's words. The character and conduct of Nero show that he was not the minister of God, but a fiend of cruelty. Other rulers have displayed a similar character. To quote the apostle as affirming the divine authority of every existing civil magistracy and laying down the universal obligation of obedience thereto as a duty which must always be performed is to make him teach what is not and cannot be true. It would place men so under the authority of the civil ruler that, no matter who he is, or how he has acquired his power, or how he uses it, they would have no alternative but to submit and obey. All resistance under any circumstances would be unlawful. The right of revolution could never exist, since it would never be consistent with the divine right of "the powers that be."

The only admissible construction of Paul's language is that which makes *all* governments "the ordinance of God" in the general providential sense, and that, too, simply because they exist, and for no other reason and in no other sense. Whether they are rightful and whether the people by virtue of their inherent sovereignty may displace them even by force are questions of natural reason, which the Bible does not undertake to decide. Human forces, under the general providence of God, without miracles, without inspiration, and without any divine selection of the form of government or of the ruler are left to settle the question as to *what* governments men shall live under and as to what persons shall conduct them. The result is the providential "ordinance of God," whether it be the government of a Nero, or that of Great Britain, or that of the United States.

Our revolutionary Fathers, in working out this providential problem, assumed that the right of government was a right inherent in *them* as a civil community, and not in the king of England; and hence, they assumed that it was *their* right not only to determine the form and objects of the government under which they should live, but also to appoint their own rulers. Their theory was that government in its principles and the ruler in his official powers are of God providentially when they are practically of the people. We can think of no better or more equitable way to secure "the ordinance of God" than to have the people establish it for themselves and invest it with their own authority. This is good theology and good democracy at the same time.

Moreover, all the considerations for obedience to the civil magistrate, founded on conscience and penalty, apply quite as forcibly when he is the choice of the people, derives his powers from the people, and acts in virtue of their delegated authority as they do when a Nero is the magistrate. In neither case does he possess any divine prerogative which is not common to all men in the relations in which they exist and act. He is simply a magistrate, and, as such, the creature of natural causes operating under the providential superintendence of God. Being such, he has certain powers to exercise and certain duties to perform. Precisely the same principles apply to a bank clerk, or the manager of an insurance company, and indeed, to all men. Any theory which makes the civil ruler specially the *elect* of God and the legate of the skies is a mere pretense, unsustained by history, with the single exception of the Jewish theocracy.

The doctrine of democracy is that the ruler represents the sovereignty of the people. The doctrine of theocracy is that he represents the sovereignty of God. The former, and not the latter, is the doctrine upon which the civil and political institutions of this country are founded. Every officer of law is the creature of the popular will; and government, in its form and in the persons who administer it, depends at last upon a prevalent public opinion expressed according to certain prescribed methods. The body politic rules itself by subjecting itself to the regulation of law and employing governmental agents for the expression of its will. Such is the theory of American democracy, and it necessarily excludes the theory of any right in the ruler other than that which the people bestow. He is a citizen, exercising their authority while in office by their will, and no longer.

This great principle of popular sovereignty, while true of the National Government, is also expressly affirmed by most of the State constitutions in respect to the governments organized under them. Thus the constitutions of Alabama (I. 3); of Arkansas (I. 1); of California (I. 2); of Connecticut (I. 2); of Florida (Declaration of Rights, 1); of Iowa (I. 2); of Kansas (Bill of Rights, 2); of Kentucky XIII. 4); of Nevada (I. 2); of New Jersey (I. 2), and of Ohio (I. 2), expressly declare that "all political power is inherent in the people." The constitutions of Missouri (I. 4); of North Carolina (I. 2), and of South Carolina (I. 3.), state the same doctrine by declaring that "all political power is vested in and derived from the people." The constitution of Vermont (I. 6), says: "That all power being originally inherent in and consequently derived from the people, therefore, all officers of government, whether legislative or executive, are their trustees and servants, and at all times in a legal way accountable to them." The constitution of Massachusetts (I. 5) declares that "all power residing originally with the people, and being derived from them, the several magistrates and officers of government vested with authority, whether legislative, executive or judicial, are the substitutes and agents, and are at all times accountable to them."

There are examples of the doctrine as to the rights of the officers of government that pervades all the State constitutions. Like the Constitution of the United States, they utterly ignore and virtually exclude the whole theory of any special divine right as being vested in the civil ruler. His authority is entirely representative, and the people, and the people only, form the party represented. He is not the vicegerent of God, and acts under no commission or inspiration from Heaven; but is simply the trustee or agent of the people for the purposes specified in the trust. The people have a right to govern themselves according to the rules of law, and, in order to the convenient and practical exercise of this right, they delegate a portion of their own powers to the officers of law, not only choosing these officers, either directly or indirectly, but also prescribing their duties. Such is the American theory of civil government. It is a theory which has the whole power of the people behind it, and would be defended at any sacrifice.

XVII.

CHRISTIANITY AND THE COMMON LAW.

The first judicial declaration that "Christianity is parcel of the laws of England" was made by Sir Matthew Hale. Lord Mansfield subsequently modified the statement by saying that "the essential principles of revealed religion are part of the common law." Lord Campbell, in his "Lives of Chief-Justices," explains the language as simply meaning that the law will not permit the essential principles of revealed religion to be ridiculed and reviled. The English Commissioners on Criminal Law, in their sixth report (1841) express the opinion that the maxim does not "supply any reason in favor of the rule that arguments may not be used against" Christianity, "provided it be not done in such a manner as to *endanger the public peace by exciting forcible resistance.*" Archbishop Whately, in his preface to his "Elements of Rhetoric," says that he had "never met with any one who could explain" to him the meaning of the maxim; yet he did not understand it as implying "the illegality of arguing" against the established religion of England. Thomas Jefferson, in an Appendix to his "Reports of Virginia Cases" says that the declaration of Sir Matthew Hale was not at the time of its utterance sustained by any authority, and that, though frequently repeated by English judges, it never had any legislative authorization. He speaks of it as resting upon the "usurpation of the judges alone, without a particle of legislative will having ever been called on or exercised towards its introduction or confirmation." He characterized it as "the most remarkable instance of judicial legislation that has ever occurred in English jurisprudence, or perhaps, in any other."

Is Christianity a part of the common law of this country, and, if so, in what sense and to what extent? There is no pertinency in this question, considered in application to the General Government, since there is no common law of the Union. The Supreme Court of the United States, in the case of Wheaton *vs.* Peters (8 Peters, p. 591), said: "There is no principle which pervades the Union and has the authority of law that is not embodied in the Constitution or laws of the Union. The common law could be made a part of our Federal system only by legislative adoption." So, also, in the case of The State of Pennsylvania *vs.* The Wheeling Bridge Company (13 Howard, p. 518), the same Court said: "The Federal courts have no jurisdiction of common law offenses, and there is no abstract pervading principle of the common law under which we can take jurisdiction." It, hence, follows that the question proposed has no reference to the United States. The law of the Union is contained in the

Constitution, and in the statutes of Congress enacted in pursuance thereof.

If, then, Christianity be a part of our common law, it must be so exclusively in relation to the State governments. How far and in what sense is this a fact, if it be a fact at all? In answer to this question, we submit the following exhibit of authorities referring to it:

Mr. Sedgwick, in his treatise on the "Construction of Statutory and Constitutional Law" (p. 14), says:

"It is often said that Christianity is part and parcel of the common law. But this is true only in a modified sense. Blasphemy is an indictable offense at common law; but no person is liable to be punished by the civil power who refuses to embrace the doctrines or follow the precepts of Christianity. Our constitutions extend the same protection to *every* form of religion and give no preference to any."

Judge Cooley, in his "Constitutional Limitations" (p. 472), observes:

"It is frequently said that Christianity is a part of the law of the land. In a certain sense and for certain purposes this is true. . . . But the law does not attempt to enforce the precepts of Christianity on the ground of their sacred character or divine origin. Some of these precepts are universally recognized as being incapable of enforcement by human laws, notwithstanding they are of continual and universal obligation. Christianity, therefore, is *not* a part of the law of the land, in the sense that would entitle courts to take notice of and base their judgments upon it, except so far as they should find that its precepts had been incorporated in and thus become a component part of the law."

In the same treatise Judge Cooley remarks: "It is not toleration which is established in our system; but *religious equality*." The doctrine of this eminent jurist is that the principles of Christianity are not *ipso facto*, in virtue of their divine origin or sanction, any part of the law of the land, and not so at all, except as they may have been legally incorporated therein; and that they cannot be thus incorporated in any sense that would be inconsistent with the fundamental principle of "religious equality."

Mr. Francis Wharton, in his work on "American Criminal Law" (vol. 3, p. 188), refers to cases in which the courts have spoken of Christianity as part of the common law, and then adds the following comment:

"But when these cases are analyzed it will be found that, though in most of them the courts throw out the declaration that Christianity is part of the common law, yet they all of them rest on grounds independent of this general position; for it is a common nuisance, and punishable as such by indictment at common law, to disturb the religious worship of others or flagrantly or indecently insult their religious belief, no matter what be their creed. Thus it would be held indictable to wantonly disturb a congregation of Mormons or Jews, or even of Mohammedans, when peaceably engaged in their religious rites. . . . Infidel and skeptical opinions are only indictable when publicly and grossly expressed in such a way as to become a *common nuisance, or to provoke a breach of the peace.* We may, therefore, conclude that, while the spiritual element of Christianity is protected by the common law, the former does not so enter into the latter as to place matters of religious faith within the jurisdiction of the civil authority, either for vindication or enforcement."

Justice Story, in delivering the opinion of the Supreme Court of the United States in the case of Vidal *vs.* Girard's Executors (2 Howard, p. 127), referred to Christianity as being "a part of the common law of Pennsylvania," and then immediately added: "But this proposition is to be received with its appropriate qualifications and in connection with the bill of rights found in its constitution of government." After quoting the section of the constitution relating to the rights of conscience, he proceeded to say:

"Language more comprehensive for the complete protection of *every* variety of religious opinion could scarcely be used; and it must have been intended to extend equally to *all* sects, whether they believed in Christianity or not and whether they were Jews or infidels. So that we are compelled to admit that, although Christianity be a part of the common law of the State, yet it is so in this qualified sense, that its divine origin and truth are admitted, and, therefore, it is not to be *maliciously and openly reviled and blasphemed against, to the annoyance of believers or the injury of the public.* Such was the doctrine of the Supreme Court of Pennsylvania in Updegraph *vs.* The Commonwealth."

In the case here referred to by Justice Story, and found in 11 Sergeant and Rawle's Reports, p. 394, the Supreme Court of Pennsylvania held the following language:

"Christianity, general Christianity, is and always has been a part of the common law of Pennsylvania; . . . but with liberty of conscience. . . . . No preference is given by law to any particular religious profession. Protection is given to all by our laws. . . . It is only the *malicious reviler* of Christianity that is punished. . . . It is open, public *vilification* of the religion of the country that is punished, . . . to preserve the *peace* of the country by an outward respect to the religion of the country. . . . If, from a regard to the *decency* and *good order* of society, profane swearing, breach of the Sabbath, and blasphemy are punishable by civil magistrates, these are not punished as sins or offenses against God, but crimes *injurious to and having a malignant influence on society.*"

Chief-Justice Kent, in delivering the opinion of the Supreme Court of the State of New York in the case of The People *vs.* Ruggles (8 Johnson's Reports, p. 290), said :

"The authorities show that blasphemy against God and contumelious reproaches and profane ridicule of Christ or the Holy Scriptures (which are equally treated as blasphemy) are punishable at common law, whether by words or writings. The consequences may be less extensively pernicious in the one case than in the other ; but in both instances the reviling is still an offense *because it tends to corrupt the morals of the people and to destroy good order.* Such offenses . . . are treated as affecting the essential interests of civil society. . . The free, equal, and undisturbed enjoyment of religious opinion, whatever that may be, and free and decent discussions on any religious subject are granted and secured ; but to revile with *malicious* and *blasphemous* contempt the religion professed by almost the whole community is an abuse of that right. . . . Wicked and malicious words, writings, and actions, which go to *vilify* those Gospels, continue, as at common law, to be an offense against *the public peace and safety.*"

The Massachusetts case of the Commonwealth *vs.* Kneeland (20 Pickering, p. 206) was not a case at common law, but under a statute which provided that "if any person shall wilfully blaspheme the holy name of God by denying, cursing, or contumeliously reproaching God, his creation, government, or final judging of the world ; or by cursing or reproaching Jesus Christ or the Holy Ghost; or by cursing or contumeliously reproaching the Holy Word of God," he shall be punished in the manner prescribed. The question before the Supreme Court was whether the language charged in the indictment—and which the jury in the court below found Kneeland to have published—was blasphemy within the meaning of the above statute, and, if so, then whether the statute itself was consistent with the constitution of Massachusetts. This question in both of its branches was answered affirmatively by Chief-Justice Shaw, who delivered the opinion of the majority of the Court. The statute, he said, was not "intended to prevent or restrain the formation of any opinions or the profession of any religious sentiments whatever; but to restrain and punish acts which have a *tendency to disturb the public peace.*"

Judge Morton in a dissenting opinion, said: "It [the statute] was not intended to punish a denial of the existence of God; but only such a denial when made in a *manner calculated to give just offense to others and with a bad intent.*" He also said: "When he [the citizen] engages in the discussion of any subject in the honest pursuit of truth, or endeavors to propagate any opinions which he sincerely entertains, he is covered by the ægis of the constitution; but when he *wantonly and maliciously assails the rights and privileges of others or disturbs the public peace* he is the proper subject of punishment." He held that the instruction to the jury in this case was incorrect, and, hence, that the defendant was entitled to a new trial.

Justice Clayton, of the Supreme Court of Delaware, in the case of The State *vs.* Chandler (2 Harrington's Reports, p. 553), gives an elaborate opinion as to the question how far and in what sense Christianity is to be deemed a part of the law of the land. We quote as follows from this deliverance:

"The common law was, as Lord Coke expressed it, . . . the preserver of the common peace of the land; and, therefore, we find it punished outrages on, or breaches of the peace of society, and also acts whose tendency was to disturb that peace. . . . But, even in England, Christianity was never considered a part of the common law, so far as that for a violation of its injunctions, independent of the established laws of man, and without the sanction of any positive act of Parliament made to enforce these injunctions, any man could be drawn to answer in a common law court. . . . It [the common law] adapted itself to the religion of the country just so far as was necessary for the peace and safety of civil institutions; but it took cognizance of offenses against God only where, by their inevitable effects, they became offenses against man and his temporal security. . . . If in Delaware the people should adopt the Jewish or Mohammedan religion, as they have an unquestionable right to do, if they prefer it, this Court is bound to take notice of it as their religion and respect it accordingly. . . . It [the common law] sustained indictments for *wantonly* and *maliciously* blaspheming God or the Founder of the Christian religion, because such blasphemy tended to subvert the *peace* and *good order*, which it was bound to protect. But it sustained no indictment for a mere sin against God as a common law offense where *these* objects of its care were not affected. . . . The common law only punished it [blasphemy] when it tended to create a riot or break the peace in some other way, or subvert the very foundation on which civil society rested. . . . It will be seen that, in our judgment, by the constitution and laws of Delaware the Christian religion is a part of those laws so far that blasphemy against it is punishable *while the people prefer it as their religion, and no longer*."

The doctrine of Justice Clayton is that, Christianity being the religion which the great mass of the people of Delaware prefer, the courts of that State are bound to treat as an offense against civil society an act of blasphemy against that religion which outrages the sense of decency and is calculated to provoke a breach of the public peace and order. The same doctrine would equally apply, as he distinctly says, if Judaism or Mohammedanism were the religion professed by the people. It is only when acts which are offenses against God have the character of offenses against the peace and good order of society that they are punishable at common law, and even then they are not punishable as *religious* offenses, but solely as crimes against society.

The Supreme Court of Ohio, in the case of Bloom *vs.* Richards (2 Ohio State Reports, p. 387), said:

"Neither Christianity nor any other system of religion is a part of the law of this State. We sometimes hear it stated that all religions are tolerated in Ohio; but the expression is not strictly accurate. Much less accurate is it to say that *one* religion is a part of our law, and all others only tolerated. . . . We have no union of Church and State, nor has our government ever been vested with authority to enforce any religious observance simply because it is religious. . . . Thus the statute upon which the defendant relies, prohibiting labor on the Sabbath, could not stand for a moment as a law of this State if its sole foundation was the Christian duty of keeping that day holy and its sole motive to enforce the observance of that duty. . . . We are, then, to regard the statute under consideration as a *mere municipal or police* regulation, whose validity is neither strengthened nor weakened by the fact that the day of rest which it enjoins is the Sabbath day."

Two years afterward, the same Court, in the case of McGatrick *vs.* Wason (4 Ohio State Reports, p. 571), spoke as follows:

"The act [the Sabbath law] does not to any extent rest upon the ground that it is immoral or irreligious to labor on the Sabbath any more than upon any other day. It simply prescribes a day of rest, from motives of public policy and as a civil regulation. . . . The day of rest prescribed by the statute is the Christian Sabbath; yet so entirely does the act rest upon grounds of public policy that . . . . it would be equally constitutional and obligatory did it name any other day, and it derives none of its force from the fact that the day of rest is Sunday."

In the case of The Board of Education of Cincinnati *vs.* Minor and others (23 Ohio State Reports, pp. 246, 247), the same Court said:

"We are told that this word 'religion' must mean 'Christian religion,' because 'Christianity is a part of the common law of this country,' lying behind and above its constitutions. Those who make this assertion can hardly be serious and intend the real import of their language. If Christianity is a *law* of the State, like every law, it must have a *sanction.* Adequate penalties must be provided to enforce obedience to all its requirements and precepts. No one seriously contends for any such doctrine in this country, or, I might almost say, in this age of the world. The only foundation (rather, the only excuse) for the proposition that Christianity is a part of the law of this country, is the fact that it is a Christian country and that its constitutions and laws are made by a Christian people."

The Superior Court of New York City, in the case of Andrew *vs.* The New York Bible and Prayer-Book Society (4 Sandford's Superior Court Reports, pp. 180–184), said:

"The maxim that Christianity is part and parcel of the common law has been frequently repeated by judges and text writers, but few have chosen to examine its truth and attempt to explain its meaning. . . . If Christianity is a municipal law in the proper sense of the term, as it must be if a part of the common law, every person is liable to be punished by the civil power who refuses to embrace its doctrines and follow its precepts; and if it must be conceded that in this sense the maxim is untrue it ceases to be intelligible, since a law without a sanction is an absurdity in logic and a nullity in fact."

It will readily be seen in the light of these authorities, that those who affirm Christianity to be a part of the common law do not use the term *law* in its usual sense. They so modify the import of the term as virtually to deny what in strictness of language they affirm. The maxim does not mean that Christianity in this country is an established religion; or that its precepts, by the force of their own authority, form any part of our system of municipal law; or that courts are entitled to base their judgments upon the Bible; or that any religious observances or duties are to be penally enforced; or that any legal discrimination in favor of Christianity is allowable. All such constructions are excluded by our State constitutions. Laws against blasphemy and labor on the Christian Sabbath are not based upon the theory that Christianity possesses any *civil* authority, or upon the fact that these acts are offenses against God. Mr. Pomeroy, in his "Introduction to Municipal Law" (p. 392), says that such laws "stand on exactly the same footing as those forbidding disorderly houses, public intemperance, and all other acts which disturb the peace."

Should a person attempt to walk the streets of a city in the state of absolute nudity, the indecency and offensiveness of the act to others and its tendency to disturb the public peace would make the act a crime against society. So blasphemy is punishable as a crime because it is indecent and offensive to man, or, as Mr. Wharton says, a "common nuisance," or, as Justice Story said, an "annoyance" to others and an "injury" to the public; and, hence, punishment, whether under statute or common law, is not designed to enforce the requirements of Christianity, but rather to protect the people and preserve good social order. The law pays this respect to the religious sensibilities of believers and the demands of public propriety; and, as Justice Clayton says, it would do the same thing if Mohammedanism or Judaism were the prevalent religion of the land. It does not establish or give any authority to the religion which it thus protects against wanton and malicious insult. It does not make the religion in any proper sense a part of the law, since it neither compels its acceptance nor forbids its rejection.

The maxim, then, which we have been considering is certainly a very unfortunate choice of words. Its apparent meaning has to be almost entirely explained away. Being necessarily subjected to so large a depletion, in order not to be utterly false, it might well, at least in this country, pass into disuse among writers and judges. At the most there is but a fragment of truth in it, and that truth is not aptly expressed. Much more accurate would it be to say that the common law takes notice of Christianity as an existing fact founded on the choice of the people, and seeks to protect them in its enjoyment against such blasphemous aspersions as violate the sense of decency and endanger the peace of society. This is the sense in which Justice Clayton explains and affirms the maxim, and this is really all the import which Chief-Justice Kent attached to it. Neither of these learned jurists declares what the Supreme Court of Ohio so emphatically denies. The subject-matter of the affirmation, on the one hand, and of the denial, on the other, is not the same; and this clearly shows that the words of the maxim are not fitly chosen.

Christianity, as a *legalized* system, is unknown to our laws. As a *protected* system it stands on the common footing of all other religious systems. Judge Appleton, of the Supreme Court of Maine, in the case of Donahoe *vs.* Richards (38 Maine Reports, p. 379), said in regard to the constitution of that State that it "does not recognize the superiority of any form of religion or of any sect or denomination," and that it "regards the Pagan and the Mormon, the Brahmin and the Jew, the Swedenborgian and the Buddhist, the Catholic and the Quaker as possessing equal rights." What is thus affirmed of Maine is simply a fundamental principle pervading our American constitutions.

XVIII.

THE NATIONAL CONSTITUTION.

The Constitution of the United States declares itself to be "the supreme law of the land." By "land," as here used, is meant not only the territory embraced within the limits of the several States, but also any territory belonging to the United States and not organized into States. Over this entire domain and the people resident therein the Constitution asserts its jurisdictional supremacy in respect to all the objects and purposes set forth in the instrument itself.

The same Constitution also declares the source

of its authority as the fundamental law. "The people of the United States" ordained and established it in the first instance, and provided by the peaceful process of amendment for any changes therein which they might see fit to make. The sovereign authority of this people, taken collectively, and not as separate individuals, is hence, the sole foundation of all the powers conferred and all the restraints imposed by the Constitution. Their authority is the only authority upon which it rests. It contains not the slightest intimation of any *theocratic* element as lying at its basis, or of any *divine* right relating to the powers which it bestows. It is a human constitution, originated and adopted by men, and built upon the self-assumed and self-asserted sovereignty of "the people of the United States."

So, also, the agency, provided for carrying into effect the purposes of this Constitution, is simply a government of appointees, directly chosen by the people or selected by those thus chosen. It is a purely representative agency. No one holds or can hold any office under the Constitution except as he derives the right from the action of the people, either directly electing him or indirectly appointing him to the office. The ruler, whether legislative, executive, or judicial, is, hence, the servant of the people, entirely dependent upon them for his power to rule and responsible to them for the manner in which he exercises this power. The people, taken in their collective and corporate character, are the only sovereign known to the Constitution.

The objects to be attained by the adoption of the Constitution, as comprehensively summarized in its preamble, were "to form a more perfect union, establish justice, insure domestic tranquillity, provide for the common defense, promote the general welfare, and secure the blessings of liberty to ourselves and our posterity." The legal machinery provided for in the three co-ordinate departments of the General Government is adjusted to the accomplishment of these ends and these only. It looks no further. The avowed purpose of the Constitution, is, hence, wholly *secular,* since it relates exclusively to the temporal interests of the body politic known as "the people of the United States." The purposes of a bank corporation or a railway company are not more strictly temporal and secular than those set forth in the preamble of the Constitution, and to secure which a governmental agency is chartered, with powers appropriate to the end.

The Constitution thus appears as "the supreme law of the land," enacted by the sovereign authority of "the people of the United States," containing provisions for the organization and continuance of a government, vesting in that government certain powers, and by the nature of the powers bestowed and also the recitals of the preamble limiting itself exclusively to the attainment of purely temporal ends. The conclusion to be drawn from these facts is that those who framed and those who adopted the Constitution meant to exclude religion wholly from its scope, and thus make the instrument entirely secular and political in its objects. Whatever may have been their belief or practice as religionists, they did not think it necessary or wise to incorporate their religion or any of its doctrines into the "supreme law of the land."

The only provisions in which any reference is made to religion in the Constitution, as originally adopted, are those that relate to the oath of office prescribed to be taken by the President, by Senators and Representatives in Congress, and by officers of the United States and of the several States. In respect to the President, it is required that before entering upon the execution of his office he shall take the following oath or affirmation :

"I do solemnly swear (or affirm) that I will faithfully execute the office of President of the United States, and will to the best of my ability preserve, protect, and defend the Constitution of the United States."

The last clause of the sixth article reads as follows :

"The Senators and Representatives before mentioned, and the members of the several State legislatures, and all executive and judicial officers, both of the United States and of the several States, shall be bound by oath or affirmation to support this Constitution ; but no religious test shall ever be required as a qualification to any office or public trust under the United States."

The promissory oath for which provision is here made is a solemn appeal to the Supreme Being in respect to the sincerity of the party taking the oath, and a virtual imprecation of the divine curse if he speaks falsely. Recognizing the fact that men so regard it, as well as the general practice of governments in regard to oaths, the Constitution provides for an official oath. It does not require that this oath shall be a Christian oath, or that in its administration any use shall be made of the Sacred Scriptures. It does not absolutely require any oath at all, since the person to be inducted into office may simply affirm that he will support the Constitution. A solemn affirmation to this effect is, at his option, the constitutional equivalent of an oath. The first section of the Revised Statutes of the United States provides that "the requirement of an oath shall be deemed complied with by making affirmation in judicial form." An affirmation is distinguished from an oath in containing no appeal to God, or any sanctions growing out of his existence and attributes. In administering an affirmation the officer simply says to the party making it: "You do solemnly, sincerely, and truly declare and affirm that," etc. Whether, then, a person, in entering upon the duties of any office to which he may have been elected or appointed, shall make an appeal to God in the form of an oath, or affirm without such an appeal, is a question which the Constitution leaves him to decide for himself. It does not force an oath upon him as a condition of receiving office, and performing its duties. If he were an atheist, he is competent to affirm, and, hence, he would not, by his faith or want of faith, be excluded from any office on account of a constitutional requirement.

Moreover, to guard against the possibility of any exclusion from office on religious grounds, whether in an oath or an affirmation, the Constitution immediately adds these very significant words: "But no religious test shall ever be required as a qualification to any office or public trust under the United States." Religious tests, in respect to matters of faith, or modes of worship, or both, or in respect to adherence to some specific sect of religionists, form one of the means by which tyrannical governments have proscribed and excluded certain classes of persons, otherwise qualified, from holding office and enjoying the emoluments thereof. This had been done in England by what were called test-acts; and as learned a jurist as Blackstone defends such acts. The framers of the Constitution designed to cut up the whole principle, root and branch, so far as the General Government is concerned; and, hence, they provided that "no religious test"—that is to say, no test of any kind founded upon religion, or having reference thereto—"shall ever be required as a qualification to any office or public trust under the United States." Congress is thus deprived of all power to pass any religious test-act in respect to qualifications for office. The design, as stated by Justice Story in his "Commentaries on the Constitution," was "to cut off forever every pretense of any alliance between Church and State in the National Government."

The exclusion of all religious tests was urged as an objection to the Constitution in the convention of Massachusetts called to act upon the question of its adoption. It was said that the effect would be to permit irreligious men and even Infidels to hold office, and that this might work serious harm to the public welfare. The Rev. Mr. Shute, who was a member of the Convention, forcibly said, in reply to this objection: "In this great and extensive empire there is, and will be, a great variety of sentiments in religion among its inhabitants. Upon the plan of a religious test the question, I think, must be: Who shall be excluded from national trusts? Whatever answer bigotry may suggest, the dictates of candor and equity, I conceive, will be: *None!*" ("Elliot's Debates," vol. IV. pp. 118, 119.) The Rev. Mr. Payson, another member of the Convention, said: "Had there been a religious test as a qualification for office, it would, in my opinion, have been a great blemish upon the instrument." (p. 120). The Rev. Mr. Backus also said: "The imposing of religious tests hath been the greatest engine of tyranny in the world." (p. 148).

In the plan of a Constitution submitted to the Federal Convention by Mr. Charles Pinckney, on the 29th of May, 1787, it was provided that "the United States shall pass no law on the subject of religion." ("Madison Papers," vol. II. p. 741). This provision not having been included in the Constitution as finally adopted, the omission was soon after supplied by the First Amendment, in which it is expressly declared that "Congress shall make no law respecting an establishment of religion, or prohibiting the free exercise thereof." There was nothing in the Constitution to imply that, in the absence of this prohibition, Congress would have power to pass such a law; yet it was thought expedient to deny the power in express language, and thus put the matter beyond doubt or controversy. The denial is made in the broadest terms. Not only is Congress forbidden to establish any system of religion, or do anything involving this legal result; but it is also forbidden to prohibit, or in any way interfere with, the free exercise of religion by the people. "It was," as remarked by Justice Story, "deemed advisable to exclude from the National Government all power upon the subject;" and, as the result both sought and attained, "the Catholic and the Protestant, the Calvinist and the Arminian, the Jew and the Infidel may sit down at the common table of the national councils, without any inquisition into their faith or mode of worship." As citizens of the United States, they stand upon the same level and enjoy precisely the same rights. The whole subject of religion is totally withdrawn from the jurisdiction of the General Government, not only by not being included in its powers, but by being expressly excluded therefrom.

So far, then, as the National Government is concerned, "the people of the United States," considered as a body politic, have no religion to teach, no doctrine of God to promulgate, and no form of worship to sustain or enforce. Their Constitution is purely secular in its objects, and its authority entirely human, without any pretense of any divine right. It is an organic expression of the theory set forth in the Declaration of Independence, that governments are instituted among men to secure the rights of men, and that they derive their just powers from the consent of the governed. Those who framed the Constitution designed to make it exclusively a *political* instrument, and nothing else. It was not by accident, but by intention, that they omitted to embody any religious doctrine in it, that they prohibited all religious tests, and that the First Congress proposed, and the people ratified, an amendment that expressly denies any power to Congress on this one subject.

Very soon after the adoption of the Constitution and the ratification of this amendment—namely, on the 4th of November, 1796—a treaty was concluded with Tripoli, in the eleventh article of which occurs the following declaration :—

"As the Government of the United States is not *in any sense founded on the Christian religion;* as it has in itself no character of enmity against the laws, religion or tranquillity of Mussulmans; and as the said States never have entered into any war or act of hostility against any Mohammedan nation, it is declared by the parties that no pretext arising from *religious* opinions, shall ever produce an interruption of the harmony existing between the two countries."

This disclaimer by Washington in negotiating, and by the Senate in confirming, the treaty with Tripoli, was not designed to disparage the Christian religion or indicate any hostility thereto; but to set forth the fact, so apparent in the Constitution itself, that the Government of the United States was not founded upon that religion, and, hence, did not embody or assert any of its doctrines—and, hence, again, that, as a government, it had and could have no hostility to a "Mohammedan nation" on account of its religion. The language of this article in the treaty was used for a purpose, and that purpose was in exact correspondence with the fact as contained in the Constitution itself. Christianity, though the prevalent religion of the people when the Constitution was adopted, is unknown to it. The Constitution says that it shall be unknown as having any place in the organic law of the United States, or in the legislative powers of Congress.

Those who, in the discussion of the School question, speak of Christianity as being a part of the common law of the land are entirely mistaken, so far as the statement refers to the Government of the United States. The only common law of the United States is that which is found in the Constitution, and in laws enacted and treaties made in pursuance thereof; and it so happens that neither Christianity, nor any other system of religion, is any part of this law, or can be, so long as the Constitution itself shall remain unchanged. Congress cannot establish Christianity, and the Constitution has not done so, and, hence, it is no part of the law of the land, either statute or common, except as it may have been made such by the action of the respective States; and how far this is a fact, if so at all, is not the matter of our present inquiry. We are now dealing simply with the Government of the United States, and with "the people of the United States," considered in their federal and national character as a political corporation. As such they have no religion, either Christian or Pagan, Catholic or Protestant. Their Government is not a *Christian* government in the sense of giving any legal preference to, or sanction of, Christianity, or resting its authority upon any of its doctrines. It is simply a political organization, for secular and temporal ends, based upon the principle of popular representation, and upon nothing else, and formally and intentionally excluding religion from its scope.

It is on this ground that a portion of the people desire to have the Constitution so amended that the government under it will become a Christian government. The character of the amendment which has been suggested for this purpose, will be considered in the next article.

XIX.

RELIGIOUS AMENDMENT OF THE CONSTITUTION.

It is the opinion of a portion of the American people that our National Constitution ought to be so amended as to establish "a Christian government." The amendment proposed for this purpose, if adopted, would make the preamble read as follows:

"We, the people of the United States, *acknowledging Almighty God as the source of all authority and power in civil government, the Lord Jesus Christ as the ruler among the nations, and his revealed will as of supreme authority,* in order *to constitute a Christian government,* to form a more perfect union, establish justice, insure domestic tranquillity, provide for the common defense, promote the general welfare, and secure the blessings of liberty to ourselves and our posterity, do ordain and establish *the following* Constitution for the United States of America."

The words in italics are the ones which the advocates of a religious amendment to the Constitution desire to insert in its preamble. The object is to make the government "a Christian government," and the method of doing it is to assert these three propositions: 1. That God is the source of all authority and power in civil government. 2. That the Lord Jesus Christ is the ruler among the nations. 3. That his revealed will is of supreme authority.

It is undoubtedly true that neither the Constitution nor the Government is now Christian in the sense contemplated by this amendment. It is, however, true that the Constitution establishes "a Christian government" in the sense of providing for those great *moral* ends that refer to the present welfare and happiness of society. Unity among the people, justice, tranquillity, the common defense, the general welfare, and the blessings of liberty are enumerated as ends to be attained. These, surely, are not anti-Christian ends; and it is not straining the import of the term to say that they are Christian, considered with reference to that department of Christianity which relates to the interests and duties of time. In this sense the Constitution already provides for "a Christian government."

Let us then see in what further sense the Constitution would establish "a Christian government" if the preamble were amended in the manner proposed. What would be the *legal* effect? In answering this question, it is important to remember that the preamble to the Constitution is simply an *enacting* clause, analogous to the title of a legislative act; and that in itself considered, it makes no grants of power, imposes no restraints, and contains no provision for the organization and administration of a government. Except in connection with what follows in the several articles of the Constitution, it is as meaningless and powerless as would be a legislative act if the whole of it consisted in its title. The preamble, for example, declares the establishment of justice to be one of the ends sought, yet this mere statement would be utterly inoperative if the Constitution, in the legislative, executive, and judicial grants of power to the General Government, contained no provisions for the attainment of the end. The same would be true of all the other objects specified in the preamble, if divorced from those provisions which are designed and adapted to secure them. Justice Story, in his "Commentaries on the Constitution" (section 462), says:

"And here we must guard ourselves against an error which is too often allowed to creep into discussions upon this subject. The preamble never can be resorted to to enlarge the power confided to the General Government or any of its departments. It cannot confer any power *per se;* it can never amount by implication to an enlargement of any power expressly given. It can never be the legitimate source of any implied power when otherwise withdrawn from the Constitution."

It, hence, follows that, if the preamble were amended as proposed, not the slightest practical change would be made in the Constitution itself or in the character of the Government. The added words would be in the preamble ; but the Government would be no more " Christian " than it is without them. It would still be true that " no religious test shall ever be required as a qualification to any office or public trust under the United States ;" that " Congress shall make no law respecting an establishment of religion, or prohibiting the free exercise thereof;" and that " the powers not delegated to the United States by the Constitution nor prohibited by it to the States are reserved to the States respectively or to the people." These provisions would remain in the body of the Constitution ; and unless we adopt the false doctrine that the preamble is itself a grant of powers to the General Government the words proposed to be added to it would be legally a dead letter. The Constitution is not constructed to give any effect to such words or the ideas which they convey. There is nothing in it corresponding to them or that furnishes any method or legal machinery for their application. In this sense they would be perfectly useless.

The proper mode of making the Government " a Christian government " according to the model proposed is to adopt an amendment that would substantially read as follows :

SECTION I. It is hereby declared that God is

the source of all authority and power in civil government, that the Lord Jesus Christ is the ruler among the nations, and that his revealed will is of supreme authority.

SECTION 2. Congress shall have power, by appropriate legislation, to enforce the provisions of this article.

This, which might be called the Sixteenth Amendment, would certainly gain the end proposed on the basis of the three religious doctrines affirmed. But, in securing the end, it would fundamentally change the whole theory of the Constitution in regard to religion and, in the powers of Congress, establish a complete religious despotism. The doctrines, being thus constitutionally affirmed and thus accompanied with an enforcing power in Congress, would "constitute a Christian government" in a sense that might well fill the country with alarm. If, however, these doctrines were simply in the preamble, dissevered from any enforcing power, they would have no more legal significance than if they were found in a treatise on theology.

Moreover, if these propositions were added to the preamble, and all the other parts of the Constitution were left uchanged, there would be no *authoritative* method of determining their meaning, or in what sense they would make the Government "a Christian government." Congress could not legislatively express any opinion on the subject, since it would have no power of legislation in reference to it. The Supreme Court of the United States could not judicially expound or apply the propositions, since no case under them could arise over which it would have jurisdiction. Ecclesiastical courts could not determine their meaning, since they are not the authorized interpreters of the Constitution. Their meaning would be purely a matter of *private* interpretation, and no such interpretation would have any authority. The *words* would be in the preamble; but, as a national confession of faith, they would be accompanied by no legislative or judicial commentary on their import.

Whether God is the source of all authority and power in civil government, merely in the general sense of creation and providence, or in the special sense of investing such government with a portion of his own authority; whether the Lord Jesus Christ is the ruler among the nations in any other sense than that in which he is the ruler over the fowls of the air and the beasts of the field; where his revealed will is to be found, and for what purposes, and in what relations it is to be applied—these and the like questions would be open to all sorts of answers according to the varying notions of different persons, with no tribunal and no authority anywhere to give the true answer. The words themselves are sufficiently elastic to be capable of different interpretations; and hence, in the absence of an authentic expounder, there would be no means of deciding in what sense the people use them in the preamble.

Nor do we see any reason why, if the door is to be opened sufficiently wide to admit these three religious dogmas, it may not be opened wide enough to admit forty—indeed to permit the ingress of all the cardinal doctrines of Christianity. Why not also declare that Christ died for our sins, according to the Scriptures; that he rose again on the third day; that he ascended into heaven; and that he will come again to raise the dead and judge the world? These and the like are certainly Christian truths; and the theory which demands the utterance of three such truths may just as well be extended to the whole system. It imposes upon itself no limitation. Indeed, it would be a question of interpretation, without anybody authorized to answer it, whether the phrase "His revealed will" would not by implication embrace the whole circle of Christian doctrine and precept as given in the Bible. Words, when used in constitutions, are generally interpreted to include every thing to which, being taken in their natural sense, they are applicable; and under this rule the phrase referred to would have a very broad import.

What practical service would the insertion of these words in the preamble, with no power in the Government either to explain them or put them into legal execution, render to either God or man? A Church creed is operative for its appropriate purposes, because behind the creed we have a Church organization to work it; but such a creed, either in whole or in part, in the constitution of a government, without the power to work it, would be of no productive value. It might gratify the wishes of a certain class of the people, while it would be contrary to the convictions and wishes of a much larger class ; but it would not make one Christian more or one sinner less. It would not increase the religious zeal of the people or add to the general influence of Christianity upon the popular mind. It would not make the careless thoughtful, or convert Atheists and Deists to the faith. It would not build a church or raise a dollar for religious purposes. It would not control the legislation of the Government or furnish any guaranty that the legislation would be just and right. It would not add to the sense of God in the councils of the nation or in individual hearts. It would not purify political parties or make office-holders more circumspect.

We are at an utter loss to see how the simple creed contained in the words proposed—unaccompanied by any enforcing power, as it would be if found merely in the preamble, and as it must be, or be the basis of a most dangerous religious despotism—would secure any desirable result that would not just as well and just as certainly be secured without it. There is not a solitary thing which the creed in this form of utterance would or could do to make the Government "a Christian government" in any sense not now real, or to make the people any more Christian than they now are. Some might think it a religious ornament to the Constitution; yet a much greater number would regard the ornament as not being in its proper place.

The one great objection to the amendment, though as we have shown, it would be legally meaningless and powerless, consists in the *principle* which underlies it and which those who framed the Constitution meant utterly to exclude. The American people, so far as they are religious at all, are Christian, by a very large preponderance, and in this sense they may be justly spoken of as being a Christian people; and yet nothing is more conspicuous in their political and civil institutions than their general refusal to incorporate *pro forma* their Christianity into the language of their constitutions or laws. The great idea which they have sought to realize is that of the most perfect religious liberty and equality among all the citizens of one common government; and, in order the more effectually to gain this end, they have denied to civil government any jurisdiction in matters of religious faith and practice beyond that of extending an impartial protection to all the people. Adopting this principle, they have, with scrupulous care, limited their constitutions and legal systems to the attainment of purely temporal ends, and, hence, omitted to place in them any affirmations or denials of religious dogmas.

There can be no doubt that the amendment proposed, though confined to the preamble of the Constitution and really granting no power to the General

Government, would nevertheless, be a departure from this principle. By it, the people of the United States, not as individuals, but in their political and corporate capacity, would place a confession of religious faith in their National Constitution. This would be a step in the wrong direction, provided the doctrine of absolute religious equality is to be maintained. The next step would be to clothe the Government with power in respect to this confession; and this would at once erect a religious despotism. The safe course for the people is not to take the first step; and if they do not propose to take the second step there is no occasion for taking the first. When they are prepared to make Christianity a *legalized* system, then, and not till then, will it be seasonable to stamp its doctrines with a constitutional affirmation.

Looking, finally, at the process by which the proposed amendment must be adopted, if at all, we cannot resist the conviction that its advocates are engaged in the most hopeless of all undertakings. In order to succeed, they must persuade *two-thirds* of both Houses of Congress to propose the amendment, or *two-thirds* of the legislatures of the several States to ask Congress to call a convention to propose it. And when they have gained this end, they must persuade *three-fourths* of the legislatures of all the States or conventions in *three-fourths* of the States to ratify the proposition. This is the constitutional method of changing the fundamental law of the land. Does any man in his senses suppose that the amendment in question can be carried through this process? Nothing short of a largely predominant public sentiment could secure the result. No such sentiment now exists, and there is not the remotest probability of creating it by any amount of discussion. The tendency of discussion would be in the opposite direction. A political party organized on the basis of such an amendment would not live long enough to be entitled to a name, and any existing party adopting it as an article of its political creed would be crushed by its weight. The advocates of the amendment may as well save their time and money and apply both to the attainment of more practical objects.

XX.

THE GUARANTY OF RELIGIOUS LIBERTY.

The Constitution of the United States declares that "no religious test shall ever be required as a qualification to any office or public trust under the United States," and that "Congress shall make no law respecting an establishment of religion, or prohibiting the free exercise thereof." These provisions guarantee religious liberty against encroachments by the General Government; yet neither of them imposes any limitation upon the powers of the States.

So, also, the Constitution declares that "the United States shall guarantee to each State in this

Union a republican form of government," and that "the citizens of each State shall be entitled to all the privileges and immunities of citizens in the several States." These clauses have no relation to the question of religious liberty as it may be affected by State constitutions and State laws. A State might be republican in the form of its government and yet practice religious oppression upon a portion of its citizens. The rule adopted by the Supreme Court of the United States in interpreting the provision that relates to "the privileges and immunities of citizens in the several States" makes it inapplicable to the religious liberty or any other right of the citizen as determined by the State of which he is a resident. The Court, in the cases of Paul *vs.* Virginia (8 Wallace, p. 168), and of the New Orleans Slaughter-house (16 Wallace, p. 36), laid down the principle that this provision does not "control the power of the State governments over the rights of its own citizens."

There is nothing in the last three amendments to the Constitution that reaches the question of religion, and nothing anywhere else in this instrument that places the States under the slightest restraint with reference to this subject; and, hence, it is true, as remarked by Justice Story, in his Commentaries on the Constitution (section 1879), that "the whole power over the subject of religion is left exclusively to the State governments, to be acted upon according to their sense of justice and the State constitutions."

The States, moreover, by the express language of the Tenth Amendment, retain all "the powers not delegated to the United States by the Constitution, nor prohibited by it to the States." These are called "reserved" State powers; and among them is that of dealing with religion and the religious rights and liberties of the people in such manner as each State shall think most expedient. State power in this respect is plenary and complete, subject to no limitation by the National Constitution.

It is well known, as a matter of history, that long after the Constitution went into operation the power of taxation for the support of religion in the Protestant form was actually exercised in some of the States. That power still exists, and might be exercised by any State to any extent, and in favor of Christianity or any other religious system. New Hampshire, Pennsylvania, North Carolina, South Carolina, Mississippi and Tennessee have to-day religious tests in their respective constitutions with reference to the qualifications for holding office. Maryland has such a test in her constitution in respect to the qualifications of witnesses and jurors. Delaware, Kentucky, Maryland and Tennessee exclude clergymen from civil office, on account of their ecclesiastical functions. These examples, though exceptional to the general character of the State constitutions, are a practical commentary upon the statement of Justice Story that "the whole power over the subject of religion is left exclusively" with the respective States. They may, if they choose, establish religion, support it by taxation, and enforce it by test-acts or by pains and penalties.

The States cannot coin money, or emit bills of credit, or make anything but gold and silver coin a tender in payment of debts, or pass a bill of attainder or an *ex-post facto* law or any law impairing the obligation of contracts, or grant any title of nobility, or exercise any of the powers exclusively delegated to the United States. These and other abridgments of State power were made to secure the harmony and good of the whole as one people. If the sacred rights of religious liberty were included, and the States dispossessed of all power to interfere with these rights, this would be simply according to the analogy of the Constitution. These rights are not inferior to those which arise from contracts, or those which may be affected by *ex-post facto* laws, or those which relate to property. Religious liberty is very intimately allied with free government. Our general theory is that the citizen, subject to the limitation of decency and good order, should be absolutely free as to his religion, and that on this account no legal preferences should be granted to him and no discriminations made against him. This doctrine surely needs no defense in this country. Why, then, should it not be incorporated into the fundamental law of the land in such a form as to be restrictive not only upon the powers of the General Government, but equally so upon those of all the States? Why should not so vital an interest as that of religious liberty be committed to the custody of the whole people in their collective character, and be thus guarded in the best possible manner against the "accidents of ignorance," the passions of zealots, and, indeed, all causes of peril? It seems to us that the proper place for the assertion and guaranty of the principle is in our national Magna Charta. The principle is quite as important as the obligation of contracts or the protection of the citizen against *ex-post facto* laws.

We see no reason why Congress should by the Constitution be placed under restraint as to religious tests, as to the establishment of religion, and as to the free exercise thereof, that is not equally good to show that the States should in the same constitution be placed under a similar restraint. If the *whole* people, as represented in Congress, cannot be safely trusted on this question without a Constitutional restraint, can the people in parts and as organized into separate communities be trusted with any more safety? The whole body politic composing the nation with its diversity of sentiments, its broader comprehension of interests, and more extended view of what is best for the whole—is less likely to err than any local sections of the whole.

If a religious test would be objectionable in the General Government, it is equally so in a State Government; and if on this subject the former cannot be trusted without restraint, then the latter ought not to be trusted without the same restraint. It is not enough to deny the power of a religious test to the one and leave it to the discretion of the other. It is not enough to say that "Congress shall make no law respecting an establishment of religion, or prohibiting the free exercise thereof," and then leave the States to make as many such laws as they please. On this great subject we should be absolutely *one* people in our policy and assert this policy in our organic law. No State should deem it a hardship to be deprived of the power to impose a religious test, or to establish a religion, or to prohibit the free exercise thereof, any more than it is to be deprived of the power to impair the obligation of contracts, or to do various other things forbidden to the States by the Constitution. All persons who are not short-sighted bigots must see that all the people have a common interest in extending to the religious liberty of all the highest possible security.

The population of this country, religiously considered, and considered in reference to the question of race and nativity, is exceedingly mixed in its constituent elements, and such it will remain for many years to come. It contains a large amount of foreign-born persons. Roman Catholicism, representing the ignorance, the poverty, the bigotry, and superstition of Catholic countries, and owing spiritual allegiance to a foreign hierarchy, has become not only a strong ecclesiastical, but also a strong

political power on this soil. Some of our large cities, looked at with reference to the voting power that controls their local administration, are already foreign, if not Catholic cities. The population of the Southern States is made up of two races that cannot readily, if at all, be fused into each other. European immigration pours in upon us on the Atlantic seaboard, and the prospect is that in the future we shall receive a very considerable Asiatic immigration on our Pacific coast. We are but a young nation, and have hardly yet, as a whole, acquired a distinctively national character. It is by no means certain that we have finished our growth in the acquisition of territory. There is nothing improbable in the supposition that we may add Mexico, the States of Central America, and a part if not all of the adjacent islands to the territory of the United States.

No one looking at the spectacle of our national life as it now presents itself to the eye, is to-day wise enough even to conjecture the possibilities and contingencies that lie in the bosom of the unrevealed future. What is before us we do not know. Let us, then, as germane to the purpose of this article, indulge in one or two suppositions that may become realities.

Suppose that in a given State there should arise an intense and bitter politico-ecclesiastical struggle between Catholics and Protestants, and that the former should constitute the majority of the people. This would only be what has often happened in other countries and what may happen here. Is there anything in the Constitution of the United States to protect the religious rights of Protestants in such an event? Nothing whatever. The Catholics, being the majority, might alter the constitution of the State, make Catholicism a State religion, tax the people to support it, exclude all but Catholics from office, and enforce the Catholic faith by legal sanctions. The whole range of possibilities in reference to religious preferences, discriminations, and proscriptions would be entirely open to their choice, without any limitation imposed by the National Constitution or any corrective remedy in the powers of the General Government. This is but a supposition: yet nothing is wanting but voting power and the disposition, with suitable attendant circumstances, to convert it into a reality in any State of the Union, and it is by no means insupposable that the requisite conditions might be supplied in at least some of the States. The Constitution, as it is, would not meet such an order of things with any remedial power.

We may also suppose that Protestants, in such a religious contest, would, by reason of their number, be the political victors. What, then, would prevent them from making the State a Protestant State and committing all its legal functions and powers exclusively to Protestants, and even establishing a religious test in respect to the right of suffrage? Nothing but their own choice. The religious rights of Catholics, in every State of the Union in which they are in the minority, are to-day completely at the disposal of a majority that is non-Catholic; and if those rights are not invaded, it is not for the want of power to do so. The constitution of New Hampshire now provides that no one, unless he is of "the Protestant religion," shall be eligible to the office of governor or to either house of the State legislature. The principle of this provision, so far as the National Constitution is concerned, may be incorporated into every State constitution and put into practice to any extent

One of the territories of the United States is inhabited chiefly by a Mormon population, gathered from various countries. Let us suppose this territory to be organized into a State and admitted into the Union, and, consequently, clothed with the autonomy and powers of every other State. Whatever its constitution might be at the time of admission, it would, like the constitutions of all the other States, be subject to any change within the limits of a republican form of government which the majority might choose to make; and by such a process Mormonism, being the religion of the majority, might be made the religion of the State. Nothing is needed to make this supposition real but the admission of Utah into the Union. Congress would have no power in the terms of the admission to establish a permanent guaranty against such a result. It can refuse to admit a State; but it cannot govern an admitted State or dispossess it of the powers common to all the States. If Protestants, being the majority in any State, could establish Protestantism as a State religion, then Mormons, being the majority, could establish Mormonism as such a religion; and in neither case would there be any remedy in the Federal Constitution. Once in the Union, every State is self-governing, except as limited by this Constitution; and in respect to religion no State is thus limited at all. State constitutions are purely the creatures of State public sentiment and are what that sentiment makes them.

We give these suppositions—which in kind might be indefinitely multiplied—simply as illustrations of what is possible under our present constitutional system. It is possible that an Asiatic and heathen population may acquire the control of one or more of the Pacific States. It is possible that Mexico and the States of Central America, with their almost exclusively Catholic population, may become members of the Union. We do not now know where the doctrine of "manifest destiny" in these and other respects will ultimately conduct us as a people. We do not know what shape the School question will finally take, or to what collisions it may yet lead. What we do know is that our National Constitution, except as against encroachments by the General Government, does not stand guard over the religious liberties of the people. It affords them no protection. The whole subject is left exclusively with the States, and over their action in regard to it the Constitution asserts no control.

Would it not, then, be wise so to amend the Constitution that this great question of religious liberty in all its phases and applications shall be settled by the fundamental law of the land, and so settled that the whole people as one political organism, shall be charged with the protection of such liberty? Would it not be wise to make religious liberty in every State a national idea? The obligation of contracts, the right of protection against an *ex-post facto* law and bills of attainder, the rights of life, civil liberty, and property, as guarded against any deprivation, except by due process of law, the equal protection of the laws, the right of the United States citizen to become a citizen in any State by residence therein and there to enjoy all the privileges and immunities granted to its own citizens, the right in every State to a republican form of government, the rights of United States citizenship in each State—these and the like are already national ideas. The Constitution asserts them and protects them. Why not place religious liberty in the same category? It is a right second to no other in the whole circle. There is nothing in it to make it a local idea or require that it should be remitted to the exclusive jurisdiction of the States.

The amendment to the Constitution proposed by ex-Speaker Blaine looks in the right direction and covers the ground in part. In 1870, the Hon. E. P. Hurlbut, formerly a judge of the Supreme Court of the State of New York, published a pamphlet entitled "A Secular View of Religion in the State," in which he suggested an amendment with a view to the same general end. Combining the propositions of both these gentlemen, with some modifications and additions, we submit the following draft of an amendment that would meet the whole case :

SECTION 1. No State shall make any law respecting an establishment of religion, or prohibit the free exercise thereof, or establish any religious test as a qualification to hold any office, or to discharge any political or civil duty, or to exercise and enjoy any political or civil right, privilege, or immunity whatsoever.

SECTION 2. Neither the United States nor any State, territory, municipality, or any civil division of any State or territory, shall levy any tax or make any gift, grant or appropriation for the support or in aid of any church, religious sect, or denomination, or any school, seminary, or institution of learning in which the faith or doctrines of any religious order or sect shall be taught or inculcated, or in which religious rites or practices shall be observed, or for the support or in aid of any religious charity or purpose of any sect or denomination whatsoever.

SECTION 3. Congress shall have power, by appropriate legislation, to enforce the provisions of this article.

The phraseology of this amendment may, perhaps, be improved ; yet the ideas, if incorporated into the Constitution of the United States, would put an end to the School question and all other questions that contemplate any alliance, whether direct or indirect, between civil government and religion. Religious liberty, untaxed, uncoerced, without any patronage from the State, but simply enjoyed and protected, without any discriminations or preferences and without any encroachment by governmental power, would have its basis in the National Constitution, and would, hence, be the universal inheritance of all the people, whether they were Christians or Infidels, Catholics or Protestants, Mormons or Jews. The best ideas of the State constitutions would be nationalized, and the defects and inconsistencies which exist in some of them would be removed. The future would be guaranteed by the consolidated strength of the whole people. Ecclesiasticism would have nothing to gain by becoming a political power. Religious factions could never bring civil government within the circle of their objects, and foreign hierarchies could obtain no foothold on this soil. The divorce between Church and State would be absolute, universal, and radical. The axe would be laid at the root of the tree. Such an amendment would guarantee impartial and perfect religious liberty in all the forms and applications of the idea. And in this respect it would be simply a true and full expression of one of the essential principles of AMERICAN DEMOCRACY.

XXI.

STATE CONSTITUTIONS.

The several States of the Union exist and operate under written constitutions, which, subject only to the Constitution of the United States, form their supreme law. All of these constitutions, while substantially similar in the powers of government and the manner of their distribution, contain provisions relating to religion, designed, for the most part, to protect the religious liberty of the people against encroachments by governmental agency. Some of the provisions, however, found in the constitutions of some of the States are exceptions to this statement and to the general character and scope of the constitutions of the American States. They appear as inconsistencies and deformities, and also vestiges of ideas once entertained, but now generally obsolete.

The constitution of New Hampshire, (I., 6) furnishes one of these exceptions, in empowering "the legislature to authorize from time to time the several towns, parishes, bodies corporate, or religious societies within this State to make adequate provisions, at their own expense, for the support of public *Protestant* teachers of piety, religion, and morality;" and, also, in providing (II, 14, 29, 42) that "every member of the House of Representatives . . . shall be of the *Protestant* religion;" that "no person shall be capable of being elected a senator who is not of the *Protestant* religion;" and that no person shall be eligible to the office of governor unless "he shall be of the *Protestant* religion." The legislature is here authorized to grant to the towns, parishes, bodies corporate, or religious societies within that State the compulsory power of taxation for the support of *Protestant* teachers of religion. The constitution also establishes a religious test as a qualification for the office of representative, senator, and governor.

The constitution of Pennsylvania, (I., 4) declares that "no person who acknowledges the being of a God and a future state of rewards and punishments shall, on account of his religious sentiments, be disqualified to hold any office or place of trust or profit under this commonwealth." This immunity against disqualification does not, by its very terms, apply to those who deny the existence of God, or deny a future state, or deny the doctrine of rewards and punishments in that state. All such persons it leaves exposed to the liability of a religious test by the will of the legislature, and protects only those who acknowledge the doctrines recited.

The constitution of North Carolina (VI., 5) provides that "all persons who shall deny the being of Almighty God" "shall be disqualified for office." The constitutions of South Carolina (XIV., 6), of Mississippi (XII., 3), and of Tennessee (IX., 2), contain a similar provision, with the extension of the exclusion in the last of these constitutions to any person who denies a "future state of rewards and punishments." The constitution of Maryland (Declaration of Rights, 36, 37) declares that no person, "otherwise competent," shall "be deemed incompetent as a witness or juror on account of his religious belief, *provided* he believes in the existence of God, and that under his dispensation such person will be held morally accountable for his acts and be rewarded or punished therefor either in this world or in the world to come," and also declares that "no religious test ought ever to be required as a qualification for any office of profit or trust in this State, *other* than a declaration of belief in the existence of God." These provisions are religious tests, and, as Judge Cooley, in his "Constitutional Limitations" (p. 468) remarks, "show some traces of the old notion that truth and a sense of duty are inconsistent with skepticism in religion." They exclude persons from office on religious grounds. Maryland has quite an extended religious belief as a qualification to be a witness or perform the duty of a juror.

So, also, some of the State constitutions exclude clergymen, priests, and teachers of any religious sect from civil office. The constitution of Delaware (VII., 8) provides that "no ordained clergyman or ordained preacher of the Gospel of any denomination shall be capable of holding any office in the State, or of being a member of either branch of the legislature while he continues in the exercise of the pastoral or clerical functions." The constitution of Kentucky (II., 27) declares that "no person while he continues to exercise the functions of a clergyman, priest, or teacher of any religious persuasion, society, or sect . . . shall be eligible to the general assembly." The constitution of Maryland (III., 11,) says that "no minister or preacher of the Gospel, or of any religious creed or denomination . . . shall be eligible as senator or delegate." The constitution of Tennessee (IX., 1,) declares that "no minister of the Gospel or priest of any denomination whatever, shall be eligible to a seat in either house of the legislature." These are examples of constitutional exclusion of persons from the exercise of civil functions on account of their ecclesiastical character and office; and, so far, examples of proscription on religious grounds. The reason of the exclusion and the fact itself involve the practical results of a religious test.

These provisions are the exceptions, rather than the general rule, in the constitutions of the American States. The great mass of these constitutions exclude all religious tests as qualifications to hold office, or to perform any civil duty or exercise any political or civil right or privilege; and also exclude the power to levy taxes for the support of religion, and guarantee to each person the full enjoyment of the rights of a religious conscience within the limits of decency and public order. It would be tedious to go through the whole list of provisions that secure these results, and, hence, a few examples must suffice.

The constitution of Illinois (II., 3,) declares that "the free exercise and enjoyment of religious profession and worship, without discrimination, shall forever be guaranteed, and no person shall be denied any civil or political right, privilege, or capacity on account of his religious opinions," and that "no person shall be required to attend or support any ministry or place of worship against his consent, nor shall any preference be given by law to any religious denomination or mode of worship." The constitution of Iowa (I., 3, 4) declares that "the general assembly shall make no law respecting an establishment of religion, or prohibiting the free exercise thereof; nor shall any person be compelled to attend any place of worship, pay tithes, taxes, or other rates for building or repairing places of worship, or the maintenance of any minister or ministry. No religious test shall be required as a qualification for any office or public trust, and no person shall be deprived of any of his rights, privileges, or capacities, or disqualified from the performance of any of his public or private duties, or rendered incompetent to give evidence in any court of law or equity, in consequence of his opinion on the subject of religion." The constitution of Michigan (IV., 39, 41) declares that "the legislature shall pass no law to prevent any person from worshipping Almighty God according to the dictates of his own conscience, or to compel any person to attend, erect, or support any place of religious worship, or to pay tithes, taxes, or other rates for the support of any minister of the Gospel or teacher of religion. The legislature shall not diminish or enlarge the civil or political privileges and capacities of any person on account of his opinion or belief concerning matters of religion." The constitution of New Jersey (I., 4) provides that "no religious test shall be required as a qualification for any office or public trust, and no person shall be denied the enjoyment of any civil right merely on account of his religious principles." The constitution of Oregon (I., 3, 4, 6) says: "No law shall, in any case whatever control the free exercise and enjoyment of religious opinions or interfere with the rights of conscience. No religious test shall be required as a qualification for any office of trust or profit. No person shall be rendered incompetent as a witness or juror in consequence of his opinions on matters of religion, nor be questioned in any court of justice touching his religious belief to affect the weight of his testimony."

Similar provisions, more or less full, are found in the constitutions of most of the other States, and in all the States there are constitutional restrictions designed to protect the right of a religious conscience against encroachment by legislative power.

Some persons are conscientiously averse to bearing arms; and in many of the States we find constitutional provisions granting them an exemption from this service. Thus the constitution of Indiana (XII., 6) says: "No person conscientiously opposed to bearing arms shall be compelled to do militia duty; but such person shall pay an equivalent for exemption, the amount to be prescribed by law." The constitution of Alabama (X., 1) says: "All citizens of any denomination whatever who, from scruples of conscience, may be averse to bearing arms shall be exempt therefrom, upon such conditions as may be prescribed by law." Provisions of the same general character occur in the constitutions of many of the other States.

So also some persons are conscientiously opposed to taking a legal oath, and, hence, provision is made that they may simply affirm, as the equivalent of an oath. On this point the constitution of Missouri (II., 12) says: "If any person shall declare that he has conscientious scruples against taking an oath or swearing in any form, the said oath may be changed into a solemn affirmation and be made by him in that form." The constitution of Indiana (I., 8) says: "The mode of administering an oath or affirmation shall be such as shall be most consistent with, and binding upon, the conscience of the person to whom such oath or affirmation may be administered." Like provisions are found in the constitutions or statutes of other States.

Some of the State constitutions expressly prohibit the appropriation of any public funds or property for religious or sectarian uses. Thus the constitution of Illinois (VIII., 3) says: "Neither the general assembly, nor any county, city, town, township, school district, or other public corporation, shall ever make any appropriation or pay from any public fund whatever, anything in aid of any church or sectarian purpose, or to help support or sustain any school, academy, seminary, college, university, or other literary or scientific institution controlled by any church or sectarian denomination whatever; nor shall any grant or donation of land, money, or other personal property ever be made by the State or any such public corporation to any church or for any sectarian purpose." The constitution of Missouri (IX., 10) contains a similar provision. The constitution of Indiana (I., 6) declares that "no money shall be drawn from the treasury for the benefit of any religious or theological institution." The constitution of Oregon (I., 5) provides that "no money shall be drawn from the treasury for the benefit of any religious or theological institution, nor shall any money be appropriated for the payment of any religious service in either house of the legislative assembly." The constitution of Michigan (IV., 40) declares that "no money shall be appropriated or drawn from the treasury for the benefit of any religious sect or society, theological or religious seminary, nor shall property belonging to the State be appropriated for any such purposes." The constitution of Minnesota (I., 16) and that of Wisconsin. (I., 18) contain a similar provision.

Looking, then, at these various constitutional provisions as a whole, and as indicating the general policy of the American States in regard to religion, Judge Cooley, in his "Constitutional Limitations" (chapter xiii.), says that "those things which are not lawful under any of the American constitutions may be stated thus":

1. "Any law respecting an establishment of religion." 2. "Compulsory support, by taxation or otherwise, of religion." 3. "Compulsory attendance upon religious worship." 4. "Restraints upon the free exercise of religion according to the dictates of the conscience." 5. "Restraints upon the expression of religious belief."

"These," he adds, "are the prohibitions which in some form of words are to be found in the American constitutions and which secure freedom of conscience and of religious worship. No man in religious matters is to be subjected to the censorship of the State; and the State is not to inquire into or take notice of religious belief, when the citizen performs his duty to the State and to his fellows." He also says that "it is not toleration which is established in our system, but religious equality." The exceptions to this principle referred to and illustrated by citations in the commencement of this article he treats as exceptions not often put into practice and by no means representing the general character of our American State constitutions. They are, rather, the relics of ideas once prevalent, but now for the most part discarded in this country. They are, moreover, generally found in the older constitutions, and not in those of more recent date. The American people have outgrown the doctrine of religious tests and that of taxation for religious purposes. The tendency of public thought has been toward a complete severance of Church and State.

Mr. John Norton Pomeroy, in his "Introduction to Municipal Law" (p. 292), states as follows, the general theory in regard to religion on which our national and State constitutions are built:

"The theory of our national and State constitutions is that the State, as an organic body, has nothing whatever to do with religion, except to protect the individuals in whatever belief and worship they may adopt; that religion is entirely a matter between each man and his God; that the State, as separated from the individuals who compose it, has no existence except in a figure; and that to predicate religious responsibilities of this abstraction is an absurdity. Whatever, then, the State does, whatever laws it makes touching religious subjects, are done and made not because the State is responsible, but simply that the people may be secure in the enjoyment of their own religious preferences. Public labor is forbidden by law on Sunday, not because the State, as such, respects the sacredness of the day or attempts to enforce its observance; but because a large portion of its worthy citizens do regard the day as sacred and employ it for public and private worship, and have a right to be protected in the quiet use of the time for these purposes. So far as the State is concerned, the laws forbidding public labor on Sunday stand on exactly the same footing as those forbidding disorderly houses, public intemperance, and all other acts which disturb the peace. The same may be said of laws against profane swearing."

Reasoning from these principles, Mr. Pomeroy says: "Indeed, although the people composing our body politic are doubtless as much impressed with Christian ideas as those of any other nation, our governments, both State and National, by ignoring the whole subject, can hardly be called Christian." This is undoubtedly the truth. Neither Christianity nor any other religious system forms any part of the Constitution of the United States. The same is true of the State constitutions, as a general fact. The exceptions are such as were specified in the first part of this article; and even these exceptions are limited to a few particulars and in practice are mostly obsolete.

The all-pervading principle, then, of our American constitutions is that the State, as such, has nothing to do with religion, beyond affording to the people protection in the enjoyment of their religious rights, and that, too, with no discrimination among them. It is difficult to see how a State established upon this principle, and for reasons of State policy conducting a school system at the public expense, can make that system the instrument of religious instruction or worship in any form. It manifestly cannot do so without contradicting the fundamental law of its own organic life.

XXII.

CONSTITUTIONAL RIGHTS OF CONSCIENCE.

The following citations present the several clauses of the American State constitutions, which in express words refer to the rights of conscience and guarantee their peaceable exercise and enjoyment :—

ALABAMA (I., 4) : "No person shall be deprived of the right to worship God according to the dictates of his conscience."

CALIFORNIA (I., 4) : "The free exercise and enjoyment of religious profession and worship, without discrimination or preference, shall forever be allowed in this State ; . . . but the liberty of conscience hereby secured, shall not be so construed as to excuse acts of licentiousness, or justify practices inconsistent with the peace or safety of the State."

CONNECTICUT (VII., 1): "It being the duty of all men to worship the Supreme Being, the great Creator and Preserver of the Universe, and their right to render that worship in the mode most consistent with the dictates of their conscience, no person shall by law be compelled to join or support, or be classed with, or associated to, any congregation, church, or religious association."

DELAWARE (Preamble): "Through divine goodness all men have, by nature, the rights of worshipping and serving their Creator according to the dictates of their consciences. No power shall or ought to be vested in or assumed by any magistrate that shall in any case interfere with, or in any manner control the rights of conscience in the free exercise of religious worship" (I., 1).

FLORIDA (I., 5): "The free exercise and enjoyment of all religious profession and worship shall forever be allowed in this State; . . . but the liberty of conscience hereby secured, shall not be so construed as to justify licentiousness or practices subversive of the peace and safety of the State."

GEORGIA (I., 6): "Perfect freedom of religious sentiment shall be and the same is hereby secured, and no inhabitant of this State shall ever be molested in person or property, or prohibited from holding any public office of trust on account of his religious opinion; but the liberty of conscience hereby secured shall not be so construed as to excuse acts of licentiousness, or justify practices inconsistent with the peace or safety of the people."

ILLINOIS (II., 3): "The free exercise and enjoyment of religious profession and worship, without discrimination, shall forever be guaranteed; . . but the liberty of conscience hereby secured shall not be construed to dispense with oaths or affirmations, excuse acts of licentiousness, or justify practices inconsistent with the peace or safety of the State."

INDIANA (II., 2, 3): "All men shall be secured in the natural right to worship Almighty God according to the dictates of their own consciences. No law shall in any case whatever control the free exercise and enjoyment of religious opinions, or interfere with the rights of conscience."

IOWA (I., 3): "The General Assembly shall make no law respecting an establishment of religion, or prohibiting the free exercise thereof."

KANSAS (Bill of Rights, 7): "The right to worship God according to the dictates of conscience shall never be infringed; . . . nor shall any control of or interference with the rights of conscience be permitted."

KENTUCKY (XIII., 5): "All men have a natural and indefeasible right to worship Almighty God according to the dictates of their own consciences. . . . No human authority ought in any case whatever to control or interfere with the rights of conscience."

LOUISIANA (I., 12): "Every person has the natural right to worship God according to the dictates of his conscience."

MAINE (I, 3): "All men have a natural and unalienable right to worship Almighty God according to the dictates of their own consciences; and no person shall be hurt, molested, or restrained in his person, liberty or estate, for worshipping God in the manner and season most agreeable to the dictates of his own conscience, nor for his religious professions or sentiments, provided he does not disturb the public peace nor obstruct others in their religious worship."

MARYLAND (Declaration of Rights, 36): "That, as it is the duty of every man to worship God in such manner as he thinks most acceptable to him, all persons are equally entitled to protection in their religious liberty; wherefore, no person ought by any law to be molested in his person or estate on account of his religious persuasion or profession, or for his religious practice, unless, under the color of religion, he shall disturb the good order, peace, or safety of the State, or shall infringe the laws of morality, or injure others in their natural, civil, or religious rights."

MASSACHUSETTS (I., 2): "It is the right as well

as the duty of all men in society, publicly and at stated seasons, to worship the Supreme Being, the great Creator and Preserver of the Universe. And no subject shall be hurt, molested, or restrained in his person, liberty, or estate for worshipping God in the manner and season most agreeable to the dictates of his own conscience, or for his profession or sentiments, provided he doth not disturb the public peace or obstruct others in their religious worship."

MICHIGAN (IV., 39): "The legislature shall pass no law to prevent any person from worshipping Almighty God according to the dictates of his own conscience."

MINNESOTA (I., 16): "The right of every man to worship God according to the dictates of his own conscience shall never be infringed, . . . nor shall any control of, or interference with, the rights of conscience be permitted; . . . but the liberty of conscience hereby secured shall not be so construed as to excuse acts of licentiousness, or justify practices inconsistent with the peace or safety of the State."

MISSOURI (I., 9): "All men have a natural and indefeasible right to worship Almighty God according to the dictates of their own consciences. . . No human authority can control or interfere with the rights of conscience. . . . But the liberty of conscience hereby secured shall not be so construed as to excuse acts of licentiousness, nor to justify practices inconsistent with the good order, peace, or safety of the State, or with the rights of others."

NEBRASKA (I., 16): "All men have a natural and indefeasible right to worship Almighty God according to the dictates of their own conscience; . . . nor shall any interference with the rights of conscience be permitted."

NEVADA (I., 4): "The free exercise and enjoyment of religious profession and worship, without discrimination or preference, shall forever be allowed in this State; . . . but the liberty hereby secured shall not be so construed as to excuse acts of licentiousness, or justify practices inconsistent with the peace and safety of the State."

NEW HAMPSHIRE (I., 4, 5): "Among the natural rights some are in their very nature unalienable, because no equivalent can be given or received for them. Of this kind are the rights of conscience. Every individual has a natural and unalienable right to worship God according to the dictates of his own conscience and reason; and no subject shall be hurt, molested, or restrained in his person, liberty, or estate for worshipping God in the manner and season most agreeable to the dictates of his own conscience, or of his religious profession, sentiments, or persuasion, provided he doth not disturb the public peace, or disturb others in their religious worship."

NEW JERSEY (I., 3): "No person shall be deprived of the inestimable privilege of worshipping Almighty God in a manner agreeable to the dictates of his own conscience."

New York (I., 3): "The free exercise and enjoyment of religious profession and worship, without discrimination or preference, shall forever be allowed in this State to all mankind; . . . . but the liberty of conscience hereby secured shall not be so construed as to excuse acts of licentiousness, or justify practices inconsistent with the peace or safety of this State."

North Carolina (I., 26): "All men have a natural and unalienable right to worship Almighty God according to the dictates of their own consciences, and no human authority should in any case whatever control or interfere with the right of conscience."

Ohio (I., 7): "All men have a natural and indefeasible right to worship Almighty God according to the dictates of their own conscience; . . . . nor shall any interference with the rights of conscience be permitted."

Oregon (I., 2, 3): "All men shall be secured in their natural right to worship Almighty God according to the dictates of their own consciences. No law shall in any case whatever control the free exercise and enjoyment of religious opinions, or interfere with the rights of conscience."

Pennsylvania (I., 3): "All men have a natural and indefeasible right to worship Almighty God according to the dictates of their own consciences. . . . No human authority can in any case whatever control or interfere with the rights of conscience."

Rhode Island (I., 3): "Every man shall be free to worship God according to the dictates of his own conscience and to profess and by argument to maintain his opinion in matters of religion."

South Carolina (I., 9): "No person shall be deprived of the right to worship God according to the dictates of his own conscience, provided that the liberty of conscience hereby declared shall not justify practices inconsistent with the peace and moral safety of society."

Tennessee (I., 3): "All men have a natural and indefeasible right to worship Almighty God according to the dictates of their own consciences. . . . No human authority can in any case whatever control or interfere with the rights of conscience."

Texas (I., 4): "All men have a natural and indefeasible right to worship God according to the dictates of their own consciences. . . . No human authority ought in any case whatever to control or interfere with the rights of conscience in matters of religion."

Vermont (I., 3): "All men have a natural and inalienable right to worship Almighty God according to the dictates of their own consciences and understandings, as in their opinion shall be regulated by the Word of God. . . . No authority can or ought to be vested in or assumed by any power that shall in any case interfere with or in any manner control the rights of conscience in the free exercise of religious worship."

VIRGINIA (I., 18) : "All men are equally entitled to the free exercise of religion according to the dictates of conscience."

WEST VIRGINIA (III., 15) : "Nor shall any man be enforced, restrained, molested, or burdened in his body or goods, or otherwise suffer, on account of his religious opinions or belief; but all men shall be free to profess and by argument to maintain their opinions in matters of religion."

WISCONSIN (I., 18) : "The right of every man to worship God according to the dictates of his own conscience shall never be infringed. . . . Nor shall any control of, or interference with, the rights of conscience be permitted."

Here are thirty-five State constitutions that in express language, somewhat various in the words used, yet essentially identical in substance, formulate a definite doctrine in regard to the rights of conscience and give to it the authority of constitutional law. The same doctrine is implied, but not so fully expressed, in the constitutions of Arkansas and Mississippi; and, hence, they are not quoted in the above list. What then is this doctrine? We answer as follows:

1. These provisions assume the existence of

conscience as an attribute of human nature. They also assume the doctrine of a God as existing in the faith of men, and the fact of worship or religious service rendered to God as a prevalent practice among the people. These facts are not created by being thus assumed and implied. They are simply recognized as existing antecedently to, and independently of, all constitutions; and what and all that is sought to be accomplished by the above provisions is to establish certain guaranties in respect to the rights of conscience.

2. These rights are simply those that relate to religion, to the faith involved, to the various modes of expressing that faith, and the duties by which men may deem themselves bound to God. They are purely and exclusively *religious* rights. They are not the rights which law creates, or which grow out of the relations that men hold to each other as members of the State. They spring from the relations which men hold to God, as the creatures of his power and the subjects of his moral government. Outside of this sphere of rights, the provisions have no application.

3. These rights are referred to as existing by nature—as being natural, indefeasible, and inalienable—and as being universal, or equally common to all men. These four conceptions are, in our State constitutions—in some by express words, and in others by implication—associated with the rights of conscience.

4. The phrase, "dictates of conscience,"—a phrase implying command, precept, or an authoritative rule of action—is the common form in which these constitutions express the voice or requirement of conscience. They mean thereby the affirmation and sense of obligation, as existing in the individual soul, and in respect to that soul prescribing a law which cannot be disregarded without self-condemnation. This deeply-rooted and universal fact of our nature is designated by the phrase "dictates of conscience."

5. These rights and these dictates of conscience in respect to religion are constitutionally withdrawn from the jurisdiction of civil government. The form of the withdrawal varies somewhat in different constitutions, yet the thing aimed at is the same in all. The reader, by simply casting his eye over the provisions previously quoted, will readily see the different modes of expression by which the State constitutions exempt the rights of a religious conscience from regulation, control, interference, restraint, or constraint by civil government. Their design is to secure religious freedom, by imposing limitations upon the civil power. On this vital question they all hold and all assert one doctrine.

6. The guaranty thus afforded, makes no distinction between different kinds of consciences. The conscience of a Protestant, and that of a Catholic, stand on the same footing. Neither, for the purposes of the guaranty, is any better than the

consciences of a Jew, a Deist, a Rationalist, a Swedenborgian, a Mormon, a Hindu, or a Chinaman. The guaranty does not inquire into the correctness of these several consciences, or pronounce any judgment upon them. It leaves each one to judge for himself as to what his religion shall be, and then declares that he shall not only not be interfered with, but that he shall be protected in the peaceable exercise of that judgment. It is not religious liberty for Christians, or for Protestants merely, but religious liberty for *all* the people, that the State constitutions undertake to secure.

7. The limitation upon this liberty, expressed in some of these constitutions and implied in others, is that it must be so exercised as to be consistent with the rights of society. The theory of the limitation is, that there can be no right of a religious conscience to commit trespasses against the peace, good order, and safety of the social system. Thus the constitution of Missouri declares that "the liberty of conscience hereby secured shall not be so construed as to excuse acts of licentiousness, nor to justify practices inconsistent with the good order, peace, or safety of society, or with the rights of others." Such a limitation, whether expressed or not, necessarily exists. Society has the right to protect itself and to protect all its members by just and wholesome laws; and this right it cannot surrender to any abuse or misuse of the rights of conscience. The fact that polygamy is made a part of

one's religion will not, if he practises it, exempt him from punishment in a community that treats the practice as a criminal offense. It is the right and the duty of civil society to judge for itself as to what is demanded by good morals and the general interests of the public ; and there can be no right in the individual conscience to subvert and contravene this judgment.

These seven particulars are submitted as a generalized statement of the doctrine in respect to the rights of conscience, as found in the constitutions of thirty-five States of this Union and as implied in those of the other two States. Though independent of each other and in their sphere of legal action independent of the General Government, these States exhibit a remarkable unity of opinion and purpose when dealing with religion considered in relation to the individual conscience. This fact very strikingly appears when we compare their respective constitutions with reference to this subject.

How, then, does such a constitutional system harmonize with the theory of those who demand that our public schools shall be made the instrumentality of religious propagandism? In respect to private schools there is no such question to ask, since the State has no control over them and taxes nobody for their support. But when the State interposes by its authority, establishes an educational system, and makes religion a part of it by its authority, and taxes the people for its support by the same authority, then it coerces the taxpayer to contribute his money for the maintenance and propagation of that religion. Suppose that his conscience regards the religion as a gross heresy and forbids him to do anything for its support. This will be true of the Catholic if the religion is Protestant, and true of the Protestant if the religion is Catholic, and true of the Jew if the religion is either Protestant or Catholic. Is it, then, consistent with the constitutional doctrine of the American States as to the rights of conscience to force the taxpayer to pay his money for the propagation of a religious system which his conscience condemns and which, as he believes, the God of that conscience condemns? The Protestant would instantly answer in the negative if the religion to be thus taught and made a compulsory charge upon him were Roman Catholicism, or Mohammedanism, or any form of idolatry. He would protest against it as an infringement upon his rights of conscience and as inconsistent with the spirit, if not the letter, of those provisions in our State constitutions which protect these rights.

The same protest and the same argument, coming from a Catholic, a Jew, or a Deist, are just as good as when coming from a Protestant. It matters not who makes the protest or who uses the argument. The principle is the same in all cases. The rights of conscience in respect to religion are, in this country, constitutional rights, and that, too, without any discrimination or distinction among different consciences. The necessary inference is that no State should, and that no State consistently can, compel anybody to contribute a penny for the support or propagation of any form of religion. Public schools, established by State authority and supported at the public expense, ought to be so regulated as to avoid this result ; and the only regulation which secures the end is the exclusion of religion from their educational programme. This and this only makes the schools consistent with the rights of conscience as laid down in the fundamental law of the States.

Those who have any controversy with the inference have the same controversy with this law. That man certainly is not free in the exercise of his religion who is by law forced to support a religion, and especially so if he condemns and rejects the religion he is thus compelled to support. The compulsion, whether it relates to the public school or church worship, is an abominable tyranny. It flies directly in the face of the very first principles of our constitutional system of State Governments.

XXIII.

TAXATION AND RELIGIOUS CORPORATIONS.

Seventeen of the State constitutions—namely, those of California, Connecticut, Delaware, Georgia, Iowa, Kentucky, Maine, Maryland, Massachusetts, Michigan, Mississippi, Nebraska, New Hampshire, New Jersey, New York, Rhode Island, and Vermont—contain no express provisions relating to the taxation of religious corporations. The whole question is, therefore, by implication, left to the discretion of the legislatures of these States.

The constitutions of Florida (XII., 1), Illinois (IX., 3), Indiana (X., 1), Louisiana (VI., 118), Nevada (X., 1), North Carolina (V., 6), Ohio (XII., 2), Oregon (IX., 1), Pennsylvania (IX., 1), South Carolina (IX., 1), Tennessee (II., 28), Texas (XII., 19), Virginia (X., 3), West Virginia (X., 1), and Wisconsin (VIII., 1)—fifteen States in all—expressly remit the question of taxation in respect to these corporations to legislative determination.

The constitution of Minnesota (IX., 3), declares that "all churches, church property used for religious purposes, and houses of worship . . . shall by general laws, be exempt from taxation." That of Arkansas (X., 2) provides that "houses used exclusively for public worship . . . shall never be taxed. That of Kansas (XI., 1) also provides that "all property used exclusively for" religious purposes "shall be exempted from taxation." The legislatures of these States have no power to impose any tax upon property owned and used for public worship.

The constitution of Alabama (XIII., 4) declares that "the property of corporations now existing or hereafter created shall forever be subject to taxation the same as property of individuals, except corporations for educational and charitable purposes." Unless religious corporations are included under the title of "corporations for educational and charitable purposes"—a construction that would not be according to the general usage of State constitutions—it then follows that such corporations cannot be exempted in Alabama from taxation on the property owned by them. The constitution of Missouri XI., 16) provides that "no property, real or personal, shall be exempt from taxation, except such as may be used exclusively for public schools, and such as may belong to the United States, to this State, to counties, or to municipal corporations in this State." The property of religious corporations is not included in these exceptions, and hence, the legislature has no power to exempt it from taxation.

Thus we have thirty-two States in which the

question of taxing religious societies is left to the legislative will, three States in which the power of taxing these societies is denied to their respective legislatures, and two States whose constitutions in effect deny the power of exempting church property from taxation. The general fact in this country is that all property which is directly used for religious worship is thus exempted. No discrimination is made beween the different Christian sects or between Christian and other religious corporations.

A society of Jews, or of Mormons, or of Swedenborgians, or of Mohammedans, or of Pagans, if owning property directly used for religious purposes, would enjoy the benefit of the exemption. The Revised Statutes of New York State provide that "every building for public worship" shall be exempt from taxation. This applies to a Jewish synagogue as really as to a building owned and used for public worship by a Christian society. Neither the character of the worship nor the tenets and doctrines involved therein, furnish any rule of exemption. "Houses of worship," "buildings for public worship," "property exclusively used for religious purposes," "churches and church property used for religious purposes,"—such are the constitutional or statutory designations of the property to be exempted. It is not the intention of law to confine the exemption to buildings or houses for Christian worship. Such a limitation would make a discrimination between religious sects; and this would be inconsistent with a fundamental principle of our political system.

According to the census of 1870, the amount of property belonging to the different religious denominations in the United States was then $354,-483,581, against $171,397,932 in 1860 and $87,328,-801 in 1850—showing that, for an average, it had doubled in each of the last two decades. The following table gives the result at this rate of increase in sixty years from 1870.

Years.	*Amount.*
1870	$354,483,581
1880	708,967,162
1890	1,417,934,324
1900	2,835,868,648
1910	5,671,737,296
1920	11,343,474,592
1930	22,686,949,184

Thus the aggregate of property, mainly belonging to Christian sects, would in sixty years, at this rate of increase, reach the stupendous sum of nearly twenty-three billions of dollars. The same rate may not be continued ; yet no one doubts whether there will be an immense increase of property vested in structures and their appurtenances used for religious worship. This will by no means be an evil, if considered in a moral and religious aspect, but rather a great blessing to the country ; yet it does raise the question whether the exemption of Church property from taxation is not an evil that ought to be corrected. In regard to this question we submit the following observations :

1. The general theory of all just taxation is that of reciprocal service. Judge Cooley, in his "Law of Taxation" (p. 14), says: "The protection of the government being the consideration for which taxes are demanded, all parties who receive or are entitled to that protection may be called upon to render the equivalent." The constitution of Massachusetts (I. 10) says: "Each individual of the society has a right to be protected by it in the enjoyment of his life, liberty, and property, according to standing laws. He is obliged, consequently, to contribute his share to the expense of the protection." This theory applies to corporations, as well as to individuals. Both alike need and receive the protection of government; and, hence, both come within the proper scope of the taxing power.

2. It is an acknowledged principle that taxation should, as nearly as practicable, be so distributed that all parties will contribute their appropriate share toward the expenses of government. If any are exempted from this burden, a good and sufficient reason must be shown therefor. No argument is needed to prove so plain a principle of equity.

3. Both the theory of taxation and the rule of distribution apply to religious corporations as really as to other corporations or to individuals, unless there be some special reason for making them an exception. That reason, if any such reason exists, cannot consist in the fact that these corporations are religious in their ends and objects. To make

this a reason for special privileges or immunities would be a glaring self-contradiction in an American State. It would theoretically, as well as practically adopt the principle of Church and State. Some other and different, as well as better reason must be assigned for exempting Church property from taxation. Dr. Wayland, in his "Political Economy" (Book IV., chapter 3, section 2), observes: "All that religious societies have a right to ask of the civil government is the same privileges for transacting their own affairs which societies of every other sort possess. This they have a right to demand; not because they are religious societies, but because religion is an innocent mode of pursuing happiness."

4. The direct effect of exemption is to lessen the basis of taxation to the full extent of the property exempted: and this necessitates an increase of rate on all tax-paying property. The exemption is, hence, an indirect appropriation to religious corporations, and a virtual subsidy for their support, at the expense of the general public. What is thus granted to them by not being collected from them is a gift for which the State reimburses itself by charging the amount to non-exempted property, in the form of an increased tax. It is as really a gift as would be the same amount if directly appropriated from the public treasury. What is taken off from Church property is transferred to other property not by the voluntary action of the tax-payer, but

by the compulsion of law. In this way the State avoids a deficiency in its revenues, that would otherwise occur as the consequence of exemption. Every person who pays a dollar of taxes pays a certain proportion toward the fund that must be raised to make the State good for the loss of revenue occasioned by the exemption of Church property.

5. The argument most frequently used in defending this exemption is based on the temporal benefits accruing to the State from Church property—such as improving the morals and elevating the character of the people and also enhancing the value of other property. These benefits are presented as the equivalent of the special privilege granted by the State. The fatal objection to this reasoning is that it proves too much. Nearly all kinds of private property, and especially some kinds, render an important public service. This is true of private school structures, true even of a picture gallery, true of property used for innocent public amusement, true of the property of bank corporations, railway companies, insurance companies, etc.; and yet such property cannot be exempted from taxation without starving the treasury of the State. Why, then, should Church property enjoy this favor on the ground of benefits rendered, and other property that can assign the same reason for the favor, in kind, if not in degree, be excluded therefrom? The moment we generalize the doc-

trine of uses and benefits as furnishing a reason for tax-exemption in behalf of religious corporations it refutes itself by proving more than the State can admit.

So, also, if the doctrine be good to show the propriety of tax-exemption, why is it not just as good to show that the State should directly, by formal appropriations of public money, contribute to the support of religious societies? The latter would be only a direct mode of doing what is indirectly yet really done by the former. The argument is just as strong for the one as it is for the other; and, hence, in this sense it proves too much. Church corporations do not need the exemption in order to exist, and thus afford the benefits, any more than they need direct positive support in order to exist. They could and would exist without either mode of help by the State.

6. Church property, it is said, ordinarily yields no private *income* to the corporators, and for this reason should be exempted from taxation. However plausible such an argument might be under a system of taxation based on income, it manifestly has no application to one based on the valuation of property, with a percentage of taxation on the same. The latter, and not the former, is the system on which the States rely almost exclusively for their revenue. The question of income does not and cannot enter into such a mode of taxation except as it may be incidentally involved in that of valua-

tion; and even in this collateral way it is not a ground of exemption but merely a guide in fixing the valuation. Large amounts of property from which no income is derived—as wild lands, houses, or stores not used or rented, goods unsold or on which there is a depreciation below their cost, and the like,—are, nevertheless, compelled to pay taxes. The fact of private ownership and that of an estimated value are deemed sufficient. The State, adopting valuation as on the whole the best theory of taxation, does not and cannot regulate its action by the rule of income. The property is protected by the State, whether it yields any income or not, and it has value to its owners. Why, then, should Church property be released from all tax burdens under the system of valuation because it yields no income to the corporators, even if the fact be granted? No reason can be assigned on this ground that would not equally apply to many other kinds of property; and, if it were thus applied, a still higher rate of taxation would be needed, and, as the consequence, still heavier burdens would fall upon those who pay taxes, or the revenue of the State would be insufficient for its expenses.

7. It is further said that the taxation of Church property would to the corporators be *double* taxation, and that for this reason it ought to be exempted. This is manifestly a mistake as to the meaning of a word. Double taxation is the taxation of the same property twice under one general assessment.

Church property owned by corporators jointly and their individual property certainly are not the same. If the former were taxed, the corporators, considered as individuals, would not be taxed to pay this tax, since what they paid toward the Church tax would not be compulsory, but purely a matter of their own choice. The direct effect of the tax would be simply to increase the annual expenses of the corporation, by adding thereto this item ; and the same result would ensue from raising the salary of the minister, or employing a paid choir, or contracting a loan on which interest must be paid. The tax would simply be one of the standard expenses of the corporation, and the corporators themselves would no more be taxed doubly than any other class of corporators who pay taxes on their individual property and jointly pay taxes on their corporate property.

8. But we are told that Church property is in an important sense *public* property, and that on this account it ought not to be taxed. Here is a mistake as to a fact. Such property in this country is not public property, except by the false use of a term. The public does not own it or control its uses. The public cannot use it except by the permission and at the option of the corporators. The fact that benefits to the public arise from its use does not give it the character of public property, since the same is true of the property of the merchant, the banker, and, indeed, of nearly all private property.

Public benefits are traceable to a great variety of private sources, and the use of Church property is only one of them.

9. It is also urged that taxation of Church property would be an oppressive *burden* to religious corporations. It would, undoubtedly, add a new item to their annual expenses; and this is equally true in respect to all who pay taxes, whether individuals or corporations. All taxation is a burden; yet it is the equivalent which government asks for the protection it affords. Moreover, the burden in the case of Churches, as in all other cases, would, under the rule of valuation and percentage, be simply in proportion to the amount of property owned; and this would certainly be a fair index to the ability of the corporators. The rule grades the burden to the resources of the taxpayer, and we see no reason why this rule would not be just as equitable when applied to Church property as it is when applied to any other species of property. There are hundreds and thousands of persons who find it difficult to pay their annual taxes; and yet the State cannot excuse them for this reason. Why should it on this ground excuse Churches from all participation in tax burdens, and throw the whole weight of these burdens upon property not thus exempted and excused? Why should it make Church property a virtual pensioner upon the public bounty and levy a contribution upon all other property to pay the pension? We can see no reason for so doing

in the fact that taxation is a burden. The fact is granted, and this is an important reason showing that the burden should, as nearly as possible, be distributed according to the rule of equity.

10. The courts have usually held that the exemption of Church property does not apply to *special* assessments for local improvements, as the paving or repairing of the street on which it stands and the like. The theory is that the property, though owned by a religious corporation derives a special benefit from such improvements, and, hence, that, like all other property enjoying the same benefit, it should be taxed to pay for it. If this be a sound theory, as we concede it to be, then why is not *ordinary* taxation of Church property, in common with all other property, on the ground of *general* benefits accruing from the protection afforded by government, an equally sound theory? If the State may and should tax Church property for local benefits, then why not also for general benefits? The latter are certainly more important than the former.

11. The law in this country usually limits the property which a religious corporation may acquire and hold by fixing a maximum amount or a maximum annual value or income which must not be exceeded. One of the objects is to prevent large accumulations of such property in the possession of Churches. The limitation is designed to modify in the way of restraint the effect of tax-exemption. The practical difficulty, however, is that the tax-

exemption works in all cases, and the limitation hardly in any case. The tendency of exemption, especially in cities, is to foster and encourage an extravagant and useless expenditure of the wealth of society in Church structures, without any real benefit to the community, and with a positive damage, by releasing large amounts of this wealth from any contribution toward the expenses of government. So far as taxation is concerned, property thus invested is virtually annihilated. The law of limitation does not remedy or lessen this evil, because it is not practically regarded or practically enforced. Taxation of Church property would be a perfect remedy in respect to the general public. It would, at the same time, teach religious corporations the expediency of more economy in their arrangements and facilities for public worship, and in this respect it would do them no harm.

The conclusion to be derived from these views is that, although exemption of Church property from taxation is the general practice of the country, the argument on the merits of the question is, nevertheless, adverse to the practice. We can see no sufficient reason for exemption in any case in which a direct appropriation of the public money would be improper. The two are simply different ways of doing precisely the same thing in practical effect. If the American people would not consent to be *directly* taxed to extend bounties and subsidies to religious societies, as they certainly would not, then they should not consent to an *indirect* appropriation in aid of these societies, through the process of tax-exemption. The argument which is good to prove the former proposition is just as good to prove the latter. The two propositions are essentially identical in their substance.

Religious societies, considered as civil corporations existing for lawful purposes, are entitled to the common privileges and immunities of such corporations under the authority and protection of law; and this is the sum of their just claim at the hands of government. Any legal discrimination against them would be unjust. Any such descrimination in their favor at the expense of the general public is equally unjust. Tax-exemption is such a discrimination, and is, moreover, a relic of the principle of Church and State, inherited from the past and not yet eliminated from our political system. The religious reason for such exemption would not stand the test of our institutions for a moment, and the economical and governmental reason is clearly against it. Every argument that can be urged in its favor either proves too much or is false in one of its premises. Were the American people to require religious corporations to contribute by taxation their proper share toward the expenses of government, they would not only apply to them a just theory of taxation, but would also act in perfect consistency with their own principles as a political organization.

XXIV.

SABBATH LEGISLATION.

Sunday, or "the first day of the week," is by Christians observed as a Sabbath in the twofold sense of being a day of rest from ordinary secular labor and also a period specially devoted to religious worship. The point we propose to consider is not whether this observance is obligatory under the law of God; but what is the authority, if any, of the Christian Sabbath in this country as derived from civil government.

The only clause in the Constitution of the United States that can have any possible relation to this inquiry reads as follows: "If any bill shall not be returned by the President within ten days (Sundays excepted) after it shall have been presented to him, the same shall be a law in like manner as if he had signed it," etc. This simply recognizes Sunday as one of the days of the week: and, assuming that the President would not devote it to public business, it provides that, in counting the "ten days" referred to, Sundays shall not be included. Here, clearly, is no law in respect to Sunday, except for the single purpose named.

The Revised Statutes of the United States contain four references to Sunday: In the first (section 1324), providing that cadets shall not be required to pursue their studies on Sunday; in the second (section 1526), making the same provision in regard to students at the Naval Academy; in the third (section 5013), declaring that in computing time in certain bankruptcy proceedings Sunday shall not be counted, but, like the Fourth of July or Christmas Day, shall be excluded from the computation; in the fourth (section 1125), providing that army chaplains shall, when it is practicable, hold appropriate religious services at least once each Sunday. The first three references relate to Sunday simply as a day of rest and have nothing to do with its religious uses. The fourth reference names it as the day when army chaplains shall hold religious services, because this is the common day of rest and the day usually observed for this purpose by the people, and not because Congress intended to establish any Sabbath law even for the army.

It is the practice of Congress and of the Federal courts to suspend legislative and judicial business on Sunday; yet the practice is one of usage and not of legal requirement. The same practice extends through the whole circle of government operations, with the exception of the mail. This exception was some years since the subject of very extensive discussion among the people. Numerous petitions were addressed to Congress asking for a discontinuance of the mail on the Christian Sabbath. The petitions were referred to a special committee, who reported adversely to the prayer of the petitioners. Congress, in adopting the report, declined, in respect to the transportation of the mail, to make any distinction between Sunday and the other days of the week. The Christian Sabbath is not an institution of the Government of the United States and is nowhere invested with the sanction of its authority.

In the constitutions of the several States the Sabbath is wholly unmentioned, with the exception of that of Vermont. Part I., in article 3 of that constitution, after providing for the protection of the rights of a religious conscience, adds: "Nevertheless, every sect or denomination of Christians ought to observe the Sabbath or Lord's Day, and keep up some sort of religious worship, which to them shall seem most agreeable to the revealed will of God." This language relates simply to Christian sects, and, even in reference to them, it is merely the statement of a moral obligation. No one, we presume, would claim that the legislature of Vermont could make it the basis of a statute requiring Christians religiously to observe the Lord's Day. Such a construction would be inconsistent with other parts of the same section. The constitutions of all the States leave the question of religious worship, as to time and mode, to be settled by the individual conscience, subject only to the limitation imposed by the demands of public order.

As an example of legislative action in regard to the Sabbath, we refer the reader to Part I., chapter 20, title 8, and article 8 of the Revised Statutes of the State of New York, in which he will find a series of provisions forbidding the following things to be done on "the first day of the week, called Sunday:" 1. The serving of any "writ, process, warrant, order, judgment, decree, or other proceeding of any court or officer of justice," with certain exceptions specified. 2. A variety of sports, as "shooting, hunting, fishing, sporting, playing, horse racing, gaming, frequenting of tippling houses, or any unlawful exercises or pastimes," 3. All travelling "unless in cases of charity or necessity" or for other excepted purposes named in the statute. 4. All "servile laboring or working, excepting works of necessity or charity, unless done by some person who uniformly keeps the last day of the week, called Saturday, as holy time, and does not labor or work on that day, and whose labor shall not disturb other persons in their observance of the first day of the week as holy time." 5. Public traffic in "any wares, merchandise, fruit, herbs, goods, or chattels," with the exception of "meats, milk, and fish, which may be sold at any time before nine of the clock in the morning." 6. The sale of "ale, porter, strong or spirituous liquors" by inn or tavern-keepers, "excepting to lodgers in such inns or taverns, or to persons actually travelling on that day in cases allowed by law." The title which contains these provisions relates to "the prevention and punishment of immorality and disorderly practices"; and under it we have a series of articles referring to "jugglers and the exhibition of shows, etc," "disorderly practices on public occasions and holidays," "betting and gaming," "raffling and lotteries," "the racing of animals," "profane cursing and swearing," "the disturbance of religious meetings," and "the observance of Sunday."

Part III. in chapter 3, title 1, and section 7 of the same Statutes provides that "no court shall be opened or transact any business on Sunday, unless it be for the purpose of receiving a verdict or discharging a jury."

These provisions furnish an illustration of the general scope and character of what are called "Sabbath laws." Such laws, as to their minor details, differ somewhat in the different States; yet, like the constitutions of the several States, they are in all the States substantially identical in their fundamental principle. What is that principle? In order to answer this question on the basis of judicial authority, we submit, as follows, a series of deliverances by State courts in cases referring to the Christian Sabbath:

In the case of Lindenmuller *vs.* The People (33 Barbour, p. 548), the Supreme Court of the State of New York, in expounding the Act of April 17th, 1860, forbidding theatrical and dramatic performances on the Christian Sabbath, after saying that, "as a *civil* and *political* institution, the establishment and regulation of a Sabbath is within the just powers of the civil government," held the following language:

"The act complained of here compels no religious observance, and offenses against it are punishable not as sins against God, but as injurious to and having a malignant influence on society. It rests upon the same foundation as a multitude of other laws upon our statute book—such as those against gambling, lotteries, keeping disorderly houses, polygamy, horse-racing, profane cursing and swearing, disturbance of religious meetings, selling of intoxicating liquors on election days within a given distance of the polls, etc."

In the case of the State *vs.* Ambs (20 Missouri Reports, p. 214) the Supreme Court of Missouri said:

"The Sunday law was not intended to compel people to go to church or to perform any religious act; . . . but was designed to coerce a cessation from labor, that those who conscientiously believed that the day was set apart for the worship of God might not be disturbed in the performance of their religious duties. . . . Because divines may teach their Churches that the reverential observance of the Lord's Day is an act of religious worship, it by no means follows that the prohibition of worldly labor on that day was designed by the general assembly as an act of religion."

The case of Specht *vs.* The Commonwealth (8 Pennsylvania Reports, p. 312) was that of a Seventh-day Baptist who had violated the law of Pennsylvania by working on Sunday. In regard to the statute the Supreme Court spoke as follows :

" All agree that to the well-being of society periods of rest are absolutely necessary. To be productive of the required advantage, these periods must recur at stated intervals, so that the mass of which the community is composed may enjoy a respite from labor at the same time. They may be established by common consent, or, as is conceded, the legislative power of the State may without impropriety interfere to fix the time of their stated return and enforce obedience to the direction. . . . . In a Christian community, where a very large majority of the people celebrate the first day of the week as their chosen period of rest from labor, it is not surprising that that day should have received the legislative sanction ; and, as it is also devoted to religious observances, we are prepared to estimate the reason why the statute should speak of it as the Lord's Day and denominate the infraction of its legalized rest a profanation. Yet this does not change the character of the enactment. It is still, essentially, but a *civil* regulation, for the government of man as a member of society."

In the case of The City Council of Charleston *vs.* Benjamin (2 Strobh., p. 508) the defendant was indicted for selling goods on Sunday, contrary to the ordinance of the Council. The case coming before the Court of Appeals of South Carolina, the Court, holding the ordinance to be constitutional, spoke as follows :

"If the legislature or the City of Charleston were to declare that shops within that State or city should be closed and that no one should sell any goods, wares, or merchandise on the 4th of July or 8th of January in each year, would any one believe such a law was unconstitutional ? It would not be pretended that religion had anything to do with that day. What has religion to do with a similar regulation on Sunday ? It is, in a political and social point of view, a mere day of rest. Its observance as such is a mere question of expediency."

The case of Frolickstein *vs.* The Mayor of Mobile (40 Alabama Reports, p. 725) was that of a Jew who was fined for selling goods on the Christian Sabbath. In regard to it the Supreme Court of Alabama said :

"The legally-constrained abstinence from certain worldly employments on the first day of the week cannot be justified on the ground that such abstinence is enjoined by the Christian religion. . . The legislation on the subject of abstaining from worldly employments on the first day of the week must be referred to the *police* power of the State. It has its sanction in the teaching of experience that the general welfare and good of society require a suspension of labor and business one day in seven and that the day should be of uniform observance. The exercise of the power to enforce this theory of the public good would not infringe the constitution, whether the day designated should be the Christian or Jewish Sabbath."

In the case of Bloom *vs*. Richards (2 Ohio State Reports, p. 387) the Supreme Court of Ohio said :—

"Thus the statute upon which the defendant relies, prohibiting labor on the Sabbath, could not stand for a moment as the law of this State if its sole foundation was the Christian duty of keeping that day holy and its sole motive to enforce the observance of that duty. . . We are, then to regard the statute under consideration as a mere *municipal* or *police* regulation, whose validity is neither strengthened nor weakened by the fact that the day of rest it enjoins is the Sabbath Day. . . It was within the constitutional competency of the general assembly to require the cessation of labor and to name the day of rest. It did so by the act referred to, and, in accordance with the feelings of a majority of the people, the Christian Sabbath was very properly selected. But, regarded merely as an exertion of legislative authority, the act would have had neither more nor less validity had any other day been adopted."

So also, in the case of McGatrick *vs* Wason (4 Ohio State Reports, p. 566) the same Court held as follows :—

"The act does not to any extent rest upon the ground that it is immoral or irreligious to labor on the Sabbath, any more than upon any other day. It simply prescribes a day of rest from motives of public policy and as a civil regulation. . . . Thus the day of rest prescribed is the Christian Sabbath. Yet so completely does the act rest upon grounds of public policy that . . it would be equally constitutional and obligatory did it name any other day, and it derives none of its force from the fact that the day of rest is Sunday."

The general conclusion deducible from these judicial authorities in reference to the construction of Sabbath legislation as well as from the character of the legislation itself, is that laws interdicting labor upon "the first day of the week," and prohibiting other things inconsistent with the quiet and order of the day, have nothing to do with the Christian Sabbath as a *religious* institution. They neither prescribe nor enforce any religious observance. They could not do this without conflict with those provisions found in all our State constitutions which guarantee religious freedom and equality to the people. They do not put the stamp of the state upon the Sabbath as a *divine* institution, or upon that religious system which, by its moral force, creates and perpetuates the Sabbath and of which it is so important an instrument. The Christian Sabbath is much older than the legislation that relates to it. Our forefathers brought it with them when they came to this country, and by common consent established it as a religious institution. They observed it as such, and taught their children to imitate their example. "The first day of the week," hence, came to be regarded as a sacred day, being set apart to special religious services, and to this end involving cessation from ordinary labor. If the country had been settled by Jews or was now mainly populated by Jews, Saturday, and not Sunday, would be the day marked by these characteristics. The great numerical preponderance of Christians in this country fixes the day in the usage of the people, and constitutes the reason why Sunday, rather than any other day, is the day of established usage.

Sabbath legislation finds the usage in existence, made up of the two elements of rest and religious observances. Passing by the latter element altogether, in the sense of leaving it to be regulated by the individual conscience, it places the seal of its authority upon the rest element—not for religious reasons, not to favor any system of religion in distinction from some other system, but for the twofold purpose of securing a regularly recurring period of rest and protecting those who religiously observe the day from the annoyance and disturbance which might otherwise exist. This is the whole theory of Sabbath legislation in this country, as expounded by courts and as it appears in the statutes themselves. The commands of the law on the subject are negative, and not positive; prohibitions of certain things, and not requirements of things to be done. One might keep the Sabbath very perfectly in the *legal* sense, and yet be a gross Sabbath-breaker in the religious sense. The law seeks to secure the former and does not seek to prevent the latter. It holds that a Sabbath of rest and general quietude is, on the ground of public policy, a good municipal regulation. This is just what and all that it attempts to effect.

There can be no greater mistake in logic than that which reasons from the rest element of the legalized Sabbath to the religious element, over which law exercises no jurisdiction and in respect to which determines no questions. The two elements in legal contemplation are entirely distinct and have no relation to each other except that of coincidence as to the day. With the creed of the Christian as to the religious observance of the Sabbath the law has nothing to do, any more than it would have if the period of rest were fixed on some other day of the week.

Hence, if the Seventh-day Baptist or the Jew complains of the law, because he keeps Saturday as holy time and wishes to work on Sunday, the answer is that the law cannot reasonably appoint two days of rest in one week, and that it has selected and should select the day which corresponds with the prevalent usage of the people. Let the mass of the people become Seventh-day Baptists or Jews, and then it would be very proper for the law to change its day of rest from Sunday to Saturday; and such would undoubtedly be the result. It cannot wisely appoint two rest days in each week, and it certainly cannot change the day to meet the case of that small minority of the people who keep a different day.

The Revised Statutes of New York State, however, provide that those who keep "the last day of the week, called Saturday, as holy time, and do not labor or work upon that day," shall be exempted from the statute against labor on the first day of the week, with the single qualification that their labor shall not "disturb other persons in their observance of the first day of the week as holy time." The law of the same State still further provides that those who keep Saturday "as the Sabbath of rest from labor" shall not on that day "be subject to perform military duty or jury duty in a justice's court," or on that day have any process from such a court in a civil suit served upon them or made returnable thereon. This would seem to be about as far as the law can reasonably go in accommodating its general regulations to the peculiar circumstances of Jews or other persons who observe the seventh day of the week as holy time. Such provisions show very clearly that it is not the religious element of the Sabbath which the law undertakes to decide or control, whether in respect to the Christian or the Jew.

No inference, surely, can be drawn from Sabbath legislation in respect to the question of Bible-reading or other religious exercises in our public schools.

If the legislation established the Sabbath as a sacred day and enforced its religious observance, and especially if it made that observance Christian in its form, then it might with some plausibility be said that a State doing thus much could with equal propriety engage in the work of religious propagandism in the public school. Both might be wrong; yet one would be a precedent for the other. Such, however, is not the state of the facts. There is no *religious* element in the Sabbath legislation of this country and no attempt to put any such element there, as there could not be without contradicting the theory of our political system.

Those who appeal to this legislation as an argument to support the doctrine of religious instruction and worship in the public schools, either do not understand the character of the legislation as expounded by the courts, or are lacking in logical candor. They might just as well appeal to police regulations or those that relate to banking institutions as the means of sustaining their conclusion. The fatal objection to their reasoning is that there is no connection between the conclusion and the premise.

XXV.

THE CIVIL OATH.

Bouvier, in his "Law Dictionary," defines an oath to be "an outward pledge given by the person taking it that his attestation or promise is made under an immediate sense of his responsibility to God." He quotes Starkie as declaring it to be "a solemn invocation of the vengeance of the Deity upon the witness if he do not declare the whole truth, so far as he knows it." Dr. Webster says that it is "a solemn affirmation or declaration, made with an appeal to God for the truth of what is affirmed," and then adds that "the appeal to God in an oath implies that the person imprecates his vengeance and renounces his favor if the declaration is false; or, if the declaration is a promise, the person invokes the vengeance of God if he should fail to keep it." John Milton, in his "Christian Doctrine," says: "An oath is that whereby we call God to witness the truth of what we say, with a curse upon ourselves, implied or expressed, should it prove false."

These definitions refer not to extra-legal or extra-judicial attestations, which involve no relation to law, but rather to the oath when administered by some person legally authorized, and in proceedings provided for by law. The latter only is the *civil* oath.

The fact that the National Government and all the State governments of this country make use of this oath, and that they employ the Bible, either the whole or a part of it, in administering an oath, is sometimes referred to as showing that the Christian religion, in at least a qualified sense, is a constituent element of our political system. Those who wish to incorporate Christianity into our public schools find, or rather think they find a precedent in the civil oath for their demand. If we have the oath, then why not also have the Bible and religious services in our public schools? The purpose of this article is to inquire whether the use of the oath authorizes the inference sought to be drawn from it. And, in order to determine this point, we need to know what are the provisions of our constitutions and laws in respect to the civil oath. Let this, then, be our first inquiry.

The Constitution of the United States provides that the President, before entering upon the duties of his office, shall take the following oath or affirmation: "I do solemnly swear (or affirm) that I will faithfully execute the office of President of the United States, and will, to the best of my ability, preserve, protect and defend the Constitution of the United States." It also provides that Senators and Representatives in Congress, the members of the several State legislatures, and all the executive and judicial officers of the United States, and of the several States, shall be bound by oath or affirmation to support the Constitution. Congress has enacted a series of laws respecting the oath, and the occasions of its administration, the persons by whom it shall be administered, and the penal sanctions by which it shall be enforced. This whole system of legislation provides for the alternative stated in the Constitution. The party may, at his own option, be sworn, or merely affirm, as its legal equivalent. The Revised Statutes of the United States (Section I.) declare that the "requirement of an oath shall be deemed complied with by making affirmation in due judicial form." Simple affirmation may, therefore, in every case be substituted for the oath.

Some of the State constitutions contain provisions relating to this subject. Thus the constitution of Arkansas (I., 21) declares that "the mode of administering an oath or affirmation shall be such as shall be most consistent with and binding upon the conscience of the person to whom such an oath or affirmation may be administered." The constitution of Indiana (I., 8) and that of Oregon (I., 7) contain a similar provision. The constitution of Missouri (II., 12) provides that "if any person shall declare that he has conscientious scruples against taking an oath or swearing in any form, the said oath may be changed into a solemn affirmation and be made by him in that form." The constitutions of Illinois (II., 3), of Nebraska (I., 16), and of Ohio (I., 7) provide that the liberty of conscience which they secure "shall not be construed to dispense with oaths or affirmations." Such provisions, upon their face, leave it optional with the individual whether he shall be sworn or merely affirm; and either mode of attestation is the equivalent of the other.

So, also, as to the competency of persons to be sworn or to affirm as witnesses, the constitutions of Arkansas (I., 21), of California (I., 4), of Florida (Declaration of Rights, 5), of Indiana (I., 7), of Iowa (I., 4), of Kansas (Bill of Rights, 7), of Michigan (VI., 34), of Minnesota (I., 17), of Nebraska (I., 16), of Nevada (I., 4), of New York (I., 3), of Ohio (I., 7), of Oregon (I., 6), and of Wisconsin (I., 19) expressly declare that no person shall, in consequence of his opinions on matters of religion, be disqualified as a witness in any court of law or equity. These constitutions formally exclude any religious test in application to witnesses, whether they are to be sworn or simply affirm. Their religious opinions have nothing to do with their legal competency to testify in a court of justice.

Turning then, to the question of State legislation, we refer to the Revised Statutes of New York State (Part III., chapter 7, title 3, and article 9), as an example of such legislation. We quote the following sections:

"Section 82. The usual mode of administering oaths now practised by the person who swears, laying his hand upon and kissing the Gospels, shall be observed in all cases in which an oath may be administered according to law, except in the cases hereinafter otherwise provided."

"Section 83. Every person who shall desire it shall be permitted to swear in the following form: 'You do swear in the presence of the Ever-Living God.' And while so swearing, such person may or may not hold up his right hand, in his discretion."

"Section 84. Every person who shall declare that he has conscientious scruples against taking any oath or swearing in any form shall be permitted to make his solemn declaration or affirmation in the following form: 'You do solemnly, sincerely, and truly declare and affirm.'"

"Section 86. Every person believing in any other than the Christian religion shall be sworn according to the peculiar ceremonies of his religion, if there be any such ceremonies, instead of any of the modes herein before prescribed."

These references are sufficient to give us, at least, a general idea of the oath as an institution of law. In regard to them we submit the following observations:

1. The civil oath is not absolutely required in any case, and is, hence, not made compulsory in respect to anybody. Though commonly used, because not commonly objected to, it may, never-

theless, be dispensed with, and a simple affirmation, at the option of the individual, may be substituted as its equivalent. The law assumes its right to compel witnesses to testify, and to punish them if they give false testimony ; but it does not force them to be sworn against their conscientious scruples or undertake to judge of the character of those scruples. It is well known that Quakers have such scruples ; and, hence, they are permitted to affirm, and their evidence is accepted as if it had been given under oath. And as the law deals with the Quaker, so it will with any citizen, if he desires it. Whether he shall be sworn or not is a matter for him to determine.

2. The civil affirmation is distinguished from an oath in containing no formal appeal to God and no imprecation of his curse in the event of falsehood. The affirmant solemnly, sincerely, and truly declares and affirms that he will speak the truth. He enters into such a covenant with society ; but in doing so he makes no disclosure of his religious faith or the want of such faith. His affirmation may to him, in the forum of conscience, have all the binding power of an oath, yet it is not such in form. What it is in form is a pledge of his moral nature to be truthful in respect to what he is about to say. A Deist or even an Atheist may make such a pledge as really as a Christian.

3. The constitutions of the States above referred to, distinctly declare that the opinions of a wit-

ness on matters of religion shall not affect his qualification to be sworn or to affirm, and thereafter to testify in any court of law or equity. The constitution of Oregon, for example, says that "no person shall be rendered incompetent as a witness or juror in consequence of his opinions on matters of religion, nor be questioned in any court of justice touching his religious belief to affect the weight of his testimony." So, also, that of New York says that "no person shall be rendered incompetent to be a witness on account of his opinions on matters of religious belief." An Atheist could not take an oath with any sincerity, and a Hindu could not take a Christian oath; yet either of them could in either of these States affirm and give legal evidence, and neither could be excluded from testifying on the ground of his opinions in respect to religion. The same remark applies to most of the States in the Union.

4. Those persons who do not believe in the Christian religion, but do believe in some other religion, may be sworn, if sworn at all, according to their particular faith. The law does not compel them to take any oath; and, if they do take one, it does not compel them to take a Christian oath. The form or kind of oath which corresponds with their religious faith is the one which the law will employ. Thus, as Bouvier remarks, "a Jew is sworn on the Pentateuch, or Old Testament, with his head covered; a Mohammedan, on the Koran;

a Gentoo, by touching with his hand the foot of a Brahmin or priest of his religion; a Brahmin, by touching the hand of another such priest; a Chinaman, by breaking a china saucer." The Bible, even when an oath is administered, is not an indispensable instrument of the administration, and the faith which it teaches is not an indispensable condition. In the case of The People *vs.* Cook (8 New York Reports, 4 Seld. p. 67), the Court of Appeals of the State of New York held that an oath irregularly administered by mistake, as by swearing one upon "Watts's Psalms and Hymns," instead of the Gospels, if not objected to at the time by the party taking it, is to be deemed a valid oath, rendering him liable for perjury if testifying falsely. He is presumed "to have assented to the particular form adopted," whatever it may be.

5. The fact that neither the oath itself nor the Christian form of taking it is made an absolute legal requirement conclusively shows that the State, in using the Christian oath, establishes no connection between itself and the religious system incidentally implied in the use. The whole purpose of the State is to increase the certainty that the person speaking will tell the truth. It uses his faith for civic ends, without passing any judgment upon it, and certainly without proposing first to give him a faith and then to swear him by it. The oath, in the very nature of things, if used at all, must accommodate itself to the faith of the person sworn, since here

lies all its power. The State, when it swears a Mohammedan upon the Koran, does not thereby affirm or legally adopt the Koran. So, when it swears a Jew in accordance with his own faith, it does not adopt that faith. So, also, when it swears a Christian upon the "Gospels," it does not say that these "Gospels" are true. Its act while not touching the question that relates to the truth of any religious system, refers exclusively to the assumed faith of the party sworn. The State does not coerce that faith or coerce the taking of an oath on its basis, and it does consent, at the option of the person to be affected, to accept a simple affirmation as a substitute for an oath; and, even when the oath is administered, it adapts the form to the faith of the party taking it. These legal facts clearly prove that the civil oath is not a State confession of faith or a State incorporation of religion, whether Christian or otherwise, into its own organic structure.

When, therefore, the advocate of Bible reading and religious exercises in the public schools appeals to the civil oath as a precedent for what he demands he certainly deceives himself with a totally fallacious argument. He asks that Christianity, by the authority of the State and at the public expense, shall be included in the educational system of the public school. If a Protestant, then he means Protestant Christianity; and if a Catholic, then he means Roman Catholicism. In short, he means the religion in which he believes. He means *his* religion, and he means that the State shall tax the people to propagate it. This is the substance of his demand.

One of the arguments used to sustain the demand is the civil oath. The State administers such an oath, and, hence, in the public school it may properly become a propagandist of Christianity. There would be no force in this reasoning even if the State confined the oath to the Christian form, since the two cases would not be parallel. When, however, we remember that the State not only does not require the oath at all, but also does not limit it to the Christian form when it is administered, then the logic appears so contemptible that it is really an abuse of the word to call it logic. Christianity in the public school is a *specific* thing, a definite system of religious faith, introduced by State authority and there maintained at the general expense, and, hence, a legally preferred religion. The civil oath is Christian, or Jewish, or Mohammedan, or Mormon, or even Pagan, according to the faith of the party who is to take it; and, moreover, the law, by accepting an affirmation as its substitute, does not absolutely require the oath in any form.

He who can see any analogy between these two cases, especially such as makes the latter an argumentative precedent for the former, is certainly an adept in detecting analogies. One of the incidental charms of the argument, seemingly not discovered by him, we have in the fact that it is just as good to prove that Mormonism or Mohammedanism should be taught in the public school. The State will swear a Mormon according to the faith of a Mormon. Why not, then, teach Mormonism in the public school? So, also, it will swear a Mohammedan according to the faith of a Mohammedan. Why not, then, teach Mohammedanism in the public school, and tax Christians to pay the expenses thereof? If the civil oath, administered in the Christian form, is good to prove what a certain class of Christians claim in respect to the public school, then, when administered in other allowable forms, it is just as good to prove very different conclusions. Being so exceedingly flexible, it is a very dangerous premise from which to reason.

As to the question whether the civil oath is morally lawful, and, if so, then whether it is expedient, we intentionally omit to express any opinion, since the answer has nothing to do with the matter under consideration. We accept it as an institution of our legal system. What we do not accept is the proposition that the oath involves a virtual commitment of the State to Christianity as a system of religious belief. The utmost that the State does is to use the religious faith of the person sworn, whether true or false, as the means of securing a purely temporal end; and, that it may perpetrate no injustice upon the citizen, it consents that he may, at his own option, decline even this use, and simply pledge himself by a solemn declaration of truthfulness, whether testifying as a witness or being inducted into public office. This is the whole case, and there surely is nothing in it even to suggest any legal connection between the State and Christianity.

XXVI.

NATIONAL AND STATE CHAPLAINS.

National chaplains are of three classes—namely, congressional, army, and navy chaplains. Of the first class there are two chaplains, one for each house of Congress, whose duty is simply that of opening its sessions with prayer. These chaplains are placed among " the officers and persons in the employ of the Senate and House of Representatives," and each receives a salary of nine hundred dollars a year. (Revised Statutes of the United States, sections 52, 53.) Their appointment is simply a matter of usage with each house of Congress, and all that law does is to provide a compensation for their services. The selection is not, except by usage, limited to Christian ecclesiastics, or even to ecclesiastics at all. There is nothing to preclude the suspension of the usage altogether. No such custom is adopted by the Federal courts. The practice pays a tribute of honor to the prevalent religion of the country; but it does not establish that religion, or invest it with any legal attributes. If such were the effect, it would be unconstitutional. The cost is but trifling, and hence, no question has been raised as to the power of Congress to appropriate money for such a purpose, as would doubtless have been the fact if the service involved any considerable expense. There is no reason, except that of usage, why a legislative body should have a chaplain, any more than a court of justice or a board of aldermen.

The President of the United States is authorized, with the advice and consent of the Senate, to appoint thirty post chaplains, four regimental chaplains, and " a chaplain for each regiment of colored troops," as a part of the regular Army of the United States, having the rank of a captain of infantry without command, and as to tenure of office, retirement, and pensions, standing " on the same footing with other officers of the army " and each receiving a salary of fifteen hundred dollars a year. The law provides that no person shall be appointed to this service " until he shall furnish proof that he is a regularly-ordained minister of some religious denomination, in good standing at the time of his appointment, together with a recommendation for such appointment from some authorized ecclesiastical body, or from not less than five accredited ministers of said denomination." The duties of post chaplains and chaplains of colored regiments "include the instruction of the enlisted men in the common English branches of education." All regimental and post chaplains are also required, " when it may be practicable, to hold appropriate religious services for the benefit of the commands, at least once on each Sunday, and to perform appropriate religious burial services at the burial of officers and soldiers who may die in such commands." Proper facilities for the performance of these duties must be furnished by the commanders of regiments, hospitals and posts, and monthly reports must be made by the chaplains to the adjutant-general of the army. (Revised Statutes of the United States, sections 1094, 1121–1127 and 1261.)

The same Statutes authorize the appointment of navy chaplains "for the public armed vessels of the United States in actual service, not exceeding twenty-four" in number, and "not less than twenty-one nor more than thirty-five years of age at the time of their appointment." Their rank is defined and their annual compensation fixed according as they are at sea, or on shore, or on leave, or waiting orders. They are to make an annual report to the Secretary of the Navy in regard to "the official services performed by them." These services are referred to in the provision that "every chaplain shall be permitted to conduct public worship according to the manner and forms of the Church of which he may be a member." (Sections 1395–1398 and 1556.)

Such is the law of the United States in regard to army and navy chaplains. The power of Congress to make these provisions is derived from its power "to raise and support armies" and "to provide and maintain a navy." The law certainly does not establish Christianity or place upon it the seal of governmental authority. Such a construction would make it inconsistent with the express prohibition which declares that "Congress shall make no law respecting an establishment of religion."

It is true that the army chaplain must be "a regularly-ordained minister of some religious denomination"; but this denomination is not necessarily Christian. There is no reason in the law why a Jewish Rabbi might not be appointed; and this would be eminently proper if the soldiers of a regiment or at a post were Jews. Nor is there any requirement that the navy chaplain should be an ecclesiastic at all; and whether, such or not, he is at liberty to conduct public worship "according to the manner and forms of the Church of which he may be a member." The religious services to be held by the army chaplain are described as "appropriate;" and the day specially named therefor is Sunday, not because Congress designed to establish Sunday as a sacred day but because, in the practice of the American people, it is the usual day of rest, and in that of Christians the usual day for religious services.

The obvious purpose of the entire arrangement is to promote the good of the army and navy of the United States and supply certain religious facilities to those who are in the employment of the Government, and who by the nature and circumstances of their service would otherwise be wholly deprived of them. There is no need of such provisions for those who are engaged in the civil service of the country; and, hence, none are made. The law does not establish a religion, even for the army and navy, or compel its acceptance, or require any one to attend its services; and, moreover, it carefully avoids any designation of these services as distinctively Christian. If the chaplains are usually Christian ministers, this may be sufficiently explained by the fact that Christianity is the prevalent type of religion among the American people. Let any other type be equally prevalent, and the Government would naturally recognize the fact in its chaplain appointments, as it could without any essential change in the law. Those who infer a quasi-connection between Church and State, as arising from these chaplaincies of the United States, extend their inference far beyond the premises and entirely beyond the intention of the law. No court of justice would entertain the inference for a moment.

Turning, then, to the question of State chaplaincies, we select those of the State of New York as an example. In respect to chaplains to open the sessions of the legislature with prayer the law is wholly silent. As a matter of history, this service was omitted altogether for several years prior to 1838; and at that time the clergy of Albany made an arrangement to render it without compensation, which, we believe, has continued to be the practice ever since. The practice implies the existence of the religious system represented by these clergymen; but it does not bestow upon it any legal character, and would not, even if the clergymen were formally appointed by each house of the legislature. The constitutions of Michigan (IV., 24) and of Oregon (I., 5), while not forbidding the appointment of such chaplains, expressly provide that "no money shall be appropriated for the payment of any religious services in either house" of their respective legislatures.

The act of April 23d, 1862, passed by the legislature of New York, entitled "An act to provide for the enrollment of the militia," etc., declares (section 106) that "to each regiment or battalion there shall be appointed one chaplain, who shall be a regular ordained minister of a Christian denomination." Here a Christian minister, in the character of a chaplain, is included in the organization of the staff department; and this is all that the act says about him.

The Revised Statutes of New York (Part IV., chapter 3, title 2, article 1, and sections 40, 60) provide for the appointment of a chaplain for each of the State prisons of the State and assign to him the following duties: 1. "To perform religious services in the prison, under such regulations as the inspectors may prescribe, and to attend to the spiritual wants of the convicts." 2. "To visit the convicts in their cells, for the purpose of giving them religious and moral instruction, and to devote at least one hour in each week-day and the afternoon of each Sunday to such instruction." 3. "To furnish, at the expense of the State, a Bible and hymn-book to each convict." 4. "To take charge of the library, and to take care that no improper books are introduced into the cells of the convicts; and, if any such books shall be found in the cells or in possession of any convict, to take them away, and return the same to the agent; and, for the purpose of properly discharging these duties, to visit weekly each cell in the prison." 5. "To visit daily the sick in the hospital." 6. "To make an annual report to the inspectors, up to the first of December, relative to the religious and moral conduct of the prisoners during the year."

The same Statutes (Part IV., chapter 3, title 1, article 1, and section 13) contain the following provision in respect to county prisons: "It shall be the duty of the keeper of each county prison to provide a Bible for each room in the prison, to be kept therein; and he shall, if practicable, cause divine service to be performed for the benefit of the prisoners at least once each Sunday, provided there shall be a room in the prison that can be safely used for that purpose."

Taking, then, the State of New York as an example of legislation on the subject of chaplaincies, we have a statute providing that a chaplain shall be attached to the staff department of each militia regiment, and that he "shall be a regular ordained minister of a Christian denomination." This undoubtedly implies the existence of such denominations in the State, having a recognized ministry, from which militia chaplains are to be selected; but it does not, in the remotest sense, incorporate Christianity into the law of the State. This religion being the prevalent religion of the people, and the militia being a part of the people, militia chaplains, if provided for at all, would naturally be selected from the recognized ministers of that religion. The selection incidentally recognizes this religion; but it does not legalize it or invest a solitary one of its precepts or doctrines with any civil authority.

The chaplaincies authorized in State prisons have no relation to the people at large; but are provided for *criminals*—a comparatively small class of persons who, being deprived of their liberty, cannot furnish themselves with the facilities thus afforded. They relate exclusively to prison discipline and introduce religion as one of the elements of moral influence. And because Christianity is the religion generally accepted by the people of the State it is naturally the system employed for this purpose, just as Judaism or Mohammedanism would be employed for the same purpose if either had a like prevalence. Convicts should not by any penal discipline be forced to accept these religious facilities. It is enough to supply them. In supplying them the State, while showing a merciful regard to the isolated and dependent condition of those whom it is compelled to punish, treats them as an exceptional class to all the rest of the community. It gives them a Bible and a hymn-book, which they may use or not as they please; and also provides for them, in the person of the chaplain, the ministrations of that religion which is the popular religion of the State.

Whether the arrangement adopted is the best possible in the circumstances, and whether it would not be better to leave the religious instruction of prisoners exclusively to the voluntary efforts of those who might choose to engage in it, subject to such rules as are necessary to maintain the order and efficiency of prison discipline—these are questions with which this discussion is not concerned. We are not inquiring as to the best mode of doing the work; but simply considering the mode adopted by the State, and that, too, with reference to the point whether the mode makes Christianity a legalized system under the sanction of the State. The mode certainly does not operate beyond the limits of prison discipline; and this happens to apply to a mere fragment of society. The general policy of the State in regard to religion is not changed by its special provision for this exceptional class. The provision itself is exceptional to this policy; and its only justification must be found in the particular condition of the parties for whom it is intended. That condition does not consist in their poverty, their ignorance, or their depravity; but in the fact that the State has taken the absolute control of their personal liberty and shut them out from all contact with human society, except such as it chooses to grant. They are absolutely helpless in its hands and can make no provision for themselves. For this reason the State supplies them with food and clothing, to meet their animal wants; and for the same reason it offers to them religious services in the chaplain system.

It may be said that these services are provided at the public expense, and that at last they are made a charge upon the people, through taxation. This is true, and so far as it is true it is the compulsory support of religious instruction; and this, beyond all question, is contrary to one of the standard principles of our political system. The action of the State being thus clearly exceptional to this principle, the only possible solution of the problem is wholly to abandon the chaplain policy in respect to convicts, for the sake of the principle, or to regard the peculiarities of the case as justifying the non-application of the principle. One or the other of these positions must be taken; and the latter is the theory practically adopted by most, if not all, of the States in the Union.

The constitution of Michigan (IV., 24) provides that "the legislature may authorize the employment of a chaplain for the *State prison;*" and then immediately adds that "no money shall be appropriated for the payment of any religious services in either house of the legislature." Here we have a prohibition and a permission in direct juxtaposition and seeming contrast—the one asserting in a specific application the American principle that the public money shall not be used to defray the expenses of religious services, and the other providing for an exception to this principle in the case of prison convicts. The reason for the exception must be sought in the particular condition of those in whose behalf it is made; and in this view of the case the exception proves the rule. The State virtually affirms the rule in limiting the exception to a single and small class of persons. The limitation is an indirect mode of such affirmation.

The constitution of the same State (IV., 40) says that "no money shall be appropriated or drawn from the treasury for the benefit of any religious sect or society, theological or religious seminary, nor shall property belonging to the State be appropriated for any such purposes;" and yet, to qualify the application of the principle here asserted, it also says that "the legislature may authorize the employment of a chaplain for the State prison"—clearly implying that this is regarded as an exception to its general theory in regard to religion. Whether such an exception should be made or not is not the matter of the present inquiry.

The result reached from this survey of chaplaincies, whether national or State, is that they involve no legalization of Christianity and no purpose on the part of the civil authority to patronize the system or make it a preferred religion. They cannot, therefore, be justly cited as a precedent to sustain the theory of those who demand that the State shall become a religious propagandist in its public school system. There is no analogy between the facts that respectively mark the two cases.

The chaplain service, so far as it involves religious ministrations at the public expense, is limited to a very small class of persons, whose condition is no example of the general condition of the community; and it is on this ground solely that the service is admissible at all. The public school, on the other hand, is intended for *all* the families of the State, the rich and the poor alike. It is the school of the *whole* people, supported by all who pay taxes and extending its educational advantages to all. There is nothing in it, nothing in its purposes, and nothing in the condition of those whom it seeks to educate that constitutes a reason why the State should change or omit to apply its general policy in regard to religion. The State does not take charge of the government or support of children. It does not become a parent or assume the religious obligations of the parental office. The children are left under the custody and control of family government.

The manifest absence of any parallelism between the public school and the public prison, or between such a school and the army and the navy, shows at a glance that we cannot properly reason from the one to the other. Hence, chaplaincies in respect to prisons and in respect to the army and navy, defensible under our theory of the functions of government only on exceptional grounds and confined to the merest fraction of society, furnish no precedent for the public school, since in respect to it these grounds have no existence. If the two cases were parallel in their facts, then the exception which the State makes to the application of its general theory in the one case might be cited to sustain a similar exception in the other. No principle of common sense is better settled among lawyers and judges than that the citation of precedents not analogous to the case in hand proves nothing; and this is precisely the difficulty with this chaplaincy argument as applied to the public school.

XXVII.

CRIMINAL BLASPHEMY AND PROFANITY.

The fact that blasphemy and profanity are in this country treated as penal offenses, is sometimes referred to as indicating that the law, in this instance, allies itself with religion, and enforces the injunctions thereof by its own sanctions. These offenses are forbidden by the Bible; and, moreover, they seem, in distinction from murder and theft, to be specially committed against religion. It does not, however, necessarily follow that they are punished as *religious* offenses. Though they are such, it may, nevertheless, be true that the view which the law takes of them is simply that of crimes against society, and that in this character, and this only, are they punished. This being true, then the punishment involves no legal alliance of the State with religion, and no purpose on religious grounds to give effect to its rules. Is this true? The object of the present article is to supply an answer to this question.

Dr. Theophilus Parsons, in his treatise on the "Rights of a Citizen of the United States," gives a "Glossary of Law Terms in common use," in which he defines blasphemy to be "in law any false statement or language intended as a reviling of God" (p. 681). Bouvier, in his "Law Dictionary," says that it is "a false reflection uttered with a malicious design of reviling God." He quotes Chief-Justice Shaw as declaring that "it embraces the idea of detraction when used toward the Supreme Being, as calumny usually carries the same idea when applied to an individual."

In Abbott's New York Digest, New Edition (vol. 2, p. 611), blasphemy is defined as consisting "in maliciously reviling God or religion," and reference is made to the case of The People *vs.* Ruggles 8) Johnson's Reports, p. 290), in which Chief-Justice Kent thus defined the term, and held the offense to be indictable and punishable under common law. The same Digest (Vol. I, p.549) says : "Blasphemy against God, and contumelious reproaches and profane ridicule of Christ or the Holy Scriptures, are offenses at common law, whether uttered by words or writings." The wanton utterance of words in which Christ was declared to be a bastard, "with a wicked and malicious disposition, and not in a serious discussion on any controverted point," is referred to as being "a public offense by the law of the land."

The Supreme Court of Pennsylvania, in the case of Updegraph *vs.* The Commonwealth (11 Sergeant & Rawle's Reports, page 394), said that blasphemy is the "open, public vilification of the religion of the country." The Court declared it to be punishable on the ground of its being "injurious to and having a malignant influence on society." It added that the "malicious reviler" is the only person that can be punished under the charge of blasphemy.

A very lucid statement in regard to blasphemy, especially as to the grounds of its punishment, was made by Justice Clayton, of the Supreme Court of Delaware, in the case of The State *vs.* Chandler (2 Harrington's Reports, p. 353). The learned Justice said that the common law "sustained indictments for wantonly and maliciously blaspheming God or the Founder of the Christian religion, because such blasphemy tended to subvert the peace and good order which it was bound to protect. But it sustained no indictment for a mere sin against God where these objects of its care were not affected." He added that the common law punished blasphemy only "when it tended to create a riot, or break the peace, or subvert the very foundation on which civil society rested." He further said that the common law "took cognizance of offenses against God only where, by their inevitable effects, they became offenses against man and his temporal security."

Justice Strong, of the Supreme Court of the United States, in his lectures on the "Relations of Civil Law to Church Polity, Discipline and Property" (pp. 30, 31), observes:—

"No State recognition of the Church, however, or even of religious obligation, is to be inferred from the fact that civil law punishes many offenses which are condemned by the divine law, and which the Church also condemns and punishes. Many offenses against civil society are acts prohibited by the Decalogue and by all Churches. False swearing, theft, adultery and murder are violations of municipal law, and persons guilty of them are punished by the authority of the State, not because the offenses are violations of the divine law, or the law of the Church, but because they are infractions of the rules which civil society has found it necessary to establish for its own protection. In many of the States orderly observance of the Sabbath and abstinence from unnecessary labor are enjoined by statutes. Penalties are also denounced against profaneness and blasphemy. But it would be a mistake to regard such enactments as Church recognitions. They may have been suggested by respect for religion ; but, as *civil* enactments, they are justifiable only by their tendency to protect the public peace, and preserve public decency, good order, and good morals,—objects for which civil society exists."

Judge Cooley, in his "Constitutional Limitations" (p. 471), observes :—

"Some acts, would be offensive to public sentiment in a Christian community, and would tend to public disorder, which, in a Mohammedan or Pagan country, might be passed without notice, or be regarded as meritorious. The criminal laws of every country have reference in a great degree to the prevailing public sentiment, and punish those acts as crimes which disturb the peace and order or tend to shock the moral sense of the community. The moral sense is measurably regulated and controlled by the religious belief ; and therefore it is that those things which, estimated by a Christian standard, are profane and blasphemous, are properly punished as offenses, since they are offensive in the highest degree to the general public sense, and have a direct tendency to undermine the moral support of the laws and corrupt the community."

The Judge subsequently adds (pp. 474, 475):—

"But it does not follow, because blasphemy is punishable as a crime, that therefore one is not at liberty to dispute and argue against the truth of the Christian religion, or of any accepted dogma. * * * Blasphemy implies something more than a denial of the truth of religion, even of the highest and most vital. A bad motive must exist: there must be a wilful and malicious attempt to lessen men's reverence for the Deity or for the accepted religion. But outside of such wilful and malicious attempt, there is a broad field for candid investigation and discussion, which is as much open to the Jew or the Mohammedan as to the professors of the Christian faith. * * * * It is to be collected from the offensive levity, scurrilous and opprobrious language, and other circumstances, whether the act of the party was malicious. * * * * The courts have always been careful, in administering the law, to say that they did not include in blasphemy disputes between learned men upon particular controverted points. The constitutional provisions for the protection of religious liberty not only include within their protecting power all sentiments and professions concerning and upon subjects of religion, but they guarantee to every one a perfect right to form and promulgate such opinions and doctrines upon religious matters, and in relation to the existence, power, and providence of a Supreme Being, as to him shall seem just. In doing this he acts under an awful responsibility, but it is not to any *human* tribunal."

Profane swearing in common conversation, by an irreverent, vulgar and indecent use of any of the recognized titles of the Supreme Being, is legally deemed to be an inferior kind of blasphemy. Thus Broom & Hadley, in their "Commentaries on the Laws of England" (American Edition, vol. 2, p. 375), speak of "profane and common swearing and cursing," as allied to blasphemy, "though inferior in degree." They state the law of England as follows:—

"Every laborer profanely cursing or swearing shall forfeit one shilling; every other person under the degree of a gentleman, two shillings; and every gentleman or person of superior rank, five shillings, to the poor of the parish; and on a second conviction, double, and for every subsequent offense, treble the sum first forfeited, with all the charges of conviction; and in default of payment may be sent to the house of correction for ten days. Any justice of the peace may convict upon his own hearing, or the testimony of one witness; and any constable or peace officer, upon his own hearing, may secure any offender and carry him before a justice, and there convict him."

Mr. Francis Wharton, in his "American Criminal Law" (vol 1, p. 9), classes profane swearing among misdemeanors, and places it as such in the category of nuisances and scandals to the community, analogous in this respect to public drunkenness, loud and obscene language so as to draw together a crowd in a thoroughfare, notorious lewdness, open cruelty or "any act which from its nature must prejudicially affect the morals and health of the community."

The provisions of law in regard to profanity are generally referred to what is termed the *police* power of the State. Of this power Judge Cooley, in his "Constitutional Limitations" (p. 572), says that it embraces "the system of internal regulation by which it is sought not only to preserve the public order and to prevent offenses against the State, but also to establish for the intercourse of citizen with citizen those rules of good manners and good neighborhood which are calculated to prevent a conflict of rights, and to insure to each the uninterrupted enjoyment of his own, so far as is reasonably consistent with a like enjoyment of rights by others." Chief-Justice Shaw, in the case of the Commonwealth *vs.* Alger (7 Cush., p. 84), defined the police power of a State to be "the power vested in the legislature by the constitution to make, ordain and establish all manner of wholesome and reasonable laws, statutes and ordinances, either with penalties or without, not repugnant to the constitution, as they shall judge to be for the good and welfare of the Commonwealth and of the subjects of the same." Under this general power of so regulating the conduct of individuals as to preserve the peace, good order, health and safety of society, are placed the provisions of law in relation to profanity.

Thus the Revised Statutes of the State of New York (Part I, chapter 20, title 8 and article 6,) class the law against cursing and swearing under the internal police of the State, and under the specific title that relates to "the prevention and punishment of immorality and disorderly practices." The provisions of the law are as follows :—

"Section 61. Every person who shall profanely curse or swear shall forfeit one dollar for every offense. If the offense be committed in the presence and hearing of any justice of the peace, mayor, recorder or alderman of any city, while holding a court, a conviction of the offender shall be immediately made without any other proof whatever."

"Section 62. And if at any other time the offense be committed in the presence and hearing of such justice, mayor, recorder or alderman, under such circumstances as in the opinion of the magistrate amounts to a gross violation of the public decency, such magistrate may, in his discretion, convict the offender without other proof."

"Section 63. If the offender do not forthwith pay the penalties incurred, with the costs, or give security for their payment within six days, he shall be committed by warrant to the common jail of the county for every offense, or for any number of offenses whereof he was convicted at one and the same time, for not less than one day, nor more than three days, there to be confined in a room separate from all other prisoners."

We present the above exhibit for the purpose of showing the theory of law, whether statute or common, in treating blasphemy and profanity as penal offenses. The offenses are the same in kind, and differ only in degree; and both are punishable on precisely the same ground. The courts have, in several instances, decided that the constitutional guaranty in favor of religious liberty is not violated by making these acts penal offenses, whether under the rules of common law or by specific statutes.

The theory of these decisions, expressed in some and implied in others, is that the object of the punishment is not to prevent the free discussion of any generally accepted religious doctrine, or to compel its acceptance, or to interfere with the exercise of religious liberty in the teaching of any doctrine, or to enforce any duty on religious grounds, or penally to rebuke any offense because it is a sin against God. No one of these purposes would be consistent with the constitutions of the American States. Justice Clayton is very explicit in disclaiming the idea that blasphemy is punishable as a sin against God; and with this the language of Justice Strong, as above quoted, fully accords.

It so happens, however, that while blasphemy and profanity are violations of the law of God, and in this sense sins, they are also grossly repugnant to the average moral sense of society. They constitute an indecent use of language, annoying to the sensibilities of good citizens, and tending to corrupt the public morals ; and because this is the fact, law interposes its penal and preventive power, on precisely the same theory that it punishes public drunkenness, or abates a nuisance that is offensive to our physical senses, or prejudicial to health. In doing so it deals with the acts purely in their relation to man, and not at all in their relation to God. There is no Church and State, and no legalization of Christianity, or of any other religion, and no alliance of the civil power with religion, involved in the purposes of law with respect to blasphemy and profanity.

It is quite true that the prevalence of Christianity, as the religion generally accepted by the people, is at the basis of that public sentiment which makes blasphemy offensive, and that it fixes the type of the blasphemy which is thus offensive. The same result in kind would ensue if Judaism or Mohammedanism were the religion equally prevalent. The fact of the legal blasphemy does not depend upon the truth of the religion, but upon its general acceptance. And what and all that the law says is that religion, being thus accepted, shall not be maliciously and indecently reviled to the annoyance of its receivers, and that its sacred titles shall not be profanely used in the hearing of others. It demands, as a matter of good manners and good neighborhood, that this respect shall be paid to the sensibilities of the great body of the people; and in doing so it simply applies to this specific case a principle upon which it acts in a great variety of particulars. It will not allow one to appear in the streets in the state of nudity, or publicly do anything which outrages the general sense of the community. The underlying principle in all these cases is one of the most familiar principles of municipal law.

It, hence, follows that any argument built upon the law against blasphemy and profanity, if designed to show that the State may and should establish a system of religious instruction or worship in its public school, has no validity except by a mis-statement of the premise. The premise has no religious character whatever. It would be just as reasonable to make the law against murder or theft a premise for the same inference. God forbids both of these crimes, and the law of man punishes both, not because God forbids them, but because they are offenses against those rights which it is the province and duty of civil society to protect. So God forbids blasphemy and profanity, and law in this country punishes both, not because they are infractions of the divine law, but because they are offenses against the decency and good order of society.

Whether the law punishes murder or blasphemy, it deals with the offender as a member of the State and under its authority, and not at all as a subject of the divine moral government. With the offenses as sins against God it has nothing to do. Hence, any religious inference relating to the school question, or to any other question, based upon the action of law with reference to blasphemy and profanity, assigns to it a character which it does not possess, and which, moreover, it carefully disclaims. The inference, logically considered, has no basis whatever.

XXVIII.

THANKSGIVING AND FAST-DAY PROCLAMATIONS.

The custom of public annual thanksgiving has long existed in this country. It antedates the Revolution. Its birth-place was in Massachusetts. It is certainly an appropriate custom. All persons, whether Christians or not, who have any realizing sense of the existence, attributes, government, and providential goodness of God, must heartily approve of the practice.

Society is made up of individuals ; and, when the latter jointly share the bounties of Providence they may well unite in a common service of gratitude to the Divine Source of these bounties. In order that they may thus unite in a concurrent service, and as a community render thanks to God, it is necessary that a specific time should be publicly designated for this purpose. This end is secured by what are termed Thanksgiving Proclamations.

George Washington, the first President of the United States, acting in conformity with what he knew to be the custom of the people, issued such a proclamation in 1795; and since that time, until within a comparatively recent period, these proclamations have proceeded only from governors of particular States or mayors of cities. The custom has been thus perpetuated as one of the characteristics of the American people.

What are these proclamations? It is quite true that by established usage they proceed from a *civil* and not an ecclesiastical source; yet they are merely recommendations in which a day is designated for thanksgiving, and the people advised by the President, or by the governor, or by the mayor, or by all three, to observe the day in this manner. They are not issued in the discharge of any official duty known to the constitutions or laws of the land, and are not enforced by any penalty. Whether the people shall respect the recommendation or not is a matter to be decided by each individual for himself, subject to no other constraint than that which may be imposed by his own sense of duty. He violates no human law in disregarding the proclamation, as he obeys none in observing it. It does not touch a solitary right which belongs to him as a citizen. It creates no civil duty. It makes no discrimination in respect to the religious beliefs or practices of the people, and appoints no special form of religious service. It does not pronounce any judgment as to what is the true religion, or what is the proper mode of rendering a tribute of thanksgiving to God. All such questions it leaves to the people in the fullest and freest exercise of their religious liberty.

Substantially the same remarks apply with equal truth to the appointment of Fast-days, as periods for public humiliation and confession, and the invocation of the divine favor. Such appointments, especially by the civil magistrate, are far less common than those that relate to thanksgiving: yet, like the latter, they are nothing but advice, which may be accepted or rejected according to the pleasure of the people. They are enforced by no authority, and really have no official character whatever. Whether the public designation of a fast-day, either by the civil authority or by an ecclesiastical body, establishes any religious obligation in the court of conscience is a question for each conscience to settle. Be this as it may, the designation is nothing but human counsel, and, hence, has not a single attribute which distinctively characterizes a legal statute.

Those who object to the appointment of thanksgiving and fast-days by the civil officer, because, as they allege, such appointments are a species of quasi-religious legislation, proceed upon a false assumption as to their nature. What they allege is not true; and hence the objection is not well taken. They might with more plausibility say that it is in bad *taste* for the officer of a government that exists simply for secular purposes, to designate, even by a mere recommendation, any religious services for the people or any time for such services. This is the very utmost that the truth warrants; and whether there is any force in this objection would depend on the prevalent taste of the people. The great body of the American people find no fault with the practice and, hence, we conclude that it is not offensive to them. In respect to thanksgiving proclamations, they both accept and expect it as a long established usage. They do not regard it as involving any union between Church and State, or any interference with their religious liberty.

Another class of persons, especially those who advocate Bible reading and religious instruction in our public schools, fancy that thanksgiving and fast-day proclamations may be argumentatively used as a precedent in support of their view. We remember an article published in 1870 by an eminent clergyman of this country, who appealed to Washington's thanksgiving proclamation of 1795 as furnishing a premise from which to infer that Christianity might and should be taught in our public schools, organized and conducted by the State, and supported by general taxation. This clergyman, in his haste to proceed to his inference forgot to notice the important fact that Washington was the President of the United States under a Constitution which makes legalized Christianity an impossibility in the government authorized by it; which bestows upon the President no religious power whatever; which denies all such power to Congress; and which, therefore, reduced the proclamation to the mere category of simple advice, having no more legal authority to control the action of the people than it would have had if issued by the humblest citizen in the land. Washington himself participated in the work of drafting this Constitution. He signed it as the President of the Federal Convention, and recommended the people to ratify it. To infer, as this eminent clergyman did, that the prerogatives of the President's office were attached to the proclamation is to give it a character which it did not possess, and to make Washington do what he had not the remotest idea of doing, and what he really had no power to do.

This thanksgiving and fast-day argument in regard to our public schools is so transparently fallacious that it will hardly pass muster, even as a plausible trick in logic. If great men did not sometimes use the argument, it would not be worth while to refute it. The fatal objection to it is the total want of any analogy between the two cases.

The public school is an institution of *law*, established and managed by the authority of civil government. Its expenses are paid out of the money-chest of that government: and the funds are collected from the people by compulsory taxation. To introduce religion into the school as one of the branches of education is not only to determine *what* religion shall be thus introduced, but also to compel the people to pay for its propagation. It is to this extent the coerced support of religion ; and than this nothing can be more foreign or antagonistical to the genius of our political institutions. Tested by these institutions as a standard, it is a gross heresy.

Is there anything analogous to this in a thanksgiving or a fast-day proclamation issued by the President, the governor of a State, or the mayor of a city? Nothing, absolutely whatever. To reason from the one to the other is to build an argument upon a totally false analogy. One might as well say that, because the President thanks God before eating his meals, or attends public worship on the Sabbath Day, the Bible ought to be read and religious instruction given in the public school. These acts, whether of the President or a governor, like a religious proclamation, have no official character, and, hence, furnish no precedent from which to reason in respect to a legal institution.

There can hardly be a more striking instance in which the premises utterly fail to contain the conclusion, or a more palpable confession of the extreme paucity of arguments available for its support, than that of resorting to thanksgiving and fast-day proclamations as the means of showing that Christianity is a part of our legal system, and may, hence, be introduced into our public schools. The proper mode of proof would be to appeal to the constitutions of the country, or to the laws enacted in pursuance thereof. Here, if anywhere, we are to ascertain what is the legal position of Christianity in reference to civil government. If it be a State religion in any sense, or to any extent, here is the proper place to find the evidence thereof.

A much more plausible argument might be based on the tax-exemption of Church property: yet even th s would be a failure, since the exemption is not placed at all on religious grounds.

The legislature of the State of New York, by the act of April 23d, 1870, did indeed declare that "any day appointed or recommended by the governor of this State or the President of the United States, as a day of fast or thanksgiving, shall, for all purposes whatsoever as regards the presenting for paym.nt or acceptance and of the protesting and giving notice of the dishonor of bills of exchange, bank checks and promissory notes, made after the passage of this act, be treated and considered as is the first day of the week commonly called Sunday."

This statute makes such a day a legal holiday in respect to the business matters which it recites. It treats the first day of January, the twenty-second day of February, the twenty-fifth day of December, and the fourth day of July in the same way. The statute simply postpones to the next day payments pledged to be made on any one of these days: and it does so on the general presumption that these days will not by the mass of the people be treated as ordinary business days. There is not the remotest reference to religion or to religious reasons in the statute. Its sole relation is to certain business stipulations: and in this respect it treats the first day of January, the fourth day of July, and a fast or thanksgiving day on precisely the same principle.

We are almost inclined to ask the reader's pardon for detaining him so long with this thanksgiving and fast-day question. It is, however, one of the points that has appeared in the discussion about the public schools; and this is our apology for making any reference to it.

XXIX.

PREAMBLES TO STATE CONSTITUTIONS.

Reference is sometimes made to the recognitions and acknowledgments of God found in the preambles to our State Constitutions, as evidence that the State governments are invested with a religious character, and may, hence, very properly employ the public school as an instrument of Christian instruction and worship. That the premise of this argument may have the benefit of a full statement, we submit, as follows, the preambles which contain these acknowledgments of God:—

ALABAMA.—"We, the people of the State of Alabama, * * * * invoking the favor and guidance of Almighty God, do ordain and establish the following constitution."

ARKANSAS.—"We, the people of the State of Arkansas, grateful to God for our civil and religious liberty, * * * * do ordain and establish this constitution."

CALIFORNIA.—"We, the people of California, grateful to Almighty God for our freedom, * * do establish this constitution."

CONNECTICUT.—"The people of Connecticut, acknowledging with gratitude the good providence of God, * * * * ordain and establish the following constitution."

FLORIDA.—"We, the people of the State of Florida, grateful to Almighty God for our freedom, * * * * do establish this constitution."

GEORGIA.—"We, the people of Georgia, * * * * acknowledging and invoking the guidance of Almighty God, the author of all good governments, do ordain and establish this constitution."

ILLINOIS.—"We, the people of the State of Illinois, grateful to Almighty God for the civil, political and religious liberty which he hath so long permitted us to enjoy, and looking to him for a blessing upon our endeavors to secure and transmit the same unimpaired to succeeding generations, * * * * do ordain and establish this constitution."

INDIANA.—"We, the people of the State of Indiana, grateful to Almighty God for the free exercise of the right to choose our own form of government, do ordain this constitution."

IOWA.—"We, the people of the State of Iowa, grateful to the Supreme Being for the blessings hitherto enjoyed, and feeling our dependence on him for a continuation of those blessings, do ordain and establish a free and independent government."

KANSAS.—"We, the people of Kansas, grateful to Almighty God for our civil and religious privileges, * * * * do ordain and establish this constitution."

MAINE.—"We, the people of Maine, * * * * acknowledging with grateful hearts the goodness of the Sovereign Ruler of the universe, * * * * and imploring his aid and direction, * * * * do ordain and establish the following constitution."

MARYLAND.—"We, the people of the State of Maryland, grateful to Almighty God for our civil and religious liberty, * * * * declare."

MASSACHUSETTS.—"We, therefore, the people of Massachusetts, acknowledging with grateful hearts the goodness of the Great Legislator of the universe, * * * * and devoutly imploring his direction, * * * * ordain and establish the following declaration of rights and frame of government."

MINNESOTA.—"We, the people of the State of Minnesota, grateful to God for our civil and religious liberty, * * * * do ordain and establish this constitution."

MISSISSIPPI.—"We, the people of the State of Mississippi, grateful to Almighty God for the free exercise of the right to choose our own form of government, do ordain this constitution."

MISSOURI.—"We, the people of the State of Missouri, grateful to Almighty God, the Sovereign Ruler of nations, * * * * and acknowledging our dependence upon him, * * * * ordain and establish this revised and amended constitution."

NEBRASKA.—"We, the people of Nebraska, grateful to Almighty God for our freedom, * * * * do establish this constitution."

NEVADA.—"We, the people of the State of Nevada, grateful to Almighty God for our freedom, * * * * do establish this constitution."

NEW JERSEY.—"We, the people of the State of New Jersey, grateful to Almighty God for the civil and religious liberty which he hath so long permitted us to enjoy, and looking to him for a blessing upon our endeavors to secure and transmit the same unimpaired to succeeding generations, do ordain and establish this constitution."

NEW YORK.—"We, the people of the State of New York, grateful to Almighty God for our freedom, * * * * do establish this constitution."

NORTH CAROLINA.—"We, the people of the State of North Carolina, grateful to Almighty God, the Sovereign Ruler of nations, * * * * and acknowledging our dependence upon him, * * * * ordain and establish this constitution."

OHIO.—"We, the people of the State of Ohio, grateful to Almighty God for our freedom, * * * * do establish this constitution."

PENNSYLVANIA.—"We, the people of the Commonwealth of Pennsylvania, grateful to Almighty God for the blessing of civil and religious liberty, and humbly invoking his guidance, do ordain and establish this constitution."

RHODE ISLAND.—"We, the people of Rhode Island and Providence plantations, grateful to Almighty God, * * * * and looking to him for a blessing upon our endeavors, * * * * do ordain and establish this constitution of government."

SOUTH CAROLINA.—"We, the people of the State of South Carolina, * * * * grateful to Almighty God, * * * * and imploring the direction of the great Legislator of the universe, * * * * establish the following * * * * as the constitution of the Commonwealth of South Carolina."

TEXAS.—"We, the people of Texas, acknowledging with gratitude the grace of God in permitting us to make choice of our own form cf government, do hereby ordain and establish this constitution."

VIRGINIA.—"We, the delegates of the good people of Virginia, * * * * invoking the favor and guidance of Almighty God, do propose to the people the following constitution and form of government for this Commonwealth."

WISCONSIN.—"We, the people of Wisconsin, grateful to Almighty God for our freedom,* * * do establish this constitution."

Here are twenty-eight constitutional preambles which, taken in the aggregate, are referred to as evidence that the State governments possess a religious character, and may, hence, evince the fact in their public school system by Bible reading and other religious exercises. The premise on which this conclusion is based consists in the recognitions and acknowledgments of God as found in these preambles. To this argument we submit the following reply:—

1. There are nine States of the Union to which the argument has no application. Two of these States—namely, Vermont and West Virginia—have no preamble to their respective constitutions; and seven of them,—namely, Delaware, Kentucky, Louisiana, Michigan, New Hampshire, Oregon, and Tennessee—make no reference to God in the pre-

ambles to their constitutions. The argument cannot, of course, be used in these States to decide the School question, or any other question involving the subject of religion.

2. The recognitions and acknowledgments of God contained in the above twenty-eight preambles are not distinctively and exclusively Christian. The Christian, whether Protestant or Catholic, has no monopoly in these acknowledgments. They belong to the rational Theist who is not a Christian, just as really as they do to the Theist who is a Christian. The aspect of God which they present is that which is furnished by the light of Nature, and not that special aspect for which we are indebted to the supernatural light of Christianity. No reference is made to God as "the God and Father of our Lord Jesus Christ," or to the Word of God, or to the person or offices of Christ, or to the plan of salvation, or to the doctrine of a future life, or to anything that is peculiar to Christianity. The creed which incidentally appears in these preambles is common to the Christian, the Jew, the Mohammedan, a Socrates, a Cicero, a Plato, and, indeed, all who believe in the doctrine of a personal God, and that of his providence over the affairs of men. The Christian can heartily accept the creed, since there is nothing in it repugnant to his faith; and so can Jews or Deists for the same reason, though both of them reject the distinctive doctrines of Christianity. It seems to have been the

purpose of the framers of these preambles to avoid the use of all terms that would place upon them a specifically and exclusively Christian stamp.

It is not, therefore, logically allowable for the Christian—the Protestant, for example—to claim that King James's version of the Sacred Scriptures shall be used in the public school as the means of religious instruction and worship, and then rest the claim upon these preambles. He may not say to the Catholic: "My peculiar creed is here, and yours is not; and, hence, *my* Bible, and not yours, must go into the public school." He may not say to the Jew: "These preambles are my property, and not yours; and, hence, Protestant Christianity, and not Judaism, must be taught in the public school." He may not say to the Deist: "My creed in regard to God is contained in these acknowledgments and recognitions; and, hence, my specific faith as a Christian is the form of religion that should be installed in the public school." The premise proves no such conclusions. The Catholic, the Jew and the Deist have logically the same rights in the premise that the Protestant has, and may, hence, use it with the same propriety to show that the State should establish and, at the general expense, support Catholic public schools, or Jewish public schools, or Deistical public schools. The argument is just as pertinent and as powerful when employed by the Catholic, the Jew, or the Deist, as it is when employed by the Protestant.

The fact is, the religious matters about which these parties differ are not in the preambles at all; and, hence, there is no logical proprietorship specially vested in any of them. What and all that we find is that which is their common religious property, because it is their common faith. To acknowledge God as revealed by the light of Nature is one thing: and to acknowledge him in those special aspects which are peculiar to Christianity is another and very different thing. The above preambles contain the former acknowledgment, and not the latter. They, hence, furnish no basis for any inference in respect to the latter, and give the Christian no logical advantage over the Jew or the Deist.

3. A constitutional preamble, though a form of expressing the enactment of a fundamental law by the people, either with or without the reasons for the enactment, is not upon its very face the law itself. It describes the people of a given State as ordaining and establishing "this constitution," or "the following constitution." The thing ordained and established as a fundamental law is not the preamble, but the constitution itself. The reality and validity of a constitution do not depend upon the fact that it has a preamble, formally declaring its enactment by the people, but upon the fact that it was so enacted; and the evidence, both as to what the constitution is, and as to the fact of its adoption, is preserved in the archives of the State.

The constitutions of Vermont and West Virginia have no preamble; yet this does not affect their validity. All the preambles might be stricken out, or might have been omitted altogether, without involving the slightest change in the constitutions themselves. There is no objection to them; yet they are not at all indispensable.

It is by reading "this constitution," or "the following constitution," referred to in the preamble, and not by reading the preamble, that we ascertain what is the organization of a State, what it is as a body politic, upon what principles it is constructed, what governmental agency is established, and with what powers that agency is invested. Legislative bodies acting under it, and courts of justice in applying its principles, derive their powers from the constitution itself, and not from its preamble. The latter, independently of the former, makes no grant of substantive powers. Its contents are not laws unless they are made such by the constitution enacted. It may contain reasons for the enactment of a given constitution; yet these reasons are not the thing enacted, and have no legal effect whatever unless the constitution gives them such effect.

No inference can, therefore, be drawn as to the structure and purposes of the State governments, from the mere fact that their preambles to the constitutions under which their governments are organized, recognize the existence of God, express gratitude for his favors, and invoke his guidance and direction. The mere fact itself simply proves the religious sentiments of the people as expressed: but it does not prove their purpose to ordain and establish those sentiments as fundamental laws of the body politic, to clothe them with constitutional authority, or confer any power upon State legislatures to give them legal effect. Whether these sentiments enter into the organic laws of the several States expressing them in constitutional preambles, is to be ascertained by studying these laws: and this carries us beyond the preambles into the constitutions themselves.

4. Coming, then, to these constitutions, we find, as a matter of fact, that all of them—some more fully than others—so qualify and limit the powers of the State governments in respect to religion as to secure to the people the fullest exercise and enjoyment of religious liberty, and confine the action of these governments to the attainment of merely temporal and secular ends. This is one of the most characteristic features of our American State constitutions, and that, too, whether their preambles do or do not contain recognitions and acknowledgments of God. Having presented this point at large in a previous stage of this discussion, we content ourselves here with a single illustration.

The constitution of Illinois in its preamble says:—"We, the people of the State of Illinois, grateful to Almighty God for the civil, political and religious liberty which he hath so long permitted us to enjoy, and looking to him for a blessing upon our endeavors to secure and transmit the same unimpaired to succeeding generations, * * * * do ordain and establish this constitution for the State of Illinois." So reads the preamble, acknowledging God as existing, as being Almighty, as having granted to the people civil, political and religious liberty, and as having long permitted them to enjoy it, and also adding to this acknowledgment the expression of gratitude and a prayer to God for his blessing upon the endeavors of the people.

What, then, does the constitution itself say? It says (ii., 3):—"The free exercise and enjoyment of religious profession and worship, without discrimination, shall forever be guaranteed: and no person shall be denied any civil or political right, privilege or capacity, on account of his religious opinions. * * * No person shall be required to attend or support any ministry or place of worship against his consent, nor shall any preference be given by law to any religious denomination, or mode of worship." It still further says (viii., 3):—"Neither the General Assembly nor any county, city, town, township, school district, or other public corporation shall ever make any appropriation, or pay from any public fund whatever anything, in aid of any Church or sectarian purpose, or to help support or sustain any school, academy, seminary, college, university, or other literary or scientific institution, controlled by any Church or sectarian denomination: nor shall any grant or donation of land, money, or other personal property ever be made by the State or any such public corporation to any Church or for any sectarian purpose."

Here is a State, in the preamble to its constitution certainly not lacking in devout expressions with reference to the Supreme Being, and yet in the constitution itself dispossessing its government of all religious powers and making that government exclusively secular in its purposes. It cannot establish or regulate any form of worship. It can make no discriminations on religious grounds. It cannot deny to any one any civil or political right, privilege or capacity on account of his religious opinions. It cannot interfere with the religious liberty of any person. It cannot compel any one to support any form of religion, and cannot appropriate a dollar of the public money for any such purpose. The denials of power made in this constitution leave to the government of Illinois nothing but secular power—power in relation to things temporal. The government of that State is not Christian in the sense of giving any legal preference to Christianity, or clothing it with any legal attributes, obligations or sanctions, or in any way endowing it or its institutions, or furnishing any support to these institutions, and cannot be Christian in any of these senses so long as its present constitution remains. It is not a religious government, but a republican and exclusively secular government. It is made such by the constitution of the State.

The religious sentiments found in the preamble do not in the slightest degree change this fact. They are not there for any such purpose, and are not permitted to have any such effect. Practically, the government of Illinois is just what it would be, if the preamble to its constitution had been like that to the constitution of Michigan, which simply says:— "The people of the State of Michigan do ordain this constitution."

The same general principal of constitutional restriction is found in the other State constitutions, whose preambles contain recognitions and acknowledgments of God. They all have the common purpose of so restraining the powers of the State governments as to leave the people free in the matter of religion. Religious liberty for *all* men and for *all* sects, with no endowment or support of any form of religion, and with no encroachment upon the rights of a religious conscience, is the all-pervading doctrine of our American State constitutions, no matter what religious sentiments may be expressed in their preambles. Christians have no monopoly of this liberty, and no exclusive privileges in respect to it. They are only a part of the people, and stand on the same footing with Jews, Deists, Rationalists, or any other class of citizens.

The conclusion that we derive from this survey of the recognitions and acknowledgments of God in the preambles to twenty-eight State constitutions, is that the premise thus given supplies no proof that the State should, or consistently can, undertake the work of a teacher or propagator of religion in its public schools. The governments organized under these constitutions are clearly *secular* in their objects and purposes, as abundantly shown by the limitations imposed on their powers; and this is a sufficient reason why they should be secular in any system of education which they authorize and support by compulsory taxation.

To infer the opposite from the preambles is to make these preambles contradict both the letter and the spirit of the constitutions themselves, and to give them a character which they do not possess. Especially, to infer that the religious instruction to be given in the public school should be distinctively Christian, whether of the Protestant or the Catholic type, is to assign to the preambles an import which their language does not authorize. They are not Christian preambles any more than they are Jewish or even Deistical preambles. They represent the faith of a Jew, or that of a rational Theist who is not a Christian, as really as they do the faith of a Christian. The latter, as against the former, has no special title to them, and no right to use them for purposes that are limited to his particular form of religious faith. Neither the Douay version nor King James's version of the Sacred Scriptures appears in these preambles. Nothing that is peculiar to and distinctive of the Christian faith is in them.

XXX.

THE LAW OF RELIGIOUS SOCIETIES.

Christianity exists in this country, not as a philosophical system, known only to the few, but as a popular religion, so general that it has no rival to dispute its ascendency or divide its honors. Numerous societies in the form of local Churches have been organized by its influence; and these societies by union have given birth to sects or denominations. The offerings of its receivers and adherents have accumulated a vast capital in church structures, theological seminaries, and other material appliances, which may be called the invested fund of Christianity. Nearly the sum total of the organized religion in the United States is to be found in the sects that claim to be Christian. For the result we have a religious system intimately identified with Church organisms, living in them, operating through them, and supported by them. These organisms are voluntary societies of men and women, professing the same religion, frequently meeting together, and subject to some kind of self-imposed rules which constitute their ecclesiastical government. A number of them united under the same polity, and holding the same doctrines, forms a sect or denomination of such societies.

These societies not only need protection against molestation and disturbance ; but, being the owners of property gathered by their voluntary offerings, and designed for Church purposes, they need to be clothed with legal rights in respect to its possession and use. In some way, either directly or indirectly, law must come in contact with them, and they must come in contact with law. So large a social fact as the organized religion of this country cannot exist without some form of such contact.

What we mean by the Law of Religious Societies is simply the law of the several States relating to them, and which, taken in the aggregate, may very properly be styled American Ecclesiastical Law. We mean also the law as it now is, and not as it was during the colonial period of our history. That there is such a law admits of no dispute. To state it in detail would be the work of a volume, if not many volumes. We have no such purpose. All that is proposed in this article is to give a few leading hints to some of its most general features, as the means of indicating the legal theory of the country in dealing with the subject of religion. On this point we submit the following statement :—

1. The State tolerates religious societies, whether Christian or otherwise, in the sense of not making them unlawful, or doing anything to suppress them. They are in this respect regarded as innocent organizations, as working no harm to the State, as not being contrary to public policy, and as being

an exercise of the right of voluntary association with which the State ought not to interfere. It is not necessary to spend words on this point, since the fact is one of acknowledged and universal prevalence.

2. The State protects religious societies, when met together and peaceably conducting themselves, against disturbance and interference. It will not interfere with them itself, or suffer others to do so. This protection recognizes and defends the general right of peaceable assemblage, and is simply a branch of the protection which the State extends to all persons when met together for lawful purposes, and conducting themselves lawfully. In most, if not all of the States of the Union, there are special statutes against disturbing religious meetings, defining the forms of the offense, designating penalties therefor, and providing the appropriate jurisdiction for their infliction. These statutes apply to all religious societies, no matter what may be the creed professed, or the polity adopted.

3. The State, for the purposes of its own jurisdiction and control, takes no cognizance of the Church proper, as distinguished from the incorporated religious society. It does not legislatively enter the domain of its purely ecclesiastical life, or attempt to regulate its affairs as such. Mr. Tyler, in his "American Ecclesiastical Law" (p. 128), observes :—

"Religious societies usually maintain public

worship according to some specified denominational usage; but the corporation and the Church, although one may exist in the pale of the other, are in no respect correlative. The objects and interests of the one are moral and spiritual; and the other deals exclusively with things temporal and material. The existence of the Church proper, as an organized body, is not recognized by the municipal law. (Petty *vs.* Tooker, 21 New York Reports, p. 267)."

The same author (pp. 54, 55) further remarks:—

"Over the Church, as such, the legal and temporal tribunals do not in general profess to have any jurisdiction whatever, except so far as is necessary to protect the civil rights of others and to preserve the public peace. All questions relating to the faith and practice of the Church and its members belong to the Church judicatories themselves."

Justice Strong, of the Supreme Court of the United States, in his lectures on the "Relations of Civil Law to Church Polity, &c." (p. 41), speaks of the Church "as an interior organization within a religious society," and then adds (p. 42):—

"I think it may be safely asserted, as a general proposition, that whenever questions of discipline, of faith, of Church rule, of membership, or of office have been decided by the Church in its own modes of decision, civil law tribunals accept the decisions as final and apply them as made."

It is quite true that a Church is almost always

connected with a religious society, and that the two may be largely composed of the same persons ; yet the Church itself, in distinction from the religious society of which we shall speak in the sequel, is unknown to the law for any purpose of supervision or control. The law does not appoint its officers, or prescribe any rules for their appointment, or determine what shall be its government or system of doctrine.

4. As a consequence, the State leaves the Church itself to be an entirely self-perpetuating and self-regulating organization within the limits of decency and good order. As to doctrines and government, as to the admission or exclusion of members, as to Church officers and their powers, as to the modes of worship and transacting every kind of spiritual business, as to the confederation of Churches under one system of polity and faith, as to all the religious matters and objects of the organization, the theory of American law is that the State has nothing to do with the Church. The Church can make no law for the State, and the State in regard to these subjects makes no law for the Church. As observed by Justice Strong (p. 37), the State "leaves the internal management of a Church exclusively to its own regulations."

This is but another mode of asserting the doctrine of a free Church in a free State. In the case of Harmon *vs.* Desher (1 Spear's Equity Reports, South Carolina, p. 80), the Court thus stated this doctrine:—"The structure of our government has, for the preservation of civil liberty, rescued the temporal institutions from religious interference; and, on the other hand, it has secured religious liberty from the invasion of the civil authority."

5.—It follows, as a corollary, that the State in its organic capacity has no legal opinion as to the truth of the religion professed by the Church. All creeds are in its view equally orthodox and equally heretical, since it has nothing to do with them in either aspect. If a Church chooses to adopt and preach the Mormon faith, including its doctrine in regard to marriage, the State will not concern itself with the question. If any of the members actually practise polygamy, then their external conduct, but not their articles of faith, will bring them, as individuals and members of civil society, into conflict with the law and render them liable to punishment There is no penalty against their faith, or against its peaceable propagation; but this immunity does not release them from their obligations as citizens, or exempt them from punishment if they violate the law in regard to marriage.

The underlying assumption of American law in respect to matters of religious faith is that free discussion, and not any system of legal coercion or repression, is the proper remedy for errors of faith, and the only one consistent with an equal and impartial enjoyment of religious liberty. It, hence, leaves all Church organizations to make, to administer, and defend their own creeds in their own way, alike unhindered and unhelped by the State. The creeds may be a law to the Church, but they are no law to the State. They are not co-ordinate with the civil law, and the latter never undertakes their defense.

6. The State, in order to meet certain necessities of Church organisms, provides for the incorporation and continuance of religious societies as bodies corporate; or, in the omission to do so, which is the fact in some of the States, it provides for a system of trusts, vested and perpetuated in natural persons. No religious society is compelled to incorporate itself. All that the State does is simply to furnish the opportunity. And, when such a society is incorporated, it is in legal contemplation simply a civil corporation, as much so as a bank, an insurance company, or a railway company. It is in this respect the creature of legislative authority, and subject to that authority. The method of incorporation may be through a general law, or by a special charter; yet in either case the product is a civil corporation, and nothing else. All its attributes and powers are of this character. The control of the State over it respects it solely as such.

Generally a Church proper is enclosed within the religious society, or rather exists coincidently with it: yet this is not necessarily so, and all the members of the religious society are not necessarily members of the Church, and all the members of the latter are not necessarily members of the former. The Church may have one rule of membership, and the religious society may be incorporated under another and different rule. The intimate connection between the two organizations should not lead us to confound them, or suppose them to be the same.

The Church proper, considered in its collective character, has no corporate powers which are known to the law. The religious society, when incorporated, has the general powers of a civil corporation, and also the special powers which the State may see fit to grant, as the means of attaining the special ends of its existence; and in respect to the latter powers it differs from a bank only as a bank differs from a railway company. It is a civil corporation to do a certain kind of business, which every Church needs to have done.

7. The State, in providing for the incorporation of religious societies, or adopting a system of trusts, adapts its regulations, to some extent, to the peculiarities of different Church organizations. This fact is conspicuously seen in the Act of April 5th, 1813, passed by the legislature of New York for the incorporation of religious societies, and the subsequent acts amendatory thereof. There are specialties connected with the incorporation of Episcopal Churches, Reformed Churches, Reformed Presbyterian Churches, and Roman Catholic Churches, which are intended to be suited to their respective organizations. The Quakers and the Shakers,

having no incorporated religious societies, are provided for in the laws of New York through a system of trusts vested in natural persons, and designed to serve the ends sought to be secured by incorporation. Where there are no special features of Church organization, making a special method necessary, the law has a general method of incorporation by the election of trustees in conformity with prescribed rules.

Thus the laws of New York suit themselves to the wants of particular Church organizations, and seek, without discrimination for or against any, to secure to all at their option the civil benefits of incorporation, or, in its absence, those of a system of trusts. Similar arrangements are found in other States. The incorporation of religious societies or a trust system for their benefit is, with some diversities of detail, among the standard legal usages of the American States.

8. What are called the temporalities of the Church, in distinction from things moral and spiritual that pertain to its doctrine and government, are by authority of the State assigned to the incorporated religious society, subject to regulations prescribed by law. The ownership of Church property and the power to make legal contracts are vested in this society. It is known to law as a civil corporation and can act in this capacity. It has a corporate title and seal. It can sue and be sued. It exists by perpetual succession. It acts

through a board of agents created by its own choice in conformity with law. There are differences in the laws of the different States with respect to religious corporations ; yet the one feature common to them all is that of making legal provision for the orderly and proper exercise of those civil powers that stand connected with the acquisition, possession, use, and disposal of Church property.

Property is the one temporality of the Church which forms the subject-matter of nearly all the legislation and all the judicial decisions that have any reference to the Church. Take out this one element and the rights in various ways allied therewith ; and there would hardly be a question in relation to the Church, other than that of protection, which civil tribunals would have occasion to consider. Justice Strong says (p. 40) :—" Almost all, if not all the questions mooted in the civil courts of this country relating to Church polity, discipline, officers or members, have arisen incidentally in controversies respecting Church property." This is the one point in respect to which the powers of the State come in contact with the Church ; and but for it the State, under our system of government, would have nothing to do with Churches beyond affording them protection against any improper disturbance. There must be some law in regard to Church property, and the State is the only party that can either make or administer it.

9. It is a general principle of law, subject to various qualifications in the different States, that the legal doctrine of trusts and charitable uses applies to the tenure of Church property, and that such property cannot be diverted from the use originally intended and devoted to other purposes. Justice Strong remarks (p. 77) :—" The law of trusts and the law of charities, closely connected as they are, constitute the protection of our Churches, so far as they hold and enjoy property." He observes again (pp. 86, 95) :—" Church property is regarded by law as devoted to charitable uses." " In this country gifts and settlements for religious uses have always been considered as charities." So, also, Mr. Tyler, in his " American Ecclesiastical Law " (p. 97), after saying that the trustees of a religious society simply have the custody and control of its property, but are in no sense the owners thereof, adds :—

" But should the trustees of a religious society attempt to divert the funds and property of the society from the purposes for which they were contributed by the original donors, a court of equity would intervene to prevent it. For instance, where property is conveyed to a religious corporation or a religious society which afterwards becomes incorporated, to promote the teaching of particular religious doctrines, and the funds are attempted to be diverted to the support of different doctrines, it is the duty of a court of equity, under its general jurisdiction over trusts, to interpose for the purpose of carrying the trust into execution according to the intention of the donors. (Miller *vs.* Gable, 2 Denio, p. 492.)"

This principle of trusts and charitable uses in respect to Church property, taken in connection with the powers possessed by courts of equity, constitutes the guaranty furnished by law against the misapplication and misuse of such property. The law assumes that the original donors had a right to fix and qualify the use; and when they have done so, either expressly or by legal implication, the property is assumed to have been received and to be held as a trust, subject to whatever conditions may be involved therein, provided they are legal. There is no dispute among judges as to this principle. When they have differed it has been with reference to its application in specific cases. The principle, though by no means invented for the benefit of Churches, is, nevertheless, one of immense importance in relation to the tenure and use of property acquired for church purposes.

10. Civil tribunals, for the purpose of applying this principle, or for that of determining the legal rights of litigant parties in cases properly before them, sometimes have occasion to inquire into the proceedings of the Church itself, and to judge whether they are in conformity with its own law. They do so not to review the proceedings, or to reverse them, or to change their ecclesiastical effect,

but simply as incidental to a decision upon the legal rights of the parties in controversy. A question of faith or one of Church order may be thus collaterally involved. Cases come before the courts affecting vested rights which can be disposed of in no other way.

A conspicuous example of this character is furnished by the suit in regard to the Methodist Book Concern, decided by the Supreme Court of the United States, at the December term in 1853. The Methodist Church of this country, prior to its division, had accumulated a large invested fund, entitled the Book Concern, which had been gathered by the voluntary contributions of its traveling preachers, and which, as a charity fund for the relief of these preachers and their families, was placed under the custody and superintendence of the General Conference. In 1844 this Conference adopted a plan for the division of the Church into two distinct ecclesiastical organizations, and for a division of this fund, in the event that the annual conferences at the South should approve the plan and organize themselves accordingly. These Conferences did so the next year, and, having organized themselves under the title of the Methodist Episcopal Church South, they claimed their proportion of the Book Concern.

In the case of Smith *vs.* Swormstedt (16 Howard, p. 288), the question came before the Supreme Court of the United States, whether the Methodist

Church South was legally entitled to any portion of this fund. This question the Court answered in the affirmative; and in giving the answer it was compelled to decide whether the General Conference, the highest authority in the Church, had the power to provide for the division of the Church that took place, and also whether the annual conferences at the South had acted in accordance with the provision. Both of these questions were answered affirmatively. Justice Nelson, in delivering the opinion of the Court, held the following language:—

"The division of the Methodist Episcopal Church having thus taken place in pursuance of the proper authority, it carried with it, as a matter of law, a division of the common property belonging to the ecclesiastical organization, and especially the property of this Book Concern. It would be strange if it could be otherwise as it respects the Book Concern; inasmuch as the division of the association was effected under the authority of a body of preachers who were themselves the proprietors and founders of the fund."

The sole ground upon which the Court made any decision about the authority of the General Conference was to settle the legal rights of the parties in litigation; and this is the ground, and the only ground, upon which civil courts can raise inquiries within the limits of the Church proper, as distinguished from the incorporated religious society. Whether the inquiry respects matters of faith, or those of Church order, it is not in review or correction of either, but simply for the purpose of deciding questions that relate to vested civil rights.

These general statements in regard to American Ecclesiastical Law, though but a meager sketch, must suffice to indicate its policy with reference to religious societies. It is not a policy of unfriendliness towards them, or of any discrimination among them, or of any interference with the internal and spiritual affairs of the Church proper, or of any union between Church and State. It is a policy which, in addition to complete toleration of all religious societies, and their protection against molestation and disturbance, touches them mainly, if not exclusively, in respect to the rights of property. The plan of incorporating religious societies, and thus clothing them with the rights, powers, and liabilities of bodies corporate, is the simplest way of settling the problem of their temporalities, and enabling the State to deal with those questions that relate to these temporalities.

The fact, moreover, that the State confines its jurisdiction to this sphere, and that it studiously avoids any interferenee with the spiritual part of Church life, by not administering its functions, or appointing its officers, or making any provision therefor, shows the general position which it means to take in regard to religion. The position, in the extent of it, is peculiar to this country, and differs widely from that of the colonial period. Its exact parallel is not to be found anywhere else. It is based upon the theory that the proper functions of civil government do not extend to the administration, regulation, or propagation of religion, or the control of any of its spiritual agencies. Mr. Hoffman, in his "Ecclesiastical Law in the State of New York" (p. 274), remarks: "In no part of the world is the great principle of the exclusive rule of the Church in matters ecclesiastical, and of the State in matters civil, more generally recognized than in the United States."

Very plainly, a school system governed by the State, and supported by compulsory taxation, yet in which religious instruction or worship is made an element thereof, is not in harmony with the policy and character of American Ecclesiastical Law. It violates the spirit of that law. It undertakes to do in the public school what the State utterly declines in the Church, and thus makes the State inconsistent with itself. It carries the agency of the State beyond the sphere of things temporal into that of things spiritual. It is both an abandonment and a contradiction of the general principles upon which the State elsewhere acts.

XXXI.

FRAGMENTARY THOUGHTS.

There are several fragmentary thoughts floating around the School question, whose dignity would not be very seriously compromised if they were designated as the odds and ends of the discussion. They do execution with some minds; and, hence, they are more or less used. The purpose of this article is to state some of these thoughts, and estimate their logical worth.

1. "The legislation of the Bible, and that of our civil and criminal code, are in many respects analogous, and, hence, the former is a part of the latter." It is true that many of the requirements and prohibitions of the Bible coincide, as to their subject-matter, with similar requirements and prohibitions in our legal system. Both alike forbid murder, theft, perjury, adultery, polygamy, and various other offenses; and both recognize and make prominent the marriage tie, and prescribe like rules as to the rights and duties of parents and children. The two systems of legislation contain much that is common to both. A similar fact appears in the laws of Great Britain when compared with those of this country, and, indeed, in the laws of all civilized nations when compared with each other. The

matters dealt with are similar, and, hence, it is not surprising that the legislation should be largely similar.

What is surprising is the inference, sought by some to be drawn from this fact. It does not follow, because two legislative systems are similar, that either is a part of the other. The vital element in every law is its authority, since without this there is no law; and it so happens that neither the laws of Great Britain, nor those of the Bible, considered as a *civil* code, have any authority in this country. The former have no jurisdiction within the limits of the United States, and the latter have no jurisdiction except with the individual conscience; and with this the State does not concern itself. The Bible is not the constitution or the statute-book of any State in this Union; and the fact that a given act is forbidden by it, is not recognized as a reason why it should be punished. No State undertakes to execute the laws of the Bible, or any laws but its own. Nothing is a part of its laws, or can be, except as made such by the State itself, in the exercise of its own sovereign power.

It is, of course, no objection to a human law that it agrees with the Divine law, but rather the highest possible recommendation; yet this does not confound the two systems, or make one a part of the other, or transfer their respective jurisdictions to each other. An act is not an offense against God because it is forbidden by human law, or an offense against human law because it is forbidden by the Divine law. If it is forbidden by both, then it has the double character of being a sin and a crime at the same time—an offense against two distinct systems of authority. With it as a sin against God, civil society has nothing to do; since its cognizance applies to it solely as a crime against man.

2. "The civil institutions of this country are founded upon the Bible." This is true in the sense that the influence of the Bible, in educating the people, and in elevating and purifying their character, has contributed largely to the formation of these institutions. But the proposition is not true in the sense that our legal system rests upon the authority of the Bible, or that it has borrowed any part of its authority therefrom. The Constitution of the United States, and that of every State in the Union, emphatically contradict the proposition if taken in this sense. Our civil institutions have but one basis of authority; and this is the authority of the people themselves.

Millions of the people in this country believe and respect the Bible, and worship the God therein revealed; but they have not built their governments upon its authority, and do not propose to do so. Made the wiser and the better by their knowledge of its contents, they have been taught the great wisdom of establishing civil government on the foundation of *human* authority, and confining its functions to the attainment of purely temporal ends; thus leaving questions pertaining to religion to be adjudicated in the court of the individual conscience, and not by civil tribunals. Had they built their governmental system upon the Bible, the Bible would have been its fundamental law, and the system itself would have been the legal instrumentality for its execution. Who needs to be told that this would be religious despotism? There was much in the colonial legislation of this country that partook of this character; but, ever since the Revolution, it has been a paramount object with the American people to avoid this result, and, indeed, to render it constitutionally impossible.

3. "The State has no right to deny the Word of God to the children in the public schools." Of course, the State has no such right in respect to children or adults, in the public school, or anywhere else. This, however, is not the question. The real question is this: Is it the *duty* of the State to supply the Word of God, or to preach that Word to anybody or anywhere? Is it the duty of the State to print Bibles, or to distribute Bibles among the people, or to appoint and support Bible readers for popular instruction? If it is not, as our whole American system affirms, then surely the State does not deny the Word of God to anybody by not undertaking this work, or interfere with any man's right, or any child's right, in respect

to the possession or use of this Word. The Bible is free, and the people are free to use it; and what the State does, by not using it in the public schools, is simply to decline any service in respect to the Bible. It lets the subject alone; and to call this a denial of the Word of God to anybody is a gross misuse of language.

4. "The object of using the Bible in the public school is not to teach its religious dogmas, but its morals." A serious difficulty with this idea confronts us in the fact that the dogmas and the morals go together as parts of one and the same system. Both imply inspiration, and, hence, both alike claim to rest upon the authority of God. The Bible is a book of *Divine* morals, as well as of Divine doctrines; and when these morals are taught as the morals of the Bible, whether in the public school or in the Christian pulpit, a very practical and important part of Bible religion is taught. We concede their great value, as we do that of the doctrines, and would just as soon use the Bible in the public school to teach the one, as we would to teach the other. They are so inseparable that neither is properly taught without the other. To teach the precepts of Christ, while ignoring the doctrine of his person as the Son of God and the Saviour of the world, would not half teach those precepts. The same would be true of an attempt to teach the precepts of the Apostles, while disregarding their commission as inspired

men, speaking and writing in the name and by the authority of God. The source of these precepts constitutes a most vital part of their power. They are precepts in virtue of this fact, and not merely ideas or maxims. "Thus saith the Lord" stands behind the whole of them.

The real trouble in using the Bible to teach either its doctrines or its morals in the public school, is precisely what it would be in using the Westminster Catechism for the same purpose. The laws of this country do not establish the Divine authority of either. Neither has any authority before the law. And if the morals of the Bible are to be taught in the public school by using it for this purpose, and taught as *Divine* morals, as they should be, if taught at all, then the State will be engaged in the business of religious propagandism, at the public expense; and that too, as really as if Dwight's system of theology were thus taught, or if the State did the same thing in the Christian pulpit on the Sabbath Day.

We do not escape this result by talking about the morals of the Bible in distinction from its doctrines. It is the *Divine* book in the faith of the Christian ; and those who insists upon its use in the public school expect and mean that it shall go there in this character. The Bible cannot go anywhere in its true character, without bearing upon its face the stamp of being a *religious* book ; and it cannot be used according to its own design without being used to teach religion, and that, too, whether the use respects its doctrines or its morals. Those who would use it in the public school for its morals, but not for its doctrines, not only seek to divorce what is inseparably united, but are inconsistent with themselves.

5. "But did not our Puritan fathers make the Bible a part of their school system?"—Yes: they did as a general fact, and they added the Westminster Catechism to it. They did not stop here, since they made Puritan Christianity a part of their civil system, and taxed the people for its support. They did not stop even here, since in some instances they actually became persecutors. The old fashioned New England Puritan public school, sometimes referred to as if it were a good precedent for this age, belonged to a dispensation that hung witches, whipped Quakers from town to town, and made Roger Williams an exile from his home. It suited an age in which the doctrine of religious liberty for *all* the people was not understood, and certainly not practiced. New England now, by her State Constitutions, repudiates many things which she then did.

We do not mean to disparage the Puritan Fathers. They were stern, stanch, and in the main good men. But to glorify their mistakes, or seek to make these mistakes precedents for this age, or for any age, is a species of veneration for antiquity from which we beg to be excused. The New England public school, during the colonial period, and even for some time after the Revolution, was as distinct an example of a legally preferred religion as was ever witnessed on the face of the earth. We admit the facts of history on this subject, but we wholly deny their authority as a precedent.

6.—"Is not this a Christian country?"—Yes: it is, if you mean that Christianity is the religion which has the greatest prevalence among the people, and exerts far the greatest influence upon their thoughts, habits and usages, and in this way reaches and affects the policy of the State in its legal operations. No: it is not, if you mean that the State has adopted Christianity, or clothed it with any civil power, or given it legal preference over any other religion. Christianity, as a system of religion revealed in the Bible, has no more authority over the body politic in its organic character, or through the body politic over the people, than the poetry of Virgil or Homer, or the sacred books of the heathen. The State does not know it as a law for any body. It is known as such only by individuals; and the State very wisely leaves them to judge of its claims upon their own responsibility. Any inference in respect to the public school that rests upon the assumption that Christianity is, *ipso facto*, a part of our legal system, and that in this sense this is a Christian country, rests upon a false premise.

7. "But is not this a Protestant country?" Yes; it is, if you mean that Christians form the

majority of religionists, and that Protestants form the majority of Christians. No ; it is not, if you mean that the State has set its seal to Protestantism in distinction from Catholicism, or any other type or form of religion, or that the government of the country is Protestant. If we except the Protestant office-holding test of New Hampshire, no such governmental fact exists in the United States. The people, as citizens, stand on an equal footing, no matter what may be their religion. It is one of the glories of our political system that this is not a Protestant country in any sense that legally discriminates between citizens on religious grounds. The world has had quite enough of that kind of Protestantism.

8. " These Catholics who are making so much disturbance about the public schools, being largely of foreign birth, are mere interlopers." This is simply an appeal to anti-Catholic prejudice, as anti-American as it is bigoted and ignorant. It may be well to remember that our Protestant ancestors were all of them a set of interlopers. The Puritans were interlopers. The whole people of the United States, with the exception of the Indians, are either interlopers or the descendants of interlopers. A great and powerful nation started with interloping, and interloping has been one of the elements of its rapid increase.

It is a fundamental article of our political faith that this country, on all its sides, should be open to the ingress of peaceable interlopers, whether black or white, in whatever clime born, and bringing with them whatever religion; that all these interlopers may, by naturalization, become citizens of the United States; that, being such, they are citizens of the State in which they reside; and that, possessing this double citizenship, they are entitled to all its privileges and immunities as perfectly as if they had been native-born for a dozen generations. Our political system, with the single exception of eligibility to the Presidency of the United States, makes no distinction between a naturalized and a native-born citizen.

The Fourteenth Amendment to the Constitution expressly says that "all persons born or naturalized in the United States, and subject to the jurisdiction thereof, are citizens of the United States and of the State wherein they reside." Their rights as citizens, whether such by birth or by naturalization, do not depend upon their religion, whether Protestant or Catholic. The Catholic has just as many rights as the Protestant, and no more; and the Protestant has just as many rights as the Catholic, and no more. No class has any monopoly of these rights, whether home or foreign-born, whether of this or that religious faith. That is not a true American head or heart that fails to recognize and cordially accept this principle. Our constitutions and laws do not abridge the religious liberty of anybody, and have no prejudices or spleen against the religion of anybody, and no partiality for the religion of anybody. They would not utter a word of complaint if the Pope and his whole college of cardinals were to come to these shores, and here do their utmost to propagate Roman Catholicism by methods that lie within the limits of the law. His Holiness is at perfect liberty to make the experiment whenever it may suit his pleasure. If he *can* outwork Protestants in propagating religion, then so be it.

9. "But men have no business to be superstitious Catholics, and especially to be Infidels, Rationalists, and Free Thinkers; and if they will be such, then let them take the back seat in the synagogue of citizenship." So you say; but, unfortunately for the saying, the American people, expressing their judgment through legal methods, do not agree with you. Their theory is, that whether a man shall be a Catholic, or a Protestant, or an Infidel, is, as between him and civil society, his *own* business, and the business of nobody else. If he chooses to be a fool, in the religious sense, then civil society will let him be a fool; and, so long as he does not violate the laws, afford him the same protection that it would if he were religiously wise. All questions between him and God it leaves for him to settle.

10. "Would you really expel the Bible from the public school, and thus perpetrate an outrage upon the sacred book?" There is a kind of argument which logicians call *argumentum ad reverentiam,* or

an appeal to the feeling of reverence as the means of carrying a point with any one who has the feeling. This is precisely the import of the above question.

We answer the question candidly by saying that, with a profound respect for the Bible, and a firm belief in its Divine authority, there are, nevertheless, a great many uses to which we would not apply the book. We would not consult it in solving a question of constitutional law, or in settling a problem in mathematics, or in determining the character and cure of diseases, or in deciding which is the best currency system, or in trying to find out how one can raise the largest crop from an acre of land, or in laying a plan for building a cotton factory. A man would be simply stupid who should seek these kinds of information in the Sacred Scriptures. They are not a cyclopædia of universal knowledge; and it is no disrespect to them not to use them where they should not be used. We object to their use in the public school, not for the want of faith in their doctrines, or for the want of reverence for their sacred character, but because the school in question is a civil institution of the State, supported at the general expense by compulsory taxation, and because the propagation of religion is not a proper function of the State.

For this reason we would not use the Bible in the public school, and wherever it is thus used we would discontinue that use, not simply because the

Catholic demands the discontinuance, but because it is not the business of the State to teach religion in any form, and because an American State cannot do so without contradicting one of the first principles of our system of government. This clamor about the irreverence of not thus using the Bible is but a weak and foolish bluster of words that with no sensible man will take the place of argument. The question is not at all one of reverence for the Bible, and not whether it be true, but whether an American State, in consistency with its own organic life and the principles that ought to rule in the construction of every civil government, can, at the public expense, embark in the work of religious instruction and worship. This is the question, and in respect to it our answer is an unqualified negative. Any appeal here to mere *sentiment,* as the means of supplying the lack of brains, or to substitute sentiment for brains, poorly befits the question, furnishes no rule for deciding it, and is not worthy of any one who means fairly and squarely to meet the issue. It may be a mere trick played upon human weakness.

Such are some examples of thoughts that here and there shoot themselves into the discussion of the School question, and which we have called fragmentary thoughts for the want of a better title. Their most conspicuous feature consists in the fact that they either wholly ignore the character of our governmental system, or assign to it a false character. They spring either from religious zeal not well directed, or from bigotry which in its very nature is almost sure to be wrongly directed. They are anything but safe guides in ascertaining the true solution of the School question.

CHAPTER XXXII.

THE CONCLUSION.

The present article completes the somewhat extended series which has appeared in the "INDEPENDENT" with reference to the question of religious instruction and worship in the public schools of this country. The three central topics of the series are these:—1. A statement of the question to be considered. 2. A general view of civil government in application to the question. 3. The principles of our American system of government in relation to the subject of religion. To the first of these topics the first seven articles were specially devoted, bearing the following titles:—1. The New Political Programme. 2. The Roman Catholics. 3. The Protestants. 4. The School Problem. 5. Secular Education. 6. Religious Teaching by the State. 7. The Bible in the Public Schools.

The subject, as thus explained, raised the question whether it comes within the province of civil government to undertake the work of administering, regulating, supporting, propagating, or teaching religion, or attempting to perform any function in regard to it beyond that of simply protecting the people in the peaceable and orderly exercise of their religious liberty, and especially whether such a work would be in harmony with the political and civil institutions of this country. The first or generic aspect of this two-fold question was considered in the next eight articles, whose titles are as follows:—1. The Unchristian Method. 2. Governmental Jurisdiction. 3. State Theology. 4. Civil Government. 5. The Political Value of Religion. 6. State Personality. 7. State Conscience toward God. 8. The Majority Conscience.

Each of the above articles was framed in view of the fact that the direct and immediate issue before the American people is not the general question of Church and State, but the specific question of Bible reading and religious instruction and worship in our public schools. This question is merely a branch of the larger one that relates to the attitude which civil government should assume and maintain with reference to religion. All the general principles that are applicable to the latter are equally so to the former.

The conclusion reached from the survey of the more extended field is that civil government, as such, should have nothing to do with the work of administering, sustaining, or teaching religion, and that on this subject its only legitimate function consists in affording an impartial protection to all the people in the exercise of their religious liberty, while so limiting this exercise as to make it compatible with the peace and good order of civil society. It has taken the world a long time to discover and embody this elementary truth ; and even now the discovery and embodiment are limited to a small portion of the race. It is practically an unknown truth to the greater part of mankind.

The acceptance of this general doctrine in regard to the province of civil government settles the School question and all other questions that come within the range of its application. The public school, as an institution of the State, exists and is regulated by its authority, and is, moreover, supported by compulsory taxation. To prescribe for it a religious system to be taught therein, or forms of worship to be there observed, is to determine by the authority of the State what the system or forms of worship shall be, and then to compel the people to pay the expenses thereof. Such a coerced support of religion is equivalent to a State religion in the public school, and that, too, whether the religion and the worship accord with the views and wishes of the majority or not.

All this and much more would be very proper, provided the administration or teaching of religion comes within the rightful province of civil government. But, if this province be simply that of impartial protection, and not at all that of administration or teaching, then besides being highly improper, it is a trespass upon the rights and religious liberty of the people. It is such because it compels them by law to do what should be left to their own discretion. It is especially such in a country where there is great diversity in the religious faith of the people. A school system in which a specific form of religion shall be taught or practiced at the public expense, is among such a people unjust to all who dissent from that religion, but are, nevertheless, compelled to contribute to its support. It puts civil government in a false attitude. It invests it with a function that does not belong to it. On this generic ground we believe it both impolitic and wrong to employ our public school system as the means of propagating any form of religion.

This conclusion we have endeavored to confirm by the study of the constitutional and legal system of this country. The articles relating to this branch of the argument are sixteen in number, and bear the following titles—: 1 The Divine Right of Civil Government. 2. Christianity and the Common Law. 3. The National Constitution. 4. Religious Amendment of the Constitution. 5. The Guaranty of Religious Liberty. 6. State Constitutions. 7. Constitutional Rights of Conscience. 8. Taxation of Religious Corporations. 9. Sabbath Legislation. 10. The Civil Oath. 11. National and

State Chaplains. 12. Criminal Blasphemy and Profanity. 13. Thanksgiving and Fast-day Proclamations. 14. Preambles to State Constitutions. 15. The Law of Religious Societies. 16. Fragmentary Thoughts.

The one inference sought to be derived from this part of the discussion is that we have in this country a system of *secular* governments, established by the authority of the people for secular and not for religious purposes, which, when coming in contact with religion, are planned to afford protection to the people in the peaceable exercise and enjoyment of their religion, but not to regulate, support, or teach that religion, or to make any discriminations on religious grounds. The Constitution of the United States, so far as applicable to the subject at all, is constructed on this general principle; and the same is for the most part true of the constitutions of the several States.

Any divergence from this great principle, as is the fact in some of the State constitutions, is merely exceptional to the general spirit and purpose of our governmental system. A religious test as a qualification to hold office, or to perform any political or civil duty, or to enjoy any political or civil right, is such an exception. In two of the States the power of taxation for the support of religion is granted by their constitutions; yet this, too, is an exception. So, also, in most of the States religious corporations are exempted from taxation; yet this, while an inconsistency surviving by the force of habit and usage after the theory which gave it birth is dead, is not based on religious grounds. Notwithstanding the exceptions that mar the absolute unity and harmony of the system, considered in relation to religion, it is, nevertheless, true that the system, taken as a whole, disclaims all jurisdiction over religion, all right to discriminate among the people for religious reasons, and all right to impose any tax burdens for the support or propagation of religion. We express this general fact by the oft-repeated declaration that in this country we have no union between Church and State. One need but to study its fundamental laws to see this truth.

This constitutional principle is the result of slow but steady growth. Congregational Puritanism, was once a State religion in nearly the whole of New England, as was Episcopacy a State religion in Virginia. The original settlers of this country did not in the outset understand or practice the principles of impartial religious liberty. They did not understand the proper limitations of civil government; and, hence, they were often oppressors, and sometimes persecutors on religious grounds. It has taken the lapse of time, the struggle of conflicting thought, the progress of ideas, and the intermixture of diverse religious sects in the bonds of a common citizenship, to correct the early mistakes of the fathers and their descendants, and bring us to the point where it can be truly said that we have established an American doctrine on the subject of religion, considered with reference to the State. And if there be, as there are, some things still remaining that need to be eliminated in order fully to carry out this doctrine, then judging from the past, we may anticipate that the work will go steadily forward until the last fragment of anything that partakes of the nature of State religion shall wholly disappear from our political and civil institutions. The tendency of public thought is in this direction, and has been for more than a century. The earlier State constitutions have from time to time been changed in obedience to this tendency, and those of more recent date need no change on the subject of religion.

The premise derived from the functions of civil government, especially as constitutionally defined and qualified by the American people, supplies the proper solution of the School question. That solution is clearly the one which grows out of and accords with the fundamental principles of our national and State organization. We can accept no other, and put no other into practice, without contradicting these principles. The Puritan public school, with the religious catechism and the Bible in it—which was once the public school of New England as New England then was—does not conform to the standard furnished by the American doctrine of civil government. It gave preference to a religious sect, and at the public expense inculcated the special ideas of that sect; and this is plainly contrary to the doctrine.

The same objection applies with equal force to the Protestant public school, in which King James's version of the Sacred Scriptures and religious exercises, Protestant in their type and tendency, are incorporated into its educational system. The Catholic, the Jew, the Infidel, and, indeed, all who dissent from Protestantism, being citizens in common with Protestants and having precisely the same rights, complain of the injustice done to them in taxing them for the support of such a school. Their complaint is a valid one. We do not see how it is possible to answer it without ignoring the cardinal principles upon which our national and State life is founded. The same method of reasoning is equally applicable to a Catholic public school, a Jewish public school, or any public school which is made the organ of religious instruction or worship in any form.

The fatal difficulty with all such schools consists in the fact that, while they assign to civil government functions that do not belong to it, they come into direct collision with the American doctrine as to the nature and scope of its functions. They make the State a religious teacher at the public expense, and this is just what it cannot be in consistency with its own doctrine. Shall, then, the doctrine, when applied to popular education, be abandoned as false, or shall our public school system be adjusted to it? Shall all religious and all anti-religious sects be placed on a common ground in the full and impartial enjoyment of their citizen-rights, with no discrimination against or in favor of any class? Shall the public school be the *common* school of the people, of *all* the people, and *for* all the people, and in this respect be like the government that authorizes it, and taxes the people for its support? Shall it, by a wise and just omission, remit the subject of religion in all the forms of the idea, and in all the processes of its propagation, to other agencies, neither controlled nor supported by the State, but left entirely free at their own charges to consult their own pleasure?

The design of this entire series of articles has been to supply the true answer to these questions. That answer is this:—THE PUBLIC SCHOOL, LIKE THE STATE, UNDER WHOSE AUTHORITY IT EXISTS, AND BY WHOSE TAXING POWER IT IS SUPPORTED, SHOULD BE SIMPLY A CIVIL INSTITUTION, ABSOLUTELY SECULAR AND NOT AT ALL RELIGIOUS IN ITS PURPOSES, AND ALL PRACTICAL QUESTIONS INVOLVING THIS PRINCIPLE SHOULD BE SETTLED IN ACCORDANCE THEREWITH.

We submit this answer, without qualification or reservation, as the logical result of the argument. We are quite aware that it excludes the Bible from the public school, just as it excludes the Westminster Catechism, the Koran, or any of the sacred books of heathenism. It pronounces no judgment against the Bible, and none for it ; it simply omits to use it, and declines to inculcate the religion which it teaches. This declinature, while expressing no hostility to the Bible, is founded on the fact that an American State cannot, in consistency with the principles of its own organization, and impartial justice towards all the people, undertake the work of religious teaching or worship in any form of the idea. A State differently organized, might do so in consistency with its own principles, but an American State cannot.

If there be any fault with the result to which we have come, then the fault really lies with the structure of our governmental system. The way to correct the fault is to take the back track, to reproduce and re-establish the theory that was imported from the Mother Country and generally prevailed before the Revolution, and thus radically change our present doctrine of government. This might be done if the people should so ordain ; and if it were done, then the Bible and the Catechism would be in order for the public school. Puritanism would be in order for New England, and Episcopacy for Virginia. The appointment of ministers by the civil authority and the taxation of the people for the support of religion, would be in order. Even persecution on religious grounds would not be out of order.

If, however, the people are not prepared to

abandon the doctrine in regard to religion which the last century of their history has slowly and steadily incorporated into their political system, and if, moreover, they thoroughly believe in it as the true doctrine for every government, then let them have the consistency and the courage to apply it to the public school. Let the citizen rather than the sectarian, the democrat in the true sense rather than the bigot and the zealot, decide the School question ; and there will soon be no such question to decide. The religious controversy about the public school will come to an end. It ought not to exist at all, and would not exist if the people would here apply the principles which they have placed in the fundamental laws of the land. The mere zealots on this subject can never agree because their preferences are incompatible. There is, however, no good reason why American citizens, if willing to meet each other on the basis of their common citizenship, should not come to a perfect agreement in regard to this much-disputed question.

Protestants who, as Protestants, fight Catholics and seek to resist their demands in respect to the public school, are handling very dangerous weapons, though many of them do not seem to know it. They conduct the war upon a principle which may at any time be turned against themselves.

The true ground, whether for attack or defense, is the one that places the Protestant and the Catholic on an equal footing ; and the moment the former takes this position, the whole power of our system of government at once comes to his support. The position is impregnable ; and taking it, the Protestant is sure of a victory, not as a Protestant, but as a citizen. He concedes to the Catholic all his rights and simply claims his own. He demands for himself no more than he is willing to grant to others. This position is a strong one, because it is just and because it exactly accords with the letter and spirit of our civil constitutions.

INDEX.

www.ingramcontent.com/pod-product-compliance
Lightning Source LLC
LaVergne TN
LVHW020121110826
845151LV00001B/229

* 9 7 8 1 4 2 5 5 4 1 2 8 6 *